Transpersonal B[illegible]

JAMES FAD[illegible]

Tra[illegible]
explore the ps[illegible]
and possib[illegible] [illegible]ence
through altere[illegible] consciousness,
paranormal phenomena, spiritual disciplines,
and other modes of extended awareness.

BOOKS IN THE SERIES

Awakening:
Ways to Psycho-Spiritual Growth,
by C. William Henderson

The Centering Book:
Awareness Activities for
Children, Parents, and Teachers,
by Gay Hendricks & Russel Wills

Transpersonal Education:
A Curriculum For Feeling and Being,
by Gay Hendricks & James Fadiman

The Second Centering Book:
More Awareness Activities for
Children, Parents, and Teachers,
by Gay Hendricks & Thomas B. Roberts

Feeling Good:
How To Stay Healthy,
by Emmett E. Miller, M.D., with Deborah Lueth

Precision Nirvana,
by Deane H. Shapiro, Jr.

"A splendid coalescence of Eastern and Western traditions and the first one I know of by a person who is expert in each."

Albert J. Stunkerd, M.D., Professor of Psychiatry, University of Pennsylvania

"Sparkling . . . an extraordinarily difficult task superbly done . . . a synthesis of Eastern philosophy and Western behaviorist psychology. This book has the potential of leavening the lives of thousands of Americans."

Meyer Friedman, M.D., Director, Harold Brunn Institute, Mt. Zion Hospital and Medical Center, and author of *Type A Behavior and Your Heart*

"*Precision Nirvana* is a unique synthesis of Eastern meditative disciplines and contemporary Western psychology resulting in a pragmatic approach toward achieving clarity in consciousness and in actions. Most importantly, it is based upon sound research, personal insight, and a rare sense of humor found in the smile of enlightenment."

Kenneth R. Pelletier, Ph.D., Assistant Clinical Professor, Department of Psychiatry, Langley Porter Neoropsychiatric Institute, author of *Mind as Healer, Mind as Slayer*

"A beautiful book . . . absolutely fascinating and intriguing . . . pedagogically smart, aesthetically it is attractive, philosophically it is acute, and academically it is much needed."

Peter Koestenbaum, Ph.D., Professor of Psychology, San Jose State University, author of *Managing Anxiety* and *Existential Sexuality*

DEANE H. SHAPIRO, JR.,
a Phi Beta Kappa graduate of Stanford University, is President of the Institute for the Advancement of Human Behavior, Portola Valley, California; Dean of Academic Affairs at the Pacific Graduate School of Psychology, Palo Alto, California; and a clinical instructor, Department of Psychiatry and Behavioral Sciences, Stanford University Medical School. Dr. Shapiro spent fifteen months in the Orient studying Zen and Eastern philosophy, and he is internationally recognized for his expertise in Eastern and Western self-regulation strategies.

In addition to *Precision Nirvana,* Dr. Shapiro is the coeditor of two forthcoming books, *Meditation* and *Beyond Health and Normality,* and the author of *The Psychology of Self-Control* (in preparation). He also writes Haiku poetry and Zen stories.

Precision Nirvana

DEANE H. SHAPIRO, JR.

PRENTICE-HALL, INC., *Englewood Cliffs, New Jersey 07632*

Library of Congress Cataloging in Publication Data

SHAPIRO, DEANE H.
Precision nirvana.

(Transpersonal books) (A Spectrum book)
Bibliography: p.
Includes index.
1. Self-actualization (Psychology) 2. Zen Buddhism. 3. Behaviorism. 4. East and West. I. Title.
BF637.S4S5 158'.1 78-4558
ISBN 0-13-695577-0
ISBN 0-13-695569-X pbk.

A SPECTRUM BOOK

10 9 8 7 6 5 4 3

Printed in the United States of America

PRENTICE-HALL INTERNATIONAL, INC., *London*
PRENTICE-HALL OF AUSTRALIA PTY. LIMITED, *Sydney*
PRENTICE-HALL OF CANADA, LTD., *Toronto*
PRENTICE-HALL OF INDIA PRIVATE LIMITED, *New Delhi*
PRENTICE-HALL OF JAPAN, INC., *Tokyo*
PRENTICE-HALL OF SOUTHEAST ASIA PTE. LTD., *Singapore*
WHITEHALL BOOKS LIMITED, *Wellington, New Zealand*

TO MY TEACHERS

- my family—brother, sister, mother, father—who struggled with me for the sparks of love in the long day's journey.
- those living who taught me academic knowledge and modeled the wisdom that can accompany it: Kabori Roshi, Steven Zifferblatt, Robert Kantor, Carl Thoresen, Irv Yalom, Rev. Jerry Irish, Rev. Robert McAfee Brown, Michael Novak, and to those whom I never met except through their writing: O'Neill, Kierkegaard, Kafka, Camus, Joyce, Dostoevsky.
- those whose encouragement, comments, and advice helped me compare and integrate several seemingly diverse schools of thought—

  Eastern/Humanistic/Existential: James Fadiman, Peter Koestenbaum, Rollo May, Albert Stunkard, Charles Tart, the late Alan Watts

  Behavioral/Social Learning Theory: Albert Bandura, Cyril Franks, Alan Kazdin, B. F. Skinner, Albert Stunkard, Carl Thoresen.
- Carol Smith, Lynne Lumsden, and Bill Lester for care, dedication and perseverance during times of seeming *samsara.*

- Mac, whom I met on Sixth Street in San Francisco, and who taught me that men can love each other; and who, instead of dying, bought a motorcycle and rode south to find Don Juan.
- my wife, who provides a model of a truly loving, warm, sensitive person.
- that part of myself which, even though there was no rational reason to do so, believed and had trust.
- our daughter Shauna, who teaches me anew each morning . . . to dance.
- and our daughter Jena, who was created with the Epilogue.

For permission to use the following material, grateful acknowledgement and thanks are extended to

Charles E. Tuttle Co., Inc. for permission to reprint from *Zen Comics* by Ioanna Salajan; and to reprint from Paul Reps, *Zen Flesh Zen Bones.*

United Feature Syndicate for permission to reprint the *Peanuts* cartoons by Charles Schulz.

Art Finley for permission to reprint a cartoon from *Art's Gallery* from the *San Francisco Chronicle.* 7/20/76.

Universal Press Syndicate for permission to reprint one *Doonesbury* cartoon, Copyright 1977, G. B. Trudeau, Distributed by Universal Press Syndicate; and *Herman and Ziggy* cartoons, Copyright 1977, Universal Press Syndicate.

Ashleigh Brilliant for permission to reprint three drawings, © 1974 by Ashleigh Brilliant.

Chicago Tribune and New York Syndicate for permission to reprint six *Broom-Hilda* cartoons by Russ Myers.

Playboy for permission to quote exerpts from Alan Watts, © 1971; and from Dustin Hoffman interview, © 1975; and to reproduce three cartoons.

M. Ffolkes for permission to reproduce one cartoon of his, by courtesy of the proprietors of *Punch*.

American Psychological Association for permission to reproduce a chart and excerpts from Shapiro & Ziffenblatt, "Zen Meditation and Behavioral Self-Control: Similarities, Differences, and Clinical Applications," *American Psychologist, 31,* pp. 519-532. © 1976 by the American Psychological Association.

The Consulate General of Japan for permission to reproduce two pictures, one of a monk drinking tea; one of the Shokentei tea house of the Katsura Imperial Villa in Kyoto.

King Features Syndicate for permission to reprint five *Lockhorns* cartoons.

William Hamilton for permission to reprint seven of his cartoons.

Holt, Rinehart and Winston for permission to reproduce a drawing from Adams and Biddle, *The Realities of Teaching,* 1970.

Field Newspaper Syndicate and Mel Lazarus, Jules Feiffer, and Hank Ketcham for respective permission to reprint cartoons of *Miss Peach,* Jules Feiffer, and *Dennis the Menace.*

Ken Pyre for permission to reprint his cartoon.

Pantheon Books, Inc., a Division of Random House, Inc. for permission to reprint from *The Way of Zen* by Alan W. Watts (© 1957 by Pantheon Books) and from *Zen in the Art of Archery* by Eugen Herrigel (© 1953 by Pantheon Books).

Alfred A. Knopf, Inc., for permission to quote from *The Prophet* by Kahlil Gibran (Reprinted from *The Prophet* by Kahlil Gibran with permission of the publisher, Alfred A. Knopf, Inc. Copyright 1923 by Kahlil Gibran; renewal copyright 1951 by Administrators C. T. A. of Kahlil Gibran Estate, and Mary G. Gibran.)

The Williams & Wilkins Co., Baltimore, and Arthur J. Deikman for permission to quote from "Experimental Meditation," *Journal of Nervous and Mental Disease, 136,* 1963, pp. 329-43. © 1963.

Washington Syndicate for permission to reproduce two *Val* cartoons.

Malcolm Hancock for permission to reprint one *Godfrey* cartoon.

Register and Tribune Syndicate for permission to reprint *Laughs from Europe.*

1st Communications for permission to reprint one cartoon of *Farley* by Phil Frank.

John N. Marquis, Ph.D., of the V.A. hospital in Palo Alto, California, for permission to adapt progressive relaxation exercises from his relaxation tape recording.

Scribner for permission to quote from Martin Buber's *I and Thou,* translated by Walter Kaufman (N.Y.: Scribner, 1970, pp. 58-59).

Columbia University Press for permission to quote from *Chuang-Tzu, Basic Writings* © 1964. Translated by Burton Watson.

Psychologia for permission to reprint a chart and anecdotal data from D. Shapiro, "Zen Meditation and Behavioral Self-Control Applied to a Case of Generalized Anxiety," 1976, 19(3), pp. 134-138. © *Psychologia.*

Citadel Press for permission to quote an excerpt from Frederick Spiegelberg's *Spiritual Practices In India.*

John Murray Ltd. for world rights, and Grove Press, Inc. as the U.S. publisher, for permission to quote a mondo from D. T. Suzuki's *Introduction to Zen.* © 1949 by John Murray Ltd., London, England.

University of California Press for permission to quote from Carlos Castenada, *The Teachings of Don Juan: A*

Yoqui Way of Knowledge, © 1968 by The Regents of the University of California.

Harper & Row for permission to use D. T. Suzuki's translation of Matsuo Basho's poem; and to quote from E. Fromm et al., *Zen Buddhism and Psychoanalysis.* © 1960, Eric Fromm.

Walpola Rahula and Grove Press for permission to quote from Walpola Rahula, *What the Buddha Taught.* © 1959 by W. Rahula, second and enlarged edition © 1974 by W. Rahula. All rights reserved.

Iris Verlag, Switzerland, for permission to reprint plates I, VI, XV from *Art of the Far East.*

Los Angeles Times for permission to reprint Three Smart chart cartoons

Reamer Keller for permission to reprint his 'Medicare cartoon.

New Directions Publishing Corporation and Peter Owen Ltd: Publishers for permission to quote excerpts from Herman Hesse, *Siddhartha,* translated by Hilda Resner. © 1951 by New Directions Publishing Corporation. Published in the British Commonwealth by Peter Owen, London.

Malcolm Hancock for permission to reprint his Patrick cartoon.

Harvard University Press for permission to quote from the *Baghavad Gita* translated by Franklin Edgerton. © 1944 by the President and Fellows of Harvard College. Renewed 1972 by Eleanor Hill Edgerton.

Mushinsha Ltd., Japan for permission to use poems by Matsuo Basho, *Narrow Roads to the Deep North and Other Travel Sketches.*

John M. Coronato, Rich Holeton, and Johanna Shapiro for permission to reprint their haiku poetry; Orian E.

Tolton, T. Lee, and Johanna Shapiro for the sumi-e paintings; and Duke Duisenberg for his sumi-e paintings and poetry.

Special acknowledgement to

Dr. Gerald W. Piaget for the author's photograph on the back cover.

Raymond Mullaney for handlettering the chapter-opening epigraphs.

CARE AND MAINTENANCE OF THE MIND: AN OWNER'S MANUAL FOR

- learning to use Eastern and Western self-management skills to take charge of your own life
- knowing the warmth and love in yourself and others
- preventing 1984: Becoming aware of how you have been (and are being) conditioned
- feeling the poetry and beauty of nature
- turning from external reinforcement to internal reinforcement: choosing the kind of life you want
- getting on your own team: making your thoughts your servant rather than your master
- realizing how your beliefs and preconceptions limit and distort reality
- dealing effectively with stress and tension
- attaining increased personal freedom and dignity
- exploring the power of your mind: integrating ordinary awareness with altered states of consciousness

- achieving an integrated East-West vision of excellence: the path of heart
- developing a new education: toward a harmony in mind–body–spirit
- self-celebrating: learning the art of the cosmic chuckle

Contents

Preface

Where does the Zen Master go to the bathroom? I suppose few people have ever asked themselves that question. I suppose fewer still would believe that there is a relationship between answering that question and achieving *nirvana*—a peaceful state of mind, a spiritual state of enlightenment and well-being.

One morning before sunrise, in the summer of 1970, while meditating in Daitoku-ji monastery in Kyoto, I asked myself that question. It became a kind of *koan* for me and filled my mind for many hours on many days. Finally, one morning, I decided to find out.

I followed the Master.

He goes in the toilet.

I began to wonder if there wasn't a relationship between how he had learned to go to the bathroom and how he had learned to achieve nirvana. At first this seemed like an absurd thought to me, a temptation of *makyo* (diabolical hallucinations). Yet, as I thought about it, I realized that certainly no one would disagree that the skill of learning to go to the bathroom can be taught. It seemed to me that similarly, there was an assumption being made in the monastery that nirvana could be taught. Now, this assumption was never explicitly stated. Quite the opposite. We were repeatedly told that the Master had nothing to teach; that Zen believes in neither teachings nor doctrines; that there is no goal, and that to seek a goal is already to lose it.

But then why was there a monastery to teach us how not to

rely on words; to *teach* us to learn to live in the moment, in a present centeredness, without striving for goals? And why were we taught techniques, such as meditation, to learn to achieve these goals? Likewise, I soon began to notice that the Master, by his everyday habits of eating, talking, walking, was really modeling for us the peaceful "right" attitude that we were all trying to acquire.

It became clear to me that a teaching process was occurring. This teaching was different from the rational, intellectual Western education I had received. But it was a teaching nonetheless. The Zen Masters, over the course of centuries, had developed precision methods for teaching individuals how to attain nirvana. This teaching of Zen and the Eastern tradition in general, have primarily emphasized techniques that encourage yielding, letting go, egolessness, nonattachment, present centeredness, and altered states of consciousness.

A dominant emphasis in Western psychology, on the other hand, has been the precision use of the intellect and rationality, the setting of goals, analysis, assertiveness, strong ego development, the search for causality, and the perfection of ordinary awareness.

This book attempts to combine the best of both teachings into an integrated whole: a *precision nirvana.* The essence of this book may be described as a Zen or transpersonal Behaviorism. This orientation results, in part, from my own personal and spiritual searching. This searching began nearly a decade ago, when I first read the existential writers. This reading, in turn, led to an exploration of my Judeo-Christian roots: travel to Israel, tracing Jesus' path through the Holy Land, and learning Hebrew and Greek to read the Old and New Testaments. The quest also led to the Orient, where my wife and I spent fifteen months studying Zen Buddhism.

Zen behaviorism draws from all these experiences, especially those in the Orient, and tries to integrate them with my Western psychological training in behavior therapy. Thus, the book provides a synthesis between Eastern disciplines and Western psychology. It offers a comprehensive, integrative approach to self-understanding that illustrates in practical terms ways in which the two traditions may be combined—in clinical practice, in educational settings—and above all, in dealing more effectively with our own lives.

In this latter capacity, the book serves as an owner's manual: guiding you in ways to make decisions for yourself, offering you alternatives for choosing who you want to become; and providing you with specific helpful techniques for achieving your own self-chosen goals. Also, in the process of choosing yourself and your values, the book attempts to guide you joyfully in a self-celebration.

May this owner's manual teach you to work hard, have fun, and not know the difference.

I

Teachings of the Zen Master & the Grand Conditioner

Nan-in, a Japanese tea master during the Meiji era, received a university professor who came to inquire about Zen. Nan-in served tea. He poured the visitor's cup full, and then kept on pouring. The professor watched the overflow until he could restrain himself no longer: "It is overfull, no more will go in."

"Like this cup," Nan-in responded, "you are full of your own opinions and speculations. How can I show you Zen unless you first empty your cup?"[1]

The term *Zen Master* may cause many people to conjure up an image of a person in a long robe with a shaved head. This person may be seen as one who teaches that there is nothing to teach, asks silly questions which don't have answers, and knocks people on the head if they aren't meditating correctly. The term *behavior modifier* (whom I will refer to as the *Grand Conditioner*[2]), on the other hand, may cause many people to conjure up an image of a rigid, unemotional, calculating disciplinarian. This person may be seen as one who tries to control our behavior without our knowing it, and treats people mechanistically, as if they were rats in a laboratory.

In this book, we will try to peel away whatever preconceptions we may have about these two stereotypes and the schools of thought they represent. The first part of the book (Chapters 1 and 2) describes the teachings of the Zen Master and the Grand Conditioner. Chapter 1 discusses *Meditation and the East: The Zen Master.* Zen here refers to the "spirit" of Zen. This may, but does not necessarily, overlap the type of Zen practiced in Zen monasteries.[3] This essence of Zen embodies many of the principles of humanistic psychology and may be seen as a representative and example of that school of thought.[4] Chapter 2 discusses *Behavioral Self-Management and the West: The Grand Conditioner.* I use the term *Grand Conditioner* here to symbolize the behaviorist analogue of the Zen Master: that is, the person who knows most about behavior therapy (social learning theory principles) and who applies those principles (behavioral self-management skills) to him- or herself. The second part of the book (Chapters 3 through 7) describes how the two schools of thought may be combined: that is, what happens *When the Zen Master Meets the Grand Conditioner.* As such, the second part builds on the first and attempts to provide an integration of East and West: Behaviorism, Humanism, and Beyond.

1
Meditation & the East: The Zen Master

We may laugh at our friend Charlie Brown. He admires his father's knowledge about cars. Yet we know that his father didn't fix the car, he merely avoided a problem. How often do we do the same with ourselves? How often do we get so wrapped up in our daily routines, living in the external world, that we forget to tune into ourselves; forget to evaluate our own internal motors?

All of us can see clearly that Charlie Brown's father made a mistake by trying to avoid the message the car's engine was giving him. Why then do we, who can clearly see someone else's mistakes, so often seem to make the same mistakes ourselves? Certainly we are admonished enough that we are living in a "wakeful sleep," in a "state of drunken awareness." We are told to tune in, turn on, attain higher and altered states of consciousness.

Why don't we? If it's clearly so good for us, as others say, what prevents us? Let me suggest a couple of answers that are often overlooked when people are discussing consciousness.

ORDINARY AWARENESS: AWKWARD SELF-CONSCIOUSNESS

As an introduction, let me ask you to swallow three times. Please stop reading, close your eyes, and swallow three times.

- Swallow once.
- Swallow twice.
- Swallow three times.

What did you notice as you became aware of swallowing? Was it difficult? Did your throat and jaws begin to tighten? If this happened, your reaction was normal. It appears that when we first focus on ourselves, or on a behavior that we are doing, an awkwardness occurs; a kind of self-conscious stumbling effect. This has been wisely illustrated in the poem "The Puzzled Centipede."

The centipede was happy, quite
Until the toad in fun
Said, "Pray, which foot comes after which?"
This worked his mind to such a pitch,
He lay distracted in a ditch,
Considering how to run.[1]

This stumbling self-consciousness seems to be a natural occurrence, part of the process of ordinary awareness. You have seen its effects for yourself, when you observed your swallowing. This same process of stumbling self-consciousness occurs when we, as individuals first observe ourselves and our place in the world. This initial self-conscious awareness has been referred to as existential anxiety, facing the abyss, confronting one's humanness. It has been poetically described as humans facing the emptiness of the universe, facing their human frailty, shouting to a God who is a

God of silence. It is we as individuals being forced to choose who we are, what our values are, and how, in a very fundamental sense, we fit into the world. The pain, the confusion, the "nausea" of Sartre come from this process of standing back and questioning one's place in the world. Nowhere is this more clearly illustrated than in facing one's own finiteness, one's own death, or the death of a loved one.

In the Eastern literature there is an ancient Chinese novel about a dissolute nobleman that vividly illustrates this relationship between death and consciousness. The author of the novel, according to legend, wrote the book in biographical form about a personal acquaintance whom he disliked intensely. After writing the book, he put poison on the corner of each page and gave a copy to his enemy. The nobleman, enthralled and engrossed in the story about his own life, lustfully licked his fingers to turn the pages. In so doing he poisoned himself before he could finish the last chapter. The last chapter told of the author's plot and the nobleman's subsequent death. In a sense, we are the same as that nobleman—we are conscious of the last chapter's inevitability, yet we will never have the opportunity to read it.

What good does it do us to know of the last chapter's inevitability? What good does it do us to see how frail and delicate and helpless we are? No matter how aware we are of our finiteness, this does not change either our frailty or the inevitability of our death.

Even in Western literature, awareness, or increased consciousness, is often seen as a curse. For example, in the Bible, human beings first gain awareness when Eve eats the apple (Genesis 3:7): "Then the eyes of both were opened and they knew they were naked." Is this awareness joyful? No. The increased awareness of their bodies caused Adam and Eve to "sew fig leaves together and make themselves aprons," and caused Adam to hide among the trees of the garden: "I was afraid because I was naked" (Genesis 3:10–11). Before awareness, Adam and Eve lived nonconsciously and blissfully in the Garden of Eden. After awareness, they saw their nakedness, felt awkward and self-conscious, and became afraid.

Classical psychoanalytic therapy uses different labels, but

describes a similar phenomenon. According to Freud, most individuals have little consciousness about themselves and develop elaborate defense mechanisms to avoid self-awareness.

To a certain extent, it makes sense that we don't want to tune in to the problems of our internal selves. Even though we are told that we are now in a state of drunken awareness, and should overcome that state, it appears that the act of focusing on oneself, of raising one's consciousness of oneself, is, at least initially, a more painful experience than the so-called state of lesser consciousness.

Therefore, why change? What is in it for us if we change our way of perceiving the world, if we focus in an intense and searching way, on ourselves?

MEDITATION AND CONSCIOUSNESS

> I commend you Siddhartha . . . that you have again heard the bird in your breast sing and followed it.[2]

In order for Siddhartha to hear the bird in his breast sing, he needed to tune in, in a sensitive way, to his internal self.

In this section we will discuss meditation, which is one of the more powerful Eastern techniques for attaining this increased consciousness of ourselves. In discussing this technique, we will point out some advantages of tuning in to ourselves. We will see that the first phase of meditation is similar to the previously described awkward (self) consciousness; but that this confusing first step is only temporary. It passes, and there are other, more pleasant feelings that may occur as one continues to practice meditation.

Meditation is a technique that involves learning how to pay attention. There are many different techniques of meditation; however, as will be described later, the major differences between them involve two variables: (1) *what* one pays attention to, and (2) *how* one pays attention.[3]

Zen Breath Meditation

Let us look at Zen breath meditation as an example of meditation. In Zen breath meditation, an individual is instructed to focus his attention on breathing. In the words of Walpole Rahula,

> Let your mind watch and observe your breathing in and out . . . forget all other things: your surroundings, your environment; do not raise your eyes and look at anything so that eventually you can be fully conscious of your breathing . . . when you will not even hear sounds nearby, when no external world exists for you . . . you are so fully concentrating on your breathing.[4]

What happens when we initially focus on our breathing? Let's look at the five different steps involved in breath meditation.[5] Steps One and Two describe meditation and *ordinary awareness*; steps Three and Four describe meditation as a *self-regulation strategy;* and step Five describes meditation as an *altered state of consciousness.*[6]

Meditation and Ordinary Awareness

Step One: Difficulty in Breathing. Often, when individuals first focus on their breathing, they complain that they are not getting enough air, that their breath comes more quickly than normal. Some have said that they felt as though they were drowning.

Notice the similarity between this first step of meditation and the awkward (self) consciousness described earlier. From the vantage point of step one it seems that meditation, rather than bringing a higher, or altered state of consciousness, rather than allowing one to experience a feeling of calmness and relaxation, merely makes breathing more difficult. That is particularly frustrating since before practicing meditation, all of us had been doing a superb job of breathing naturally, effortlessly, and without awareness. The first step of meditation, which involves becoming more aware, causes us nothing but trouble.

Step Two: Wandering Mind. In the second step, one's attention wanders from the task at hand—one forgets to focus on breathing, the mind wanders, thoughts arise, and one begins to enter into conversations with the thoughts, ruminating about them, having a dialogue with them. In psychological terms, this may be referred to as *habituation* to the task. An example of this second stage occurred for me during one of my early meditation sessions in the Zen monastery Daitoku-ji in Kyoto. I was practicing in the meditation room and I heard a car honk. I said to myself, "This is ridiculous—I'm in a peaceful, quiet monastery setting, and what kind of nonsense is this to hear a car honk!" A dialogue then began in my "mind" about the way civilization was encroaching upon nature. I began to feel sorry for the Zen master whose peaceful retreat was being invaded. It was only several minutes later that I realized that I was no longer focusing on the breathing.

When this nonattentive dialogue occurs, and when the individual becomes aware of it, he is asked to bring his attention back to the act of breathing. In Japan, the meditator is aided in this task by the Master, who walks around the meditation hall, literally carrying a big stick. The Master watches each of the meditators to make sure they are alert and receptive. Since sleepiness (*kanchin*) is not desirable in Zen training, when the Master sees one of the students sagging, or not concentrating, he approaches that person and bows. (The meditator, aware of his wandering mind, can also initiate the bow.) The Master then raises the stick and gives a blow (called a *kwat*, after the Zen Master Rinzai) which, I can assure you from personal experience, returns the individual to conscious alertness in a very immediate manner:

> . . . his diaphanous white robe quivered as his arm raised the stick above the closely shaved head. The candle next to me magnified his shadow on the ceiling of the meditation hall. After he hit my shoulder, we both bowed.
>
> All was then still in the hall except for the sound of raindrops striking the roof. Before my closed eyes I saw the white sand of the rock garden which lay outside the meditation hall. The sands were carefully raked to appear like the ocean. The rain mixed with the ocean of sand, and out of the union of the two bodies of water, an embryo was formed.[7]

When there is no Master present, the beginning meditator is told to be his own master: he is told to learn to identify when his attention wanders from the task of breathing and to bring it back to that task.

Step Three: Relaxation. With practice, the individual learns to focus on his breathing without the self-conscious stumbling effect of step one, and without habituating to the task as in step two. At this point, he has learned to breathe effortlessly. His air comes in and goes out. People have described this as a "sense of floating," as "air coming through my pores effortlessly." This is referred to as the third step of meditation. It is this aspect of meditation Benson refers to when he discusses the relaxation response. This step of meditation seems to be effective in reducing blood pressure (hypertension), stress and tension, and insomnia.[8]

Step Four: Detached Observation. In the fourth step of meditation, the individual maintains the kind of effortless breathing of the third step, and yet new thoughts do occur. However, when these new thoughts occur, the meditator does not enter into a dialogue with them, as I did with the honking horn; rather, the individual is instructed to "just observe them . . . and let them flow down the river."

Therefore, in the fourth step, an individual does not enter into dialogue with a thought, but merely watches it, and lets it go, while maintaining the effortless breathing of the third step. This fourth step seems to have an important effect in helping an individual overcome anxieties, phobias, and other concerns. The assumption is that whatever is important to a person at the time will come into awareness; and, since the person is in a relaxed, physically comfortable posture, whatever does come into awareness will not be seen as threatening.

An illustration from some of my research with heroin addicts vividly illustrates this fourth step.[9] One of the subjects noted that while he was meditating he saw a movie screen. On this screen flashed pictures of his life and questions such as, "Hey man, what are you doing with your life? You're really blowing it. What are you going to do with yourself?" He said that normally these questions would cause him a great deal of anxiety and turmoil, and would be the kind of thoughts that would lead him to use heroin again. However, when he became aware of these questions while meditating, there was none of the anxiety, none of the guilt: "I could merely be an observer of my own life." In other words, the fourth step of meditation serves to present whatever is of concern to the person at that time in a calming, nonemotional manner.

This observing oneself without feeling threatened is referred to as *detached observation.* This detached observation helps us obtain a perspective on our own lives. We have been told, at some time or another, that it is important to stand back and get a perspective. Yet we also know how difficult it is to get a perspective when we are in the middle of events.

The *Maitrayana-Brahmana Upanishad*, an Indian religious text, describes this state of detached observation as follows: The

ART'S GALLERY by Art Finley

Temper, temper

person of wisdom "seeming to be filled with desires, and seeming to be overcome by bright or dark fruits of action, . . . seeming to be changing, [is] in reality unchanging, free from desire, *remaining a spectator, resting in himself*" (italics mine).[10] This person of wisdom is able to act, yet always retains a perspective. This ability to remain a "spectator, resting in himself" has been called an "immovable wisdom" by Alan Watts. It is a means by which individuals practicing meditation can learn to observe without comment everything that is happening to them in their internal and external environment. This wisdom allows meditators to regard themselves dispassionately and nonjudgmentally, to detach themselves from the "self" until they realize that this self is no more than any other thing in the material world. Meditators in this step are able to stand back from their lives, their thoughts, their feelings, and merely watch them flow past, without making evaluations and judgments. As Eugen Herrigel noted in *Zen in the Art of Archery*,

> As though sprung from nowhere, moods, feelings, desires, worries, and even thoughts incontinently rise up in a meaningless jumble . . . the only successful way of rendering the disturbances inoperative is to . . . enter into friendly relations with whatever appears on the scene, to accustom oneself to it, to look at it equitably, and at last grow weary of looking.[11]

Meditation as an Altered State

Step Five: Higher State of Consciousness. Finally, there is the fifth step of meditation. This is the step that has been referred to in various Eastern literatures as *satori, nirvana, kensho, samadhi*. In the West it has been referred to as an *altered state* or *higher state* of consciousness. Research on this step of meditation, although quite difficult, is provocative and exciting. It consists primarily of understanding the relationship between meditation, self-actualization, and an altered state of consciousness. Although the altered state is often spoken of as something ineffable, something that cannot by understood by words, it is important to give at least an experiential hint of what this step is like, and how it differs from our ordinary ways of seeing the world. I would like to illustrate this step with a poem by the Japanese *haiku* poet Basho. Basho's poem translates as follows:

Over the darkened sea
Only the shrill voice of a flying duck
Is visible—
In soft white[12]

Close your eyes now and listen to the poem again in your mind. Perhaps if a friend is close, you may ask him or her to read it to you. "Over the darkened sea only the shrill voice of a flying duck is visible in soft white." Note the images that come to mind as you listen. Let me pause briefly and let you think through the images.

Often this is a very difficult poem for the Western-educated person to understand. The reason this poem is used here is to focus on the relationship between the different ways we perceive the world. For example, if it is dark, how can a voice be visible? Even if it is not dark, how can a voice be visible? How can it be visible in soft white? What this poem suggests is an openness to experience. Basho, as he walks beside the sea, is keenly aware; all his senses are open. The kinds of distinctions that we make in ordinary awareness between an eye seeing and an ear hearing are not made by Basho. He is living totally in the moment, without goals, without thought, with nothing but an openness, a present-centeredness, to what is around and within him. This nonthinking, nonlabeling openness is characteristic of the fifth step of meditation.

THE ALTERED STATE

How Does the Altered State Differ from Ordinary Awareness?

There are several important differences between the altered state and ordinary awareness. Some of these differences have been briefly mentioned already.

Timelessness

First, there is an altered sense of time. The Greeks had two words for time: *kairos* and *chronos.* Chronos refers to chronological time—that is, time as we know it, with seconds, minutes, hours, days; past, present, future. Kairos is timelessness—when chronological time literally stands still. If chronological time is represented in a linear fashion,

minutes ———————————————— *chronos*
1 2 3 4 5 6 7 8 9 10

kairos time may be represented vertically:

minutes ———————|——————— *kairos*
1 2 3 4 5 | 6 7 8 9 10

This represents a moment of timelessness, a present-centeredness, a sense of infinity. The fifth step of meditation is an example of *kairos.*

Goallessness

In the fifth step, there is also a sense of goallessness. There is no striving, no seeking, merely a receptivity and openness to what is occurring.

One of the main disadvantages to goal setting is that when an individual sets a goal for himself, he may become rigid about attaining that goal, even if the goal is inappropriate or unrealistic. Several studies on self-concept have shown that individuals who set unrealistically high goals for themselves have a low self-concept and increased feelings of depression because they can never obtain the goals they set. Thus, there may be a certain freedom in letting go of unrealistic goals.

A second disadvantage to goal setting is that once an individual has set a goal, he focuses on obtaining that goal and developing instrumental means for achieving it. This may cause that individual to put on a type of blinders such that other objects and events that do not help lead to the goal are ignored. *As long as we focus exclusively on the path, we may lose sight of the flowers that line the path.*

Third, one may become caught up in the competitiveness of

HERMAN

"If you took my advice you'd throw away those bathroom scales. You're letting this weight-loss thing become an obsession."

POT-SHOTS NO. 519

I FEEL MUCH BETTER, NOW THAT I'VE GIVEN UP HOPE.

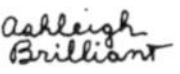

goal setting, striving, and winning. Often this is done at the expense of interpersonal relationships or other values.

Fourth, as Dollard and Miller[13] have pointed out in their personality studies, the closer we get to a reward, the more frustrated we become if we are blocked from that goal or reward. From an Eastern perspective, we need to learn to appreciate the *process* of working toward the goal.

POT-SHOTS NO. 572

Ashleigh Brilliant

TO BE SURE
OF HITTING
THE TARGET,

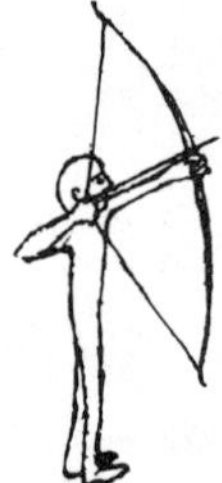

SHOOT FIRST

AND, WHATEVER YOU HIT,
CALL IT THE TARGET.

Absence of Concepts, Labels, Thinking

In the fifth step of meditation, there is an absence of language and images. The individual does not think or analyze.

Socrates noted that it was through reason, through intellect, that human beings had achieved and would continue to achieve wisdom. Beginning with the Socratic doctrine "know thyself," the history of Western science has involved using the intellect in order to gain a better understanding of human nature. This philosophy was especially evident during the period of enlightenment, when it was assumed that human beings were capable of understanding through reason and intellect whatever was necessary for their welfare. This is a viewpoint reflected in Descartes' statement, "I think, therefore I am." Education in Western society has primarily emphasized the cognitive mode, and placed a high value on the ability to think.

There are many disadvantages to labeling and intellectualizing. Part of these disadvantages are suggested by Lao'tse's student, the Chinese philosopher Chuang Tzu, who was concerned with the futility of language and consciousness. Chuang Tzu wrote,

> If there is existence, there must have been nonexistence. And if there was a time when nothing existed, there must have been a time when even nothing did not exist. All of a sudden nothing came into existence. Could one then really say whether it belongs to a category of existence or nonexistence? Even the words which I have just now uttered, I cannot say whether they say something or not.[14]

Chuang Tzu's view of the absurdity of words is echoed in Gandhi's opinion of the futility of words: "We are frail human beings. We do not know very often what we say. If we want to listen to the 'still small voice' that is always speaking within us, it will not be heard if we continually speak." This view of the limitation of words and intellect is one of the fundamental principles of Zen. The spirit of Zen, notes D. T. Suzuki, is "A special transmission outside the scriptures; [involving] No dependence on words or letters."[15] It is believed in Zen that for individuals to have true understanding, they must understand not by reason, not by intellect, but by intuition and a holistic grasp of the subject.

This *holistic mode of perceiving* may be related primarily to the right hemisphere of our brain. Research suggests that our brain may have two specialized hemispheres[16]; the left hemisphere involves the use of verbal, logical deductions and a sequential processing of information. The right hemisphere seems to grasp the relationship between parts directly, rather than by a sequence

of deductions. Meditation may involve a holistic mode of knowing primarily specialized in the right brain.

What Are the Advantages of the Altered State?

Advantages of this holistic perception of the world may be seen in our *relationship to nature*, *to other people*, and *to ourselves.*

Improved Relationship with Nature

This nonintellectual openness and receptivity may enhance our experience in nature, whereas words and labels may diminish our experience in nature. The Eastern approach emphasizes a relationship with nature that doesn't analyze, and doesn't use concepts.

This openness to nature is important in Eastern thought, especially as a way of learning about ourselves. For example, Hindu doctrines suggest that the way to be at peace with oneself is through living in concert with the natural environment. In Zen, the self is explained and understood through nature. For example, there is a Japanese poem entitled "Self" which speaks of the *cherry blossoms* in spring, the *moon* in autumn, the *snow* on Mount Fuji in winter. In the West, because of the importance of believing that the individual is in control and master of his own destiny, there has been less of an effort to look toward the environment as a way to understand ourselves and more of an emphasis on human beings conquering nature, which is considered to be an opponent. Nature is seen to exist as something to be explained, something outside ourself, and something to be overcome. As one means of understanding the difference between Eastern and Western thought let's take a look at the following two poems, the first by the Japanese *haiku* poet Basho and the second by the English poet Tennyson.[17]

When I look carefully,
I see the nazunia blooming
By the hedge!

Flower in the crannied wall
I pluck you out of the crannies
Hold you here, root and all, in my hand,
Little flower—but if I could understand
What you are, root and all, and all in all,
I should know what God and man is.

In Basho's poem, the last syllable (*kana* in Japanese) is translated by an exclamation point. *Kana* conveys a feeling of admiration, praise, sorrow. Tennyson's poem also expresses these same feelings. But Tennyson, as representative of the Western tradition, conveys the feelings by intellectualizing them. Further, he plucks the flower, he tries to capture its essence both physically and symbolically. Basho simply sees the flower. There is no need for him to think about the flower. Unlike Tennyson, he feels no need to possess it by plucking it, because he acknowledges no separation between himself and the flower.

In Zen it is believed that nature produces man out of itself. As D. T. Suzuki noted, "Man came from nature in order to see nature in himself."[18] And Alan Watts said, "The individual is a nerve ending through which the universe is taking a peek at itself."[19]

Therefore, the environment (*kyogai*) is very important in Zen. A Confucian scholar asks a Zen Master, "What is the ultimate secret of Zen?" The Master replies, "Do you hear the murmuring sound of the mountain stream?" The Scholar responds, "Yes, I do." "Then," declares the master, "I have hidden nothing from you."[20]

The openness of the fifth step of meditation helps an individual relate more fully and directly to nature, without the intervention of intellect and reason. A study by two Japanese researchers, Kasamatsu and Hirai,[21] is relevant to this point. These researchers attached experienced Zen meditators to biofeedback equipment to record their brain waves. Alpha waves (brain waves that have been subjectively correlated with a state of relaxation) were recorded in all brain regions. When a click sound was made, however, there was alpha blockage of 2 or 3 seconds. Then the alpha resumed. This click sound was repeated twenty times, and each time there was alpha blockage for 2 to 3 seconds followed by a resumption of alpha waves. This illustrates what might be called an "opening-up" meditation; that is, each time there was a sound in the external environment, the monk heard the sound as evidenced by the blockage of the alpha waves. *In opening-up meditation, the individual attempts to remain open to all stimuli in the external and internal environment.* By contrast, when the control subjects in this study heard the click, they initially had a longer alpha blockage time in response to the click. However, the third and fourth time the click occurred, their alpha blockage was much shorter. And from the fifth to the twentieth time there was no alpha blockage; that is, they did not hear the click. In psychological terms, the control subjects of the experiment "habituated" to the sounds in the external environment.

This experiment suggests an explanation for the Zen saying that one should learn to perceive a flower the five hundredth time as one perceives it the first time. In other words, the goal of opening-up meditation is to teach us to see the environment in a fresh and new way every single time. In ordinary awareness, we discriminate an object, like a flower. Once we've given the flower a label, "flower," we've put it in a category so that the next time we see it we say, "Yeah, that's a flower. I know what it is." Further, in ordinary awareness we don't *experience* the flower, but rather evaluate it and ask questions about it: e.g., Is it good, bad, pretty, ugly, etc.? Buddha taught that it was our sixth sense (the sense that is conscious of the five senses of taste, touch, smell, sight, and hearing) that formulated the categorizations, labels, and analyses involved in ordinary awareness. Meditation teaches us to see things directly—without labels, without categories, without analysis. It enables us to perceive afresh every time. Thus, the monks in this experiment perceived the clicks each time, whereas the control group habituated to the click sound.

Martin Buber has poetically illustrated this ability to see and experience the world in a fresh and altered way. He refers to this experience as an I–Thou relationship. Buber notes that the world of I–it consists of labels and categories; although these may be necessary for survival, the person who only uses labels, analysis, evaluation, who only sees people and nature as objects, "is not fully human." He illustrates poetically the experience of Thou-ness:

> I contemplate a tree. I can accept it as a picture: rigid pillar in a flood of light, or splashes of green traversed by the gentleness of blue-silver ground.
>
> I can feel it as movement: the flowing veins around the sturdy, striving core, the sucking of the roots, the breathing of the leaves, the infinite commerce with earth and air; and the growing itself in the darkness.
>
> I can assign it to a species and observe it as an instance, with an eye to its construction and its way of life.
>
> I can overcome its uniqueness and form so rigorously that I recognize it only as an expression of a law . . .
>
> Throughout all this the tree remains my object, and has its place in time and space, its kind and construction.
>
> But it can also happen . . . that as I contemplate the tree that I am drawn into a relation, and the tree ceases to be an it . . .
>
> This does not require me to forego any of the modes of contemplation. There is nothing that I must not see in order to see, and there is no knowledge that I must forget. Everything, picture and movement, law and number, species and instance are included and inseparably fused.[22]

This openness to nature is reflected in the painting below. Take a look at the painting and notice what strikes your eye first: Normally, when we first look at this painting, we see a waterfall, or

a tree, or fog going up the mountain. Do you see the two people? Notice in this picture of the Chinese landscape that the human figures are quite small. This is in contrast to the Greek concept, represented by Phidias and Praxiteles, who sculpted deities in perfect human form. Their sculpture reflected the Socratic disposition to reduce the world to the dimensions and laws of human reason, which, as noted earlier, became the basis for our Western tradition of science. Chinese painting is opposed to this anthropomorphism. Human beings disappear before nature—nature is mysterious and omnipresent and not to be understood by our intellect. At first we may feel awe when confronted by this seemingly overpowering nature. Soon, however, the awesomeness turns into a harmonious feeling that can't be understood rationally.

Let me share one more painting, one of my favorites. Look particularly at the bridge in the lower right-hand corner. There is a man crossing it and he seems to have a bundle over his shoulder. What would you guess is just to the right of the bridge?

In some ways, this painting represents life: for all our knowledge, intellect, and reason, we don't know exactly where we have come from, nor, if we look off into the mist and fog and mountains at the left, do we know where we are going. Here on earth we seem to be on a bridge, in transition, knowing neither where we have come from nor where we are going. Note the way the water and the land and the mountains all seem to merge with the fog. We don't exactly know where the land ends and the water begins. This intermingling of space and senses is an important aspect of the fifth step of meditation.

When was the last time you were alone in nature? Spend a

moment recalling the experience. You may wish to jot down a few lines describing how you felt about that time.

____

____

____

____

Improved Interpersonal Relationships

A holistic perception of the world, brought about by the altered state, may enable us to have deeper, more open interpersonal relationships. Words, categories, and labels often keep us from experiencing other individuals in all their wholeness. These tools of ordinary awareness straightjacket our perceptions, biasing the way we experience the world, limiting our freedom to experience directly.

A study was made by T. Lesh attempting to determine whether counselors who meditated were more empathetic than those who didn't. All the counselors were shown a videotape of a client telling about his or her problem. They were then told to formulate what they thought the client's problem was. Those counselors who had practiced Zen meditation for a half-hour per day for one month were found to be significantly more empathetic than those who had not practiced meditation. The meditating counselors did not project their own feelings and judgments onto what the client said, and thereby were able to hear the client's concern as it really was.[23]

Ordinary awareness, with its categories, labels, and words, causes us to have preconceptions and make projections about other people. According to Zen, this ordinary awareness not only hides reality from us, but also keeps us from experiencing reality. As Zen states, there is a danger that words may come to take the place of interpersonal experiencing. We may become more interested in analyzing, thinking, and reading about reality than living it. Therefore, the Zen way suggests that we first need to learn to be comfortable on a nonverbal, intuitive, holistic level of awareness in order ever to be able to function properly on a verbal level of abstraction.

In ordinary awareness, we make dichotomies: teacher/student;

"Knock it off! Can't you see I'm reading?"

doctor/patient; or we use labels like "waitress," "gas station attendant," "engineer." We fit people into our preconceptions of the labels and roles they fill. For example, think of the last time you looked at a grocery clerk or a gas station attendant or a teacher or a student as a *person*, quite apart from his or her role. When was the last time you looked at your spouse, or a child, in all his/her wholeness and humanness? Or caught a fresh glimpse of someone you thought you had always known well?

Just as labeling other people makes it more difficult to relate to them fully as human beings, labeling ourselves has a similar effect of removing us even further from experiencing others directly.* Thinking of ourselves in terms of the label "I" leads us to need to defend this "I" from others who might injure our prestige or lessen our reputation. Through the acquisition of wealth, credentials, social role, power, prestige, we try to build up the "I," this "ego," as a separate, fortified, indestructible "thing." In Martin Buber's terms, we come to see ourselves as an "it." We examine ourselves in terms of our property, our power, our status, our intellect. We come to see the world of nature as an "it," something to be manipulated and conquered; and we begin to see other people as objects that can either hinder us or advance us in our position, or aggrandize our ego. Thus we become incapable of allowing ourselves to see other people in all their fullness, their "Thou-ness." But the type of altered awareness experienced in the fifth step of meditation helps teach us an openness to others—a nonjudgmental, nonlabeling openness that lets us see them not as "its" but as "thous." Hence we improve our interpersonal relationships—we *live* and *experience* the reality of others.

In summary, meditation may help improve our interpersonal relationships by (1) removing our projections about others; (2) helping us see "beneath" the traits, roles, and labels we give other people; (3) allowing us to see the illusory nature of our self-label

*Buddhist tradition suggests that the formation of this self-concept "I" is a developmental process that proceeds as follows: (a) We have five senses—sight, taste, smell, hearing, and touch. With these senses we experience the world directly. (b) Soon we begin to label the world of our senses: bird, flower, song, music, soft, salty, etc. Buddha imputed this labeling of the inputs of the five senses, to the *sixth sense.* (c) Once we become aware of the sixth sense, we believe that there must be something within us—some *self*—which causes this labeling. We call this self "I," which Buddha said was the *seventh sense.*

"I," thereby freeing us from the need to defend this illusion of self from others; and (4) giving us the ability to experience reality on a direct, nonverbal level, rather than merely an analytical, thing-oriented one. Life cannot be quantified, for life, as William James suggested, is like a stream of consciousness. A stream flows and is one.

Improved Relationship with Oneself

Finally, the altered state of consciousness we can attain through meditation can help open us up to what Zen calls "direct pointing to the soul of man; seeing into one's nature . . . ,"[24] the true reality of ourselves. As we have just discussed, all of us have a self-concept, which consists of a series of labels that we give to ourselves. These concepts that we have of ourselves are long-enduring and highly resistant to change.

"Do you think yours is really necessary?"

It is often difficult for us to experience emotions and feelings that are not consistent with that self-concept. One of the goals of the fifth step of meditation is to allow ourselves to experience ourselves without any labels, and to tune into all of our emotions, experiences, sensations. In doing so, we open ourselves to the possibility of rich and rewarding *internal experiences* and we increase the chance of attaining what are called *"peak" and "mystical" experiences.*

Openness to Internal Experiences. Zen and *yoga* Masters are able to hear their internal signals clearly. They have removed the normal kinds of "internal chatter" that go on inside all of us most of the time; thus other signals that are generally drowned out may come into awareness. This has important implications for us in learning about ourselves and our bodies—for example, becoming aware of times when we are tense; when we are hungry, when we need to tune in to our bodies and our minds.

If we go back to the Charlie Brown cartoon, we realize that meditation has the effect of turning down our "radios," so that we can tune in to what is happening within us. This tuning in is crucial in the maintenance of physical and emotional health, for it allows us to see when our internal engines need to be cared for.

Openness to Peak and Mystical Experiences. During an altered state of consciousness, the individual is simultaneously acutely aware of and unable to describe what he or she is feeling.[25] Arthur Deikman has suggested that the mystic experience is brought about by what he calls the "deautomatization" of our ordinary ways of perceiving.[26] Deautomization refers to the *process by which our perception of reality loses its automatic, reflex quality.* This involves opening ourselves to experiences that cannot be described with words, and to which we are not attuned in our daily routines.

An exercise will show how difficult it is to use words to describe even the simplest experience. Let me ask you to eat (or imagine eating) a banana. Now, with words, try to describe what it tastes like to someone who has never before eaten a banana.

The Eastern tradition suggests that words, labels, *cannot take the place of even the most ordinary experiences;* evaluation and analysis can even make experiences less enjoyable. For example, as long as we are *analyzing* the taste and texture of a banana, we are not giving ourselves the opportunity to relax, let go, and *enjoy* the banana. According to Buddha, in order to become free, in order to understand our true self, we need to develop an *eighth sense* (see the footnote in the preceding section.) This eighth sense allows us to realize the illusory nature of the labels and intellectual analyses of the sixth sense and the concept of "I" of the seventh sense.

When we achieve *satori*, or enlightenment, we gain the wisdom (*prajna*) to hear our true self, "the sound of the heart." In Chinese the word "mind" or "self-nature" is composed of two characters:

The top part of character means "sound" (literally, the sun rising). The bottom character stands for "heart." When we can hear the sun rising in our heart, we will be free. We will be able to join Siddhartha in hearing the bird in our breast sing—and following it.

Meditation Instructions

It should be clear from our preceding discussion that the effects of meditation have to be experienced, they can't just be talked about. When Shinru Suzuki was asked to give a talk on meditation at Stanford, he illustrated this point effectively. He told the audience that in Zen meditation it is necessary to cross your legs in the lotus position, put your hands over your belly (*mudra* position), keep your shoulders straight but not erect, your ears in line with the shoulders, and your eyes half-closed, looking about three feet ahead. He then proceeded to take the meditation posture.

An hour later he got up and left.

As a first step in experiencing some of the concepts we've been discussing, you may wish to follow the instructions below describing Zen breath meditation.

There are four aspects of meditating: choosing a setting, choosing a position, the process of meditation, and the end of the meditation session. (At the end of the chapter is a list of books for those interested in pursuing the practice further.)

1. *Choosing a Setting.* It is best to pick a quiet room, where there will be few distractions. Let the other members in your house know that you would like a few moments to yourself, and ask them to please pick up the phone for you. You may also want to meditate outside in one of your special places in nature. The natural setting provides a way of further reducing the distractions of our daily routine.

2. *Choosing a Position.* Find a comfortable position—probably in a chair, or on a pillow on the floor. Loosen your clothing. Unbuckle your belt if you'd like, take your shoes off, and just let yourself relax. It's best not to lie down because in meditation you don't want to go to sleep; you want to be relaxed but alert. Just settle in for a second. Let go. Feel the floor or the chair holding you up. Put your legs in a comfortable position; if you are sitting on a chair, let them dangle uncrossed over the sides of the chair. If you are sitting on the floor, you may want to sit cross-legged. Put your hands in your lap so they, too, feel comfortable. Your back should be straight, but not tightly erect. The important thing is to find a posture that is comfortable for you. Although the research suggests that the full- or half-lotus position is the posture with the least muscle tension for experienced Zen Masters, it is usually not the most comfortable for those in the West who are beginning to practice meditation.

Further, the studies of Akishige[27] and his colleagues have suggested that the attitude of the meditator is more important than the actual physical posture or the environment. Alpha brain waves occurred in subjects who had the "right" attitude, even if they weren't in the lotus position. Conversely, those who were in the lotus position, but without the right attitude, didn't evidence alpha brain waves.

3. *The Process of Meditation: Attaining the Right Attitude.* Take a deep breath. Feel yourself controlling your breathing. In meditation, *you don't want to control your breathing;* you want to let it go—very naturally, just like you've been breathing all day. The only difference between the way you've always breathed and the way you're breathing now is that now you are focusing on your breathing. Yet, at the same time, you continue to breathe naturally. Breathe through your nose, letting the air come in by extending your diaphragm. Don't draw it in, don't try to control it, rather allow it to come to you—slowly—letting your diaphragm expand naturally, letting the breath in as much as you need. Then, allow the breath to go out slowly, letting all the air out of your lungs. As you exhale slowly, count 1. Now inhale again, just letting the air come to you. Then exhale and count 2. Continue focusing on your breathing, letting the air come in, letting the air go out. Take a few minutes to focus on the breathing, letting the air come naturally, exhaling, and as you exhale counting from 1 to 10. Do this up to 10, and then begin at 1 again. Don't pay attention to anything but your breathing. If your attention begins to wander, or thoughts arise, just watch the thoughts, let go of them, and return to observing your breathing. If you get lost and lose count of breaths, just return to your breathing and the count of 1 again. If you begin to feel anxious, watch this anxiousness. If you feel pleasant, watch this feeling also, while continuing to focus on your breathing. Eventually you will be able to be quiet in both mind and body. There is no goal in meditation, there's nothing you have to do except be in the moment, and let yourself relax.

4. *The End of Meditation Sessions.* As you feel comfortable doing so, gradually begin to open your eyes. Don't rush to do anything, just sit quietly for a bit and notice what you are feeling.

You may want to stop and practice a brief ten- or fifteen-minute meditation before reading any further. Following is a checklist that may be helpful.

Checklist for Meditation

1. Find a quiet setting with few distractions.
2. Sit comfortably, with your back erect, but not taut, hands in your lap, legs in a comfortable position and with your eyes closed.
3. Breathe through your nose, letting the air come to you; don't draw it in; exhale slowly and completely, and as you exhale, count 1; inhale; exhale slowly to the count of 2—up to 10, then start at 1 again.
4. Keep your mind on the breath and numbers, and do not count absentmindedly or mechanically.
5. If your mind wanders, let thoughts rise and vanish; do not become involved with them; merely watch them, relax, let go, and continue to focus on your breathing.
6. At the end, gradually and gently open your eyes, and sit quietly for a few moments.

After you have practiced a brief meditation, notice what you are feeling. Notice what you thought about, the images you had. There is a space below in which you may want to record your feelings and thoughts. Just quickly jot down a few words or phrases to describe your reactions to your first meditation experience.

____

____

____

____

At first it may be best to practice meditation for not more than forty minutes a day. Twenty minutes in the morning and twenty minutes in the evening is usually suggested. If you are interested in practicing meditation, it might be worthwhile to take a minute or two to write down where (i.e., home, office, specific site in nature, etc.) and when would be a good place and time to do so.

First Meditation

Where: ________________ When: from ________ to ________

Second Meditation

Where: ________________ When: from ________ to ________

It may seem somewhat arbitrary and formal to put down precise times and places to practice obtaining a state of awareness that is not time-oriented. However, my personal experiences, as well as those of clients and students to whom I've taught meditation, suggest that this is important for two reasons. First, it helps us arrange our schedule, thereby *preparing* us ahead of time for the practice. Second, we often place doing something nice for ourselves, like meditation, low on our priority list. Therefore, if we aren't careful, it may become the first thing to be omitted in our busy schedules. Usually schedules that are filled with pressing external demands do not provide the time or the reinforcement for our internal demands. This planning time for ourselves suggests the interrelationship between the two modes of awareness: precise chronological time is used to structure experiences that can help us attain a non-time-oriented altered state.

Additional Formal Zen Meditation Techniques

Counting 1 While Breathing

We have just described the meditation technique of counting from 1 to 10. After you have practiced and are comfortable with that, try counting just 1 during several of your sessions. This will help you get away from goal-orientedness (reaching 10) and will focus you more in the moment.

Shikan-Taza: Just Sitting

Eventually there is a technique for advanced meditators in Soto Zen, called a *Shikan-taza. Shikan* means nothing but, or just; *ta* means to hit; and *za* means to sit. Shikan-taza is a practice in which the focus is on neither breaths nor counting, and in which the mind is intensely involved in just sitting.

The Koan

The Zen *koan* is a means of tuning out the external environment by concentrating on a covert (internal; inside the head) verbal riddle. In terms of the psychology of awareness, Ornstein has pointed out that the *koan* "is an extreme and compelling method of forcing intense concentration on one single thought."[28]

As noted previously, Zen believes that in the search for enlightenment, our worst enemy is often the intellect, which insists on discriminating between subject and object. Zen Masters of the eleventh century noticed that their monks spent increasing amounts of time in intellectual argumentation. They also observed a growing tendency toward quietism and passivity during meditation. Therefore, it was necessary to develop a technique that would create a psychological impasse challenging the supremacy of reason and at the same time keep the monks alert. The *koan* satisfied both criteria: as the reason of unreason, it used intellect to show the limits of intellect; also, it engaged the monks more actively in the process of meditation. Suzuki observed that "the koan was the natural development of Zen consciousness in the history of human strivings to reach the ultimate."[29]

During formal meditation, the individual concentrates on such *koans* as the following:

- Feel your yearning for your mother before your conception.
- What is the sound of one hand clapping?

At first we attempt to find cognitive, rational answers for the questions which koans raise. But the puzzle of a koan cannot be assembled by conventional logic. The Master repeatedly rejects each solution until the disciple realizes that enlightenment can occur only when we go beyond words and reason. When this happens, we are freed from the bondage of intellect. As Watts observed, "You can still use ideas, but you no longer take them seriously."[30]

Chanting

ku fu i shiki shiki soku
ze ku ku soku ze shiki

This is an excerpt from an Indian Buddhist *sutra,** written in Chinese pictographs, chanted with Japanese words. Literally translated it reads, "Emptiness is not different from form. Form is the emptiness, emptiness is the form." Form, which involves the normal, automatic way of labeling and looking at the world, is empty. Emptiness and clarity, the nature of the mirror, are full of form and meaning. Because of its emptiness, a mirror can accept everything into itself. Its emptiness gives it the form in which to accept the world.

However, the significance of the chant is not found in the meaning of the words, but in the motion of the sounds. The above chant, called the Heart Sutra, is composed of sonorous consonants: s, z, f, k; and many vowels.[31] The meaning comes from our ability to concentrate on the sound and motion of these vowels and consonants. Again, what is important is the attitude—the capacity to give the total attention to the repetition of sound on sound. Other chants, such as the two-syllable *om*, can also be used. Chanting, like the *koan*, should completely fill the individual's mind, so that there is no room for extraneous stimuli. As a student noted about chanting:

> It was as though the essence of my head circled from deep inside and out of my mouth, first ballooning up to block out everything else, and so it became the chant.

Opening-up and Concentrative Meditation

The formal Zen meditation techniques discussed above may be classified into two types: *opening-up meditation* and *concentrative meditation.* We discussed opening-up meditation earlier, and

*A *sutra* is a discourse of the Buddha.

defined it as meditation in which the individual remains open to all stimuli in the external and internal environment. It will be helpful at this point to define concentrative meditation and then compare the two types.

Concentrative Meditation

There are almost as many different types of concentrative meditation as there are spiritual disciplines: e.g., the Taoist focuses on the abdomen; the Zen follower focuses on the koan; the Christian focuses on the cross; the Sufi focuses on the dervish call. However, there are certain elements which all types of concentrative meditation have in common. In all types of concentrative meditation, there is a *restriction of awareness by focusing attention on a single object.* Other stimuli in the environment are ignored, and complete attention is focused on the stimulus labeled "object of meditation." During the act of meditation, the object is to be perceived in a nonanalytic manner. For example, in his instructions to people focusing on a blue vase, Deikman stated:

> By concentration I do not mean analyzing the different parts of the vase, or thinking a series of thoughts about the vase, or associating ideas to the vase, but rather, trying to see the vase as it exists in itself, without any connections to other things. Exclude all other feelings or sounds or body sensations. Do not let them distract you but keep them out so that you can concentrate all your attention, all your awareness on the vase itself. Let the perception of the vase fill your entire mind.[32]

The "object" of meditation can be located in either the external or internal environment. Examples of objects in the external environment include the abdomen (Taoism), the cross (Christianity), or a vase. The meditator can also focus on internal stimuli, such as visual images: the third eye, the vault of the skull (e.g., as done by Raj yogis); or internally generated sounds, such as a mantra; a sutra; a prayer; a sentence (e.g., the Zen koan).

The element in common in all these types of concentrative meditation is the restriction of awareness to a single object, and the focus of awareness on that object over a long period of time. Here are some examples of concentrative meditation:

Overt, External Environment

Auditory	*Visual*	*Tactile*
verbal —	mandala	touching thumb to each
sufi dervish call	cross	of four fingers
mantra	vase	
	abdomen	

Internal Environment

Auditory	*Visual*	*Tactile*
verbal —	third eye	heart beat
mantra	vault of skull	breathing
koan	symbol of guru (image)	

The focusing in concentrative meditation is different from that of ordinary awareness; meditative focus involves pinpointed awareness without evaluation, and without analysis. Further, it involves focusing so intensely that other stimuli in the environment are excluded.

Ornstein has suggested that concentrative meditation is like taking a vacation, leaving a situation, turning off one's routine way of dealing with the external world for a period, later to return (after meditation) to find the world fresh and different. In the philosophy of Zen, concentrative meditation helps the person see the flower the five-hundredth time the same as he saw it the first time.

A Comparison. The difference between concentrative and opening-up meditation is best explained by comparing the results of two experiments: one involving Raj yogis practicing concentrative meditation and the other, the Kasamatsu and Hirai experiment involving Zen monks practicing opening-up meditation that we discussed earlier in "The Altered State" under "Improved Relationship with Nature."

Raj yogis practiced concentrative meditation by "pinpointing consciousness" on the back of their skulls, a third eye, or the tip of the nose. During meditation, their eyes were closed. The experimenters administered the following external stimuli to the yogis: photic (strong light); auditory (loud banging noise); thermal (touching with a hot glass tube); and vibration (tuning fork). "None of these stimuli produced any blockage of alpha rhythm when the yogis were in meditation."[33] When the yogis' hands were immersed in cold water (4° centigrade) for 45 to 55 minutes, there was persistent alpha activity both before and during the period in which their hands were immersed. In other words, the yogis did not see, hear, or feel the stimuli presented to them.

The Zen subjects of Kasamatsu and Hirai's study meditated with their eyes open. As with the Raj yogis, soon after the onset of meditation (50 seconds), alpha waves were recorded in all brain regions: frontal, central, parietal, and occipital. The longer the monk had been in training, the more pronounced the changes in his alpha activity. However, when a click sound was made, there was alpha blockage of 2 to 3 seconds. This click sound was repeated twenty times, and each time there was an alpha blocking for 2 to 3 seconds, followed by a resumption of alpha waves. This presents a marked contrast to the results of the experiment with the Raj yogis, whose alpha waves showed no blockage, even though very strong stimuli were presented.

It can be seen from the two studies that during concentrative meditation there is an effort made to reduce awareness of the environment to one specific object; in opening-up meditation, a deliberate attempt is made to remain aware of all aspects of the internal and external environment. The difference lies in tuning out within meditation in the former and opening up within meditation in the latter. Theoretically, however, both types of meditation have the same goal: to remove the automatism and selectivity of ordinary awareness.

In concentrative meditation, the individual shuts off external stimuli so that when he returns to them, he once again sees them afresh. In opening-up meditation, an attempt is made to be aware of the environment, both during and after meditation. Thus, although the techniques are different, the consequences after the person has finished meditating should be the same.

There may be some confusion about whether Zen breath meditation should be referred to as a concentrative or opening-up meditation. For example, to repeat Rahula's instructions for Zen meditation:

> Let your mind watch and observe your breathing in and out . . . forget all other things: your surroundings, your environment; do

> not raise your eyes and look at anything so that eventually you can be fully conscious of your breathing . . . when you will not even hear sounds nearby, when no external world exists for you . . . you are so fully concentrating on your breathing.[34]

However, the sitting meditation (*Zazen*) practiced by the Zen monks in Kasamatsu and Hirai's study would not fit into Rahula's paradigm. Nor would Rahula's concept of breath meditation fit into Watts' view of Zen meditation as "watching everything that is happening, including your own thoughts and your breathing.[35] In these last two examples, it is apparent that Zen breath meditation is being conceptualized and practiced as an "opening-up meditation" in which the meditator not only sees each breath afresh but also maintains receptivity to environmental stimuli (e.g., the clicks in Kasamatsu and Hirai's study).

The apparent confusion between the Rahula paradigm of concentrative Zen meditation and Watts' and Kasamatsu-Hirai's definitions of "opening-up" Zen meditation can be clarified by the analysis of Zen meditation in the diagram below.[36] At first, the beginning meditator has to learn to shut out external stimuli in order to maintain focus on his/her breathing (Steps 1 and 2;

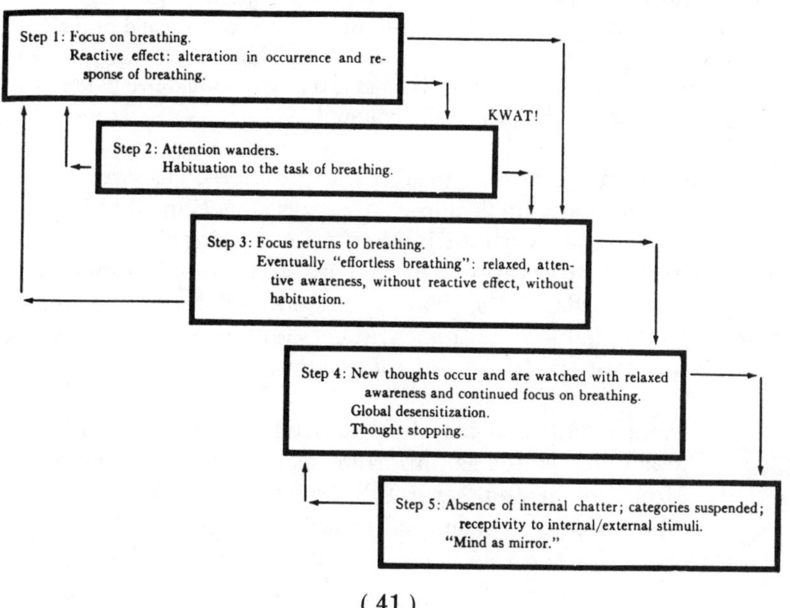

compare with Rahula). However, once he/she has learned to focus on his/her breathing (Step 3), he/she is then able to open up to *both* internal and external stimuli (Steps 4, 5; compare with Watts and Kasamatsu and Hirai). Zen meditation on breath *begins* as concentrative meditation (Steps 1 and 2) and *ends* as opening-up meditation (Steps 4 and 5). Thus, while Zen breath meditation includes concentrative meditation, its emphasis is different.

Informal Meditation

Thus far we have talked only of *formal* meditation: that is, meditation practiced at specific times during the day. Meditation may also be practiced informally throughout the day.

Informal meditation requires only that one be conscious of everything one does, to attend very closely to one's everyday actions:

> Be aware and mindful of whatever you do, physically or verbally, during the daily routine of your work in your life. Whether you walk, stand, sit, lie down, or sleep, whether you stretch or bend your legs, whether you look around, whether you put your clothes on, whether you talk or keep silent, whether you eat or drink, whether you answer the calls of nature—in these and other activities you should be fully aware and mindful of the act performed at the moment, that is to say, that you should live in the present moment, in the present action.[37]

Thus, in informal meditation, also referred to as *mindfulness meditation*, the individual merely observes all actions that he does throughout the day, without judging or evaluating. This is similar to the detached observation effected by step four of formal meditation. In the words of Alan Watts: "Listen. Listen to the sound of your own complaint when the world gets you down, when you are angry, when you are filling out income tax forms. Above all, just listen."[38]

Informal meditation may be practiced at any time and in any place. The activity is not as important as the way we observe that activity. However, in Zen, several different types of specific activities may be used as a means of ensuring proper practice of informal meditation. Two such activities are the *tea ceremony* and the *mondo.*

The Tea Ceremony

Historically, the tea ceremony was used by *samurai* warriors as a refuge from the constant strain of battle. The ceremony took place in a quiet room, apart from the outside world, to help remove the adverse stimuli of the battleground. Literally and symbolically, the warriors removed their weapons and washed themselves before entering the tea house.

Although the location of the tea house was physically different from that of the battlefield, to further assist the samurai in eliminating mental images of war, the ceremony itself was highly disciplined and ritualized. For example, the act of sipping tea was prescribed to the last detail, and did not vary from day to day. Ritualized actions induced a state of intense involvement in the moment to the exclusion of all distractions of the outside world. A contemporary reflection of this experience is Paul Reps' poem:

drinking
a bowl of green tea
I stopped the war[39]

By removing the images of the battlefield, the warrior was able to open each of his five senses to the ongoing moment: he heard the whistle of the tea kettle, smelled the incense, tasted the slightly bitter tea, and rested his eyes on the scrolls, flower arrangements, and surrounding garden. The tea garden was designed to contribute to this feeling of expansiveness and openness. The small twigs were beautiful as small twigs, and at the same time were the embodiment of mighty trees. Hillocks had meaning both as mounds of dirt and as lofty mountains. The sand, raked to give the appearance of water, was both a still lake and a vast ocean.

The entire ceremony created a feeling of the infinite by means of the finite, a feeling of eternity in the midst of time: a quiet moment of timelessness at once apart from and part of the everyday world.

In Japan, tea is a way of life, an embodiment of the Zen philosophy: a belief in the uniqueness and beauty of the moment. Its ritual and discipline are means for an individual to center and "return to the starting point."

Tea Ceremony Instructions. Although few of us will want or be able to gather together all thirty-four instruments for the tea ceremony, let me suggest that you observe yourself informally the next time you drink a hot beverage. See how closely you can stay in the moment, investing attention in the task at hand. At first, it may help to give yourself specific instructions, such as: "Let's put aside the cares of today for a while. This is a time for quiet." It may also help to pick a quiet place in the house, and a quiet time, when there will be a minimum of distractions. Tell yourself to open all your senses to what is going on—hear the whistling of the kettle, note the smell of the tea, observe your immediate surroundings.

The Mondo

Mondos are a series of questions and answers which, in their intent, are very similar to the *koan.* Because mondos appear to be ridiculous exchanges between Master and monk, they have the effect of removing the individual from the confines of conventional, logical, intellectual constructs. However, *mondos* are not used in the formal posture; instead they are the result of spontaneous interaction between Master and pupil. Whereas the *koan* is a technique of formal meditation, the *mondo* embodies the essence of informal meditation. Some examples follow:[40]

Joshu, when asked about Zen, said, "Have you had your breakfast?"

Monk: Yes.
Joshu: Then go wash your dishes.

Pupil: How can I escape the bondage of birth and death?
Master: Where are you?

A monk came to Shuzan and asked him to play a tune on a stringless harp. The Master was quiet for some while, then said, "Do you hear it?"

Monk: No, I do not hear it.
Master: Why did you not ask me to play louder?

Pupil: Whenever appeal is made to words, Master, there is a taint. What is the truth of the highest order?

Master: Whenever appeal is made to words, there is a taint.

Pupil: Where is the one solitary road to being oneself?
Master: Why trouble yourself to ask about it?

Pupil: Before my parents gave birth to me, where was my nose?
Master: When you are already born of your parents, where are you?

When Ungan was making tea, Dago asked, "To whom are you serving tea?"
Ungan: There is one who wants it.
Dago: Why don't you make him serve himself?
Ungan: Fortunately, I am here.

These questions and answers are teachings that attempt to point directly to the spirit of Zen. Since in Zen belief enlightenment does not come through rational discourse, but rather through direct action, "whenever appeal is made to words, there is a taint." Direct action takes place in everyday activities: eating breakfast, or washing dishes. Metaphysical speculation is seen as worthless. As Buddha wrote in his first sermon:

> *[Regarding] Questions which tend not to edification:* The religious life does not depend on the dogma that the world is eternal, or not eternal, or whether the saint exists after death or does not exist after death. For . . . there still remain birth, old age, death, sorrow, lamentation, misery, grief, and despair.[41]

In other words, in Zen the emphasis is not on breaking the bondage of birth and death; rather it is on "where you are now." The moment is all that is important, and in this moment, time has no relevance; neither does birth or death. In this timeless moment, subject-object dichotomies disappear. When Ungan serves himself the tea, he is both subject and object. They are one. And this one is seen, upon awakening, to be egoless. There is no path for discovering the self, for it is already within. This egoless, empty nature, however, is simultaneously rich and full: emptiness is fullness, and the stringless harp, like one hand clapping, makes sound.

Mondo Instructions. Although *mondo* has a certain logic of its own, its primary purpose is to demonstrate to us the futility of our everyday Western logic. Try pasting an appropriate *mondo* where you can read it frequently: on the bathroom mirror, above your office desk, to a clock. Note how you feel when you read it. What impact does it have when you are stuck on a business problem? Worrying about groceries? Arguing with your spouse? Hopefully, as with other kinds of informal meditation, the *mondo* will give you a perspective, a centered feeling from which to continue your everyday actions.

Additional Zen Techniques

In Zen, according to D. T. Suzuki, every person has the potential to become an "artist" of life.[42] Meditation is one means of getting in touch with this creative potential which all of us have. There are two additional Zen techniques associated with meditation which I would like to describe here—*sumi-e* and *haiku.* These techniques illustrate ways all of us can further express the creative potential within us.

Sumi-e

Sumi-e is brush-stroke painting. Initially, the artist makes the paint by stroking hard charcoal in a circular motion on a piece of stone. This process is a type of concentrative meditation in which the artist focuses on a repetitive motion over a period of time. This concentrative meditation empties his mind so that subsequently he is able to see afresh the environment he is going to paint. Then, through an informal opening-up meditation, the artist tries to penetrate, to see the spirit of the environment he is about to paint. When he executes the painting, his strokes are quick, yet deliberate, embodying both perfect spontaneity and perfect self-control.

The painting does not attempt accurate representation, but rather to capture the moving spirit, for nothing is static except that which is dead. *Sumi-e* therefore involves the unexpected. In looking at a picture of the Chinese or Japanese masters, when one expects a line, it isn't there. Whiteness (emptiness) becomes a lake, or a waterfall.

If the artist is truly like a mirror when he is painting, then the picture will reflect his spirit as well as the spirit of the object. If he allows logic or reflection to come between the brush and the paper, the whole work is spoiled. Suzuki has compared Zen and *Sumi-e* to Western philosophy and oil painting. In oil painting, there is layer upon layer of paint, reflective construction, as in Western philosophy. In Zen, "life is a *sumi-e* painting, which must be executed once for all time, without hesitation, without intellectualization. In this painting, all corrections show when the ink dries; Zen seeks to show the fleeting, unrepeatable, ungraspable character of life."[43] No corrections, erasures, or improvements are allowed: as in life, actions are irrevocable.

Sumi-e Instructions. There are several good books for instruction in *sumi-e.* The basic equipment you need is the brush, a stone, and the chalk, as well as some paper. Regarding technique, there are two schools of thought on how to hold the brush: one says you absolutely do not hold the brush like a pencil, but rather hold it upright. The second school says to hold it exactly like a pencil. Sound like a Zen koan? Let's interpret these contradictory instructions as giving us permission to hold the brush exactly as we wish. Our goal is a free-flowing stroke that allows us to catch a glimpse of the spirit of nature . . . of our spirit.

The illustrations on the following pages are paintings done by Johanna, two of my students, and myself.

Haiku

Bradford Smith[44] has conceptualized *haiku* as a form of meditation. As in *sumi-e*, the poet opens all his senses to the surrounding environment. He tries to be aware of everything, to accept all inputs without discrimination or differentiation.

In its form, the haiku is a simple, concise style of poetry, consisting of only seventeen syllables, grouped in a 5-7-5 pattern.* Its subject matter is generally derived from nature. In its tone, it is characterized by *sabi-wabi* (the spirit of eternal loneliness). As Suzuki writes, "A certain loneliness engendered by traveling leads

*These Haiku poems are not in the 5-7-5 pattern because they have been translated into English.

one to reflect upon the meaning of life, for life is, after all, a traveling from one unknown to another."[45] Let me repeat the example we have already given from Basho:

Over the darkened sea
Only the shrill voice of a flying duck
Is visible
In soft white

In addition to illustrating an intermingling of senses, this poem also illustrates a quality of egolessness. Basho never says "I." We never see him, yet he is everywhere in the poem. Although he is concealed by the dark night, we hear him, feel him, see him, "in soft white," within us.

The following haiku, again by Basho, also shares this absence of "I":

Breaking the silence
Of an ancient pond
A frog jumped into the water—
A deep resonance [46]

Where is Basho? On the surface this poem is an objective description of observable reality: a pond and a frog that sends vibrations rippling through the pond. But the pond is also a mirror held up to internally reflect the author's mind. The resonance in the ancient pond is Basho writing the poem.

In meditation, the goal is to become empty, like a mirror. To write poetry, the artist must also be like a mirror, so that "he and the object become one. If he and the object are separate, then his poetry is not true poetry, but subjective counterfeit."[47] The mirror accurately reflects and is not associated with such subjective counterfeits as "I" or ego. To meditate (action in inaction) is to write a poem (inaction in action). Creativity is an attitude, and can exist even when nothing new is created in the world of things. The person of enlightenment creates a poem by watching a sunset, even though he or she writes no words and makes no movement.*

*It may be important to note the way a literary poem seems to integrate the two brain hemispheres: the open receptivity to nature (right) with the poetic rendering of that receptivity in words (left). For further discus-

Haiku Instructions. When we write haiku we are not trying to get the exact 5-7-5 syllables but merely to see poetry as an expression of ourself; another way of interacting and relating with nature and the environment. In workshops I have people arise before dawn and go to a favorite natural spot. I instruct them to relax, enjoy, and *be* in that spot. They may just want to breathe in nature, or they may want to jot down a few lines. Let me ask you to do the same. Find a place that you particularly like in nature, whether it be by the ocean or a lake, some trees, a stream, or a particular tree or a small garden, whatever is important to you. Practice meditation there and if you'd like to write a few lines about the experience, either about meditation or about the setting in which you are, do so. Don't be worried about trying to write a poem. Here are some of the poems my students have written for workshops and classes,[48] as well as some by myself (D.) and my wife (J.).[49]

On the stark limbs
of a winter tree:
a bluebird eating
an orange persimmon
—*D.*

Many haiku poems
really are no more profound
than a blade of grass

Whiteness of birch
in a crystal wind
disturbing the silver
fragility of dusk
—*J.*

Noiselessly, the bicycle's wheel
runs over the bird's shadow
—*D.*

Blue sky, cloud wisps
in calm misty water

---

sion of this integration, see the section in the Epilogue on the care and maintenance of the mind.

The tree limb's shadows
sway on the dirt, revealing
the wind's quiet preserve
—*D.*

The puddle mirrors
rain drops dissolving in the
image they contain
—*J.*

A bubble rising
from below the surface
ripples, ripples . . .
calms

Death's wing
makes life's moment
into a soaring flight
of intensity
—*D.*

On the underside of opaque leaves
the sun reveals tiny veins
facing earthward
—*D.*

Another form of poetry called *linked verse* is a Chinese poetry form in which each stanza adds to the one preceding. You may wish to practice writing a linked verse poem with a friend—a rewarding shared experience.

Frozen snow encloses the night
—*D.*

The white candle wax cries
as the spiraling red flame
causes the wick to decay into ashes
—*J.*

The hardened remains of a
cold silent puddle lie unseen
—*D.*

SUMMARY

When we first observe ourselves or our behavior, an awkwardness occurs. This awkwardness, which may range from confusion to pain, is one of the reasons we seem to have an initial reluctance to tune in to ourselves. In the first step of meditation, there is a similar self-conscious awkwardness. However, by continuing to practice meditation, we soon learn to overcome this awkwardness. With further practice we learn to maintain an effortless breathing, to be calm when faced with fears and concerns, and eventually to have an empty mind. This empty mind, in which there is no internal chatter, is a different state of consciousness than our ordinary awareness, and has several advantages. It provides us with an openness and receptivity to the world of nature, to other people, and to our own internal world.

Several different meditative techniques were discussed, and a comparison was made between concentrative and opening-up techniques. Informal meditation was also discussed, including the tea ceremony and the *mondo.*

Finally, the techniques of *sumi-e* and *haiku* were illustrated so that we could learn to relate to and express ourselves creatively through writing or painting, as well as through our breathing.

All these techniques involve a different mode of awareness than we are used to; and provide us with a certain type of knowledge about ourselves and the world around us. This new mode of awareness can help us, like Siddhartha, clearly hear the bird in our breast sing.

2
Behavioral Self-management & the West: The Grand Conditioner

> The world is filled with two types of people: those who think there are two types of people, and those who don't.
>
> — Anonymous

If meditation, with the accompanying altered state, has so many advantages, as we have shown in Chapter 1, why do we bother with ordinary awareness? Certainly ordinary awareness seems to be considered inferior by many, who refer to it as a waking sleep, a drunken awareness; they speak of the altered state as cosmic consciousness, the higher state.

The debate over which state of awareness is *really* the higher one goes back at least to fourth-century China. Lao-tse was the principal advocate of what may be referred to as *Taoism*, or a holistic view of the world. Lao-tse proclaimed that "names imply differentiation and loss of the original state of Tao."[1] His disciple Chuang Tzu noted: "Banish wisdom, discard knowledge, and people shall profit a hundredfold."[2]

Lao-tse suggested that we are not free as long as we are bound by labels and words, as long as we seek to understand cause and effect. The seasons come and go, whether or not we understand them. The free person is one who has learned to let go of analysis, yield, and follow the way of water. As we saw in Chapter 1, this holistic view of Lao-tse is evidenced and experienced in the fifth step of meditation.

Confucius, on the other hand, believed that our problems stem from the fact that we don't have *accurate* enough names and labels. In order to restore order and harmony to living, he felt we needed more and better rules of conduct. In a sense, the contemporary content of Confucius' viewpoint may be seen in the behavioral literature, which emphasizes *precise labeling of experience* and a *sequential analysis of causality.*

Let us now look more closely at some of the components of ordinary awareness to better understand its advantages.

THE IMPORTANCE OF ORDINARY AWARENESS

Its Components and Advantages

One important component of ordinary awareness involves *naming and labeling objects* in our environment: tree, house, plant. This aspect of ordinary awareness also involves differentiating between objects (red, yellow, large, small) and between people (I/you; mine/yours). There are several advantages to this type of awareness. First and foremost, there is a *survival value* involved in assigning labels. Without the ability to sort items by means of conceptual labels (information processing), it would be impossible for the individual to deal with the variety and complexity of stimuli that surround him.[3] Second, categories, by allowing events to be placed into fewer and simpler units, make for *better memory storage*—they allow us to place events within the limited scope of memory.[4]

Further, putting a label on experiences—particularly those that are frightening or confusing—gives a type of *reassurance* by helping remove the ambiguity and allowing us to feel more in control:

In an uncertain hour,
a wise man acknowledges uncertainty.

In this regard, Dollard and Miller have noted the importance of sorting and labeling for the patient: "To contain the panicking spread of anxiety, one must be able to identify and put a comprehensive label upon one's feelings—the better to treat them again; the better to learn from experiences."[5]

Labeling others also allows us to *feel in control* and to feel we can *predict other people's behavior.* Mischel has noted that categorization and habituation give a perceived consistency which increases our feelings that we can predict other people and ourselves, thus making our world seem less chaotic. For this reason, he suggests that the construction of stereotypes about other people by assigning their diverse behaviors into a few broader categories may be highly adaptive.[6] In medical diagnosis, it is felt that if we can label a disease, we can then know better how to cure it. Labeling helps us to *discriminate between objects*—to know which foods are edible, and which are poisonous, for example. As noted in Chapter 1, research suggests that verbal analytic style may be the mode of the left brain hemisphere. It is efficient for *dealing with technological society* and for *making scientific achievements*—these depend heavily on linear analytic methods and logical approaches proceeding piecemeal and step by step.

Finally, there is another important aspect of ordinary awareness, with its labeling and sequential analysis of events. Social learning theorists believe that *a crucial first step in developing personal freedom involves gaining an intimate and precise awareness of the internal and external environments and realizing the strong influence these environments have on our behavior.** These environments include the social (i.e., interpersonal relationships), the physical, and the internal (i.e., what we say to ourselves, physiological cues). Let us look at each of them to understand better how they might influence our behavior.

The Power of the Environment

Social Environment

One of the most dramatic research studies illustrating the effect of the social environment (e.g., peer pressure) on our behavior was done by S. E. Asch.[7] Asch had an unsuspecting subject sit in a room with seven confederates whom he had previously instructed. The task given to the eight people was to answer a simple perceptual problem (e.g., to determine which among four lines was longest), as illustrated.

*Bandura says that personal freedom involves learning skills and competencies that can offer options for alternative actions (*Social Learning Theory*, Englewood Cliffs, N.J.: Prentice-Hall, 1977). Our world view is deterministic only in that there is a "production of effects by events, rather than in the doctrinal sense that the future is determined by the past" ("The Self-system in Reciprocal Determinism," *American Psychologist*, in press).

Each of the seven confederates was instructed to respond at certain times with wrong and unanimous judgments (e.g., to choose line number 2 as the longest line). Contrary to what we might predict, this situation caused a great deal of difficulty for nearly all the unsuspecting subjects. Many of them (33 percent) literally were not able to believe their own eyes and "went along with the crowd," agreeing that line number 2 was the longest. This occurred even though line 3 was longer than the other lines.

To illustrate this influence of others on our behavior, let me ask you to imagine that you have just entered a restaurant and are seated alone eating a meal. You are feeling comfortable and relaxed, ready to enjoy a nice meal alone. Someone you don't know comes in and sits down at the table directly across from you. The person is seated facing you. How do you feel? Where do you put your gaze? Do you look at a newspaper? Do you look straight at the person? Do you avoid looking at the person? All of a sudden, you are faced with a variety of decisions you didn't have before. Most of us would feel somewhat uncomfortable initially. This "self-conscious stumbling effect" suggests in a small way the influence other people can have on our behavior.

Many of us can probably think of several other examples illustrating situations in which we were influenced by those around us: e.g., we tried to exaggerate our accomplishments so as to win more approval; or we went along with social convention so as not to appear different; or maybe we used social pressure or joined a group to achieve a desirable but difficult goal. (For examples of self-observation of external cues in the social environment, see the two cartoons at the top of the next page.)

Social learning theorists believe that regardless of whether we realize it or not, the social environment influences our behavior. Therefore, one aspect of developing personal freedom is to learn when the social environment is influencing us for our benefit and when it is influencing us to our detriment.

"I WAS HAVING A NICE QUIET EVENING AT HOME AND I COULDN'T UNDERSTAND IT········THEN I REALIZED I WAS IN THE WRONG HOME."

4-25

HERMAN

"That's just his way of saying he wants you to stay!"

The Now Society

No goddam building ever dehumanized me!

Physical Environment

Similarly, regardless of whether or not we are aware of it, our behavior may be influenced by the physical environment (see the cartoon at the bottom of page 60 for an example of self-observation of external cues in the physical environment). The research of Robert Sommer and that of Adams and Biddle has shown that the physical environment has a significant effect on our behavior[8]; for example, the arrangement of seats in a classroom plays a role in determining which students participate in discussions and which do not, regardless of their actual ability. The grey shaded area accounted for virtually all responses from the students.

THE "ACTION" ZONE

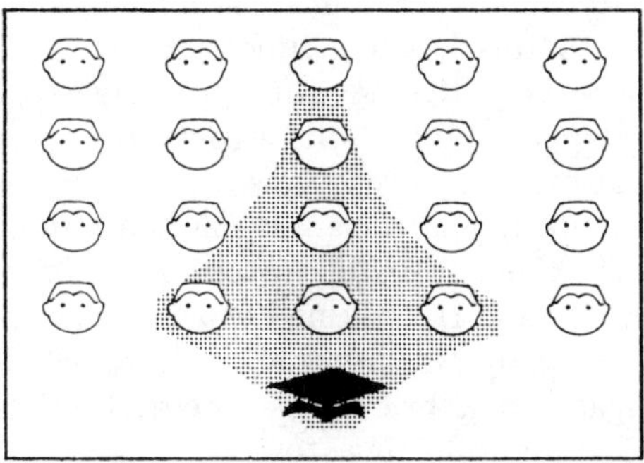

FRONT

Think about ways in which *your* physical environment has affected you. What about that quart of ice cream in the freezer? Did that influence your after-dinner snacking? When you walk into a room, how does the furniture arrangement affect where you sit, and, in turn, to whom you talk? There are many ways in which the external environment affects what we do and how we think. In the space below, jot down a few examples of the ways your environment influences you:

____

____

____

Internal Environment

Our internal environment consists of two things: (1) physiological cues from our bodies and (2) internal thoughts and images in our minds.

Research on self-perception suggests that it is often difficult to interpret the physiological cues that our body gives,[9] and that how we interpret the cues will have a strong influence on our behavior.[10] The obese person, for example, often interprets cues of anxiety and tension as signs of hunger. There is evidence that we may interpret our internal cues based on environmental stimuli. For example, when we are surrounded by angry people, and are unsure of the cause of our physiological arousal, we tend to describe what we are feeling as anger; when we are around happy people we tend to call our internal sensations joy.[11]

In addition to this labeling function (attribution of causality), our mental or cognitive environment (the kinds of things we say to ourselves—our hopes, our expectations, our hurts, our concerns) also influences our actions and feelings in other ways. This may be manifested in such ways as the intensity of our depression, our effectiveness in approaching other people, or the amount of creativity and risk-taking behavior we engage in.

To show one way the internal environment affects us, I'd like you to engage in a brief experiment. Look at the picture below and imagine the following story.

> I just obtained these pretzels from a delightful health food store in town. It's a clean, fresh place with a beautiful flower garden and a brick patio overhung by hanging baskets. There's a big black old stove in the store and the woman who serves you is a motherly type, clean and smiling. She has just baked the pretzels and they have come piping hot out of the oven. Think about how very warm and salty and crisp they are. Imagine how they would taste. Note what you are feeling. Note what you would like to do.

Now stop that imaginary scene. Look again at the picture. This time let me tell you what actually happened.

> I was at the beach recently and I found some twigs on the ground. There were bugs on them and some birds had left their droppings on them. I washed them off in salt water and saw that they were decayed, with bugs and ants crawling through them. Note again your feelings toward the picture and what you feel like doing.

Most people observe that when they have made positive statements to themselves about the picture ("How good those pretzels look!") they want to approach the pretzels and maybe eat one. Similarly, if they don't think they look very appetizing, they want to avoid them. Thus the kinds of things that we say to ourselves, our "internal environments," affect our behavior. This is one reason why it is important to get in touch with these internal self-statements.

Another example of this influence is illustrated in the following anecdote. A patient I was seeing became terrified every time he went to a party or social gathering. When we began to explore this problem, we discovered that every time he attended a party, he was having thoughts such as, "No one knows me here," "No one really cares that I'm here," "I can't really make good conversation." He would then retreat to a corner of the room, thus fulfilling his own fears about himself. I had him observe his thoughts by teaching him to first discriminate and label the negative statements and then note on a sheet when and where the thought occurred (that is, who was present, where he was), and how he responded to it.

After we had gathered this information, I pointed out that he didn't have to say those negative things to himself. They were merely statements that he had learned to make in the past, but that he didn't need to continue to make. We worked on substituting other kinds of positive self-statements, such as, "Although I don't know anybody, I have something to offer these people," and "It would be fun to meet and talk to some new people." When he began to say these things, it was like approaching the pretzels. He mingled at parties, made small talk, and felt much more comfortable and sure of himself. This clinical case illustrates the importance of tuning in to our thoughts. The labeling that occurs, often nonconsciously, is important and affects the way we live our day-to-day lives. Social learning theorists believe that it is important when we are self-observing to tune in in a precise way to our internal environment: our thoughts, feelings, body reactions, and how they affect our behavior.

Take a moment, stop, and notice what internal cues you are experiencing right at this very moment:

____

____

____

____

BEHAVIORAL SELF-OBSERVATION

The Role of Precise Awareness

Now we can see that research bears out the idea that we are strongly influenced—our behavior is determined—by our social, physical, and internal environments. This realization is the first step in learning to *develop personal freedom.* When B. F. Skinner in *Beyond Freedom and Dignity* talks of going "beyond freedom," he means that as long as we live with the illusion that we have freedom, we may fail to develop an awareness of the things that in fact are influencing our lives, and thus we may never learn to attain true freedom. As Nasudrin, the wise fool in many Sufi stories, knew, our perception of reality, though it may appear natural, is merely a perception. Until we realize how we are conditioned, we will believe in an *illusion* of freedom. *Behavioral self-management strategies involve a precise method for attaining awareness about our conditioning.* This method is called *behavioral self-observation*, and it involves performing a very careful *analysis of the relationship between our actions and the environment*—how we affect those around us, and how the environment influences us.

Developing Precise Awareness

The concept of awareness in behavioral self-management strategies refers to a very analytical way of perceiving the world. It requires that an individual choose a specific problem area to work on changing. This may be anything, such as the number of negative things I say to my spouse, my quick temper, my weight, my smoking habits, etc. Once a choice is made, there are guidelines detailing the procedures for self-observation; these involve looking for the *antecedents*, the *behavior*, and the *consequences* of any particular action (the ABC's). Let's look at each of these separately, starting with a discussion of behavior.

The Behavior

Determining When the Behavior Occurs. Before we can learn about a behavior, we have to define for ourselves *when* that behavior is occurring. How do we determine the onset and the termination of a particular behavior? This is not too difficult with a concrete behavior, such as smoking. For example, you can record the specific number of cigarettes you smoke: the onset occurs when you light the cigarette, the termination when you put the cigarette out. But with some behaviors, especially *internal* behaviors (feelings, emotions, body sensations), it can become quite difficult to determine the onset and termination, as the following anecdote on anxiety illustrates.

A person came to me complaining of "free-flowing anxiety." When I asked him to describe what this anxiety felt like, he said that he experienced a sense of loss of control, and a tension described as an "overpowering feeling of being bounced around

"Exactly what do you mean, dear, when you say our lifestyle sucks?"

by some sort of all-powerful forces, themselves neurotic." When I asked him to tell me when these feelings occurred, he said they happened throughout the day, at no particular time, in no particular situation. At this point, therefore, our task was to tune in precisely to what this individual meant by anxiety. What were the physiological cues, such as butterflies in the stomach, or tightness in the neck? What were the self-verbalizations: that is, what were the things he said to himself when he felt anxiety? Then we tried to find out about the frequency, intensity, and duration of these feelings of anxiety. How did he know when anxiety was occurring? How intense did the butterflies have to be: was a small tingle enough to signal anxiety? Did it always have to be a knot in his stomach? These are entirely subjective questions which only the individual can determine.

Labeling the Behavior. Another closely interwoven element in observing one's own behavior is labeling and defining it—there appear to be the same internal physiological reactions to the strongest love as well as the deepest hate and anger. The difference lies in how these physiological responses are labeled. This is not always an easy task, especially with internal cues. Further, there may not always be consensus about how a certain set of behaviors should be labeled. Is this cheating, or cooperation? Who decides? This is especially important for families and couples. What a mother may feel is a positive statement may be interpreted by a child as sarcastic ("*Another* glass of water?"). Even though we may agree that a certain behavior has occurred, we may not agree on how to label that behavior.

Antecedents

In developing behavioral self-observation skills, once the behavior is defined, an individual must learn to become aware of the *antecedents* to the behavior. Returning to the case of the person with the "free-floating anxiety," it was important for him to determine under what conditions this anxiety occurred. Was it in a certain type of situation? In a certain location? Was it at a certain time of the day? What else was going on? This is done in order to pinpoint the kinds of things that may be controlling or triggering the behavior. In other words, what situations or events increase the likelihood that a particular behavior will occur?

Consequences

Finally, the individual must look at the *consequences* of the behavior he or she is observing. The consequences refer to what happens as a result of the behavior. How does the person act differently? How do others act toward that person when the behavior occurs? Does the individual stay in the same situation, or leave the situation? What does the person say to himself after the behavior has occurred?

In the above case of anxiety the person found, after two weeks of self-observation, that his "generalized anxiety" was occurring at specific times in the day (upon awakening) and before an English class. Here are some of his notes:

Anecdotal Data: Daily Self-observation of Anxious Feelings

First week: I have overpowering feelings of being bounced around by some sort of all-powerful forces.

Second week: I find the anxious periods can be timed—upon awakening and before English class in the evening. As if I'm conditioned to be anxious at those times.

It is important to note that in this case of anxiety, it was the "precise awareness" of self-observation that allowed this individual to learn the antecedents of his disturbing anxiety. This probably would not have occurred as quickly, if at all, if he had used the global, non-analytical awareness of meditation discussed in Chapter 1.

Instructions for Self-observation

Research has shown that awareness is not always automatic; sometimes it does not occur unless an individual makes the decision to develop it. Behavioral self-observation is a technique concerned with making us more aware of our own lives. The emphasis of self-observation is not on changing anything—either behavior or attitudes—but rather on trying to get to know yourself better, to see exactly what it is you might want to change or what kinds of directions you might want to grow in.

It is best to practice self-observation for about a week to ten days *without trying to make any changes* in the behavior you are observing.

On the next few pages, a brief checklist is provided for the techniques of self-observation, self-evaluation, and goal setting. Also included are a data chart on which to record any selected target behavior for one to two weeks, and the beginnings of a self-observation journal. Throughout the text, suggestions are made for areas that might be interesting for you to self-observe. In addition, you may wish to observe aspects of the vision of yourself which you form in the following goal-setting section.

Checklist for Behavioral Self-observation

1. Self-observation

   - Choose an area of concern (the *behavior*).
   - Decide what you mean by that area in some precise way, so that you will be able to observe and count, when it occurs—in other words, how will you recognize this behavior? Think about the intensity of the behavior; the onset and termination of the behavior.
   - Label the behavior.
   - Note what happens right before the behavior (*antecedents*).*

*There is usually no one single antecedent or consequence, because our lives are quite complex. However, insofar as it is possible, it provides valuable information to note as accurately as possible what you believe to be the antecedents and consequences.

Who was present? What was (were) the location(s); What time did it occur?

- Note what happens right after the behavior (the *consequences*).*

2. Self-evaluation

- After the initial week to ten days of self-observation, evaluate the results of the information.

3. Goal Setting

- Set a realistic goal for yourself (both a short-term goal and a long-term goal). Do you want to increase the behavior? Decrease the behavior? Learn a new behavior? Your goal should include a *description* of the behavior; a decision as to what *extent* you want it increased or decreased; and a decision about the *conditions.*

Self-observation Journal

In this journal, you may want to record some of the specific things you observe about the behavior you are monitoring. How did you choose this particular behavior? How did you recognize it? How did you go about determining the criteria for when it occurred? You may also want to note, especially for the first week or two, additional information you learned about the relationship between your behavior and the way it is affected by, and affects, the world around you.

____

____

____

____

The following chart may be helpful to you in recording information about the behavior, what happens right before, and what happens right after.

NAME ______________________ DATE ______________

BEHAVIOR RECORDED ___________________________

BEFORE Where? Who was present? Doing what?	AFTER How did situation change as a result?	SUN	MON	TUES	WED	THURS	FRI	SAT	TOTAL PER TIME SLOT
		7-9							
		9-11							
		11-1							
		1-3							
		3-5							
		5-7							
		7-9							
		9-11							
		11-7							
	TOTAL PER DAY								

THE ELEMENT OF CHOICE

Choosing a Vision

After precise information has been obtained through behavioral self-observation, the individual is in a position to (1) evaluate the information and (2) choose a goal. *Once we have realized what kinds of things influence our behavior, we can begin to choose how we want to live.* This choice gives us the potential to free ourselves from maladaptive habit patterns, unproductive reflex emotional responses, and injurious environmental situations.

We learn to set goals for ourselves, to choose a vision of what directions we would like to grow in and what kind of person we would like to become. These goals are set through a very careful process of decision making and self-evaluation—evaluating where we are currently and where we would like to be as we look to the future.

Self-evaluation

In order to set standards, monitor progress, and compare ourselves to the vision we are seeking to attain, self-evaluation is necessary. This self-evaluation can serve several different functions. First, it can enable us to determine the discrepancy between where we are now and where we would like to be. This can help us decide how much intervention, and of what sort, may be needed to attain our goals. Second, self-evaluation can help us monitor our progress to ensure that our present course will lead to our goal. It is through evaluation or feedback that we learn when we are making mistakes and how to improve ourselves. We may find through self-evaluation that if we continue on our present path, we are likely to miss our goals, whether the goal be an interpersonal relationship, a specific task we have set for ourselves, or larger life goals and plans. Finally, self-evaluation can help us decide whether the goal itself is still worth pursuing. Perhaps we no longer wish to pursue a goal for ethical, personal, or many other reasons.

Goal Setting

Self-evaluation, as we have seen, is intimately connected with setting specific goals. In order to make your goals clear enough so that you can ultimately determine whether or not you have achieved them, it is necessary to do three things:

1. *Describe the behavior.* What is the behavior, its antecedents and consequences.?
2. *Decide on the extent of the behavior.* How much do you want the behavior to increase or decrease? Is there a deficit, an excess, or an absence (i.e., a behavior that still needs to be learned)?
3. *Decide on the conditions of the behavior.* When and where do you want the behavior to take place?

An example will illustrate a model of goal setting. Suppose your long-term goal is to improve your relationship with your spouse. You decide that in order to do this you have to increase the number of positive remarks you make to that person. You define what you mean by "positive" (*description*) and after the first week you find that you made three positive statements to your spouse. You evaluate this baseline (taking into account feedback from your spouse!) and decide you want to increase it (*extent*) during the following week when both of you will be

together (*conditions*). Your goal is stated as follows: I want to increase my positive statements to my spouse from three a week to once per day.

At the end of the second week you can evaluate this goal. Was it reached? If it was reached, did it have a positive effect on the relationship? Do you need to further increase the goal? The precision of goal setting is crucial, for it gives us a means of evaluating our progress, and, when necessary, of changing either our strategies toward that goal or the goal itself.

Realistic Goals

It is important that our goals be realistic and attainable. For example, let's say you are a woman who is monitoring weight, and your baseline shows you weigh 139 pounds, eat 2,500 calories a day, and fourteen between-meal snacks a week (in the afternoon and before going to bed). You evaluate your weight as too high and decide you want to weigh 122 pounds. So far, so good. However, you decide you want to weigh 122 pounds within one week. Not so good. Your goals have to be realistic. You may set a *long-term* goal for yourself of 122 pounds, but your *short-term* goals should be different. For example, your short-term goals may be related to caloric intake: e.g., to cut down to 1,500 calories a day; to cut down the number of between-meal snacks from fourteen to seven per week; to change the nature of the snacks from cake to celery and carrots. A realistic goal will result in satisfaction and a sense of competence. An unrealistic goal will result in continued frustration, failure, and eventual abandonment of the hope of change.

We have talked thus far about a precise goal setting for specific kinds of changes. Obviously some goals are more important than others. Setting a goal to get a philosophy paper done by next week may be valued as less important to you than the goal of developing a close interpersonal relationship. I'd like to suggest,

however, that the process of goal setting described here seems to apply to all types of goals, from the seemingly trivial to the most high-flown dreams.

To understand the heart and mind
Of a person, what matter what he has already
Achieved, but at what he aspires to do.[12]

Each of us has within the title of an unwritten book about our wisdom and our vision. Each of us has a vision of what kind of person we would like to become. For some, the vision may involve professional advancement:

"I wonder if directors ever pretend to be cleaning ladies."

For some, the vision may involve coping more effectively with daily problems:

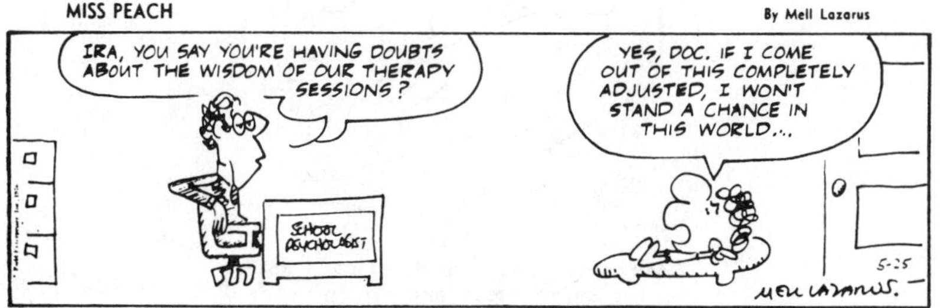

or finding a basic purpose and meaning in life:

For others, there may be a fear of reaching the vision and thereby having no vision left:

"My constant worry is that I might not always be so happy and content as I am at present."

This ability to set goals for ourselves helps determine, in a fundamental sense, *who we become* as individuals. Thus, goal setting is a necessary technique not only for choosing what we want to be in a larger sense but also for pursuing a productive and meaningful life on a daily basis.

POT-SHOTS NO. 571
Ashleigh Brilliant

ONE POSSIBLE REASON WHY THINGS AREN'T GOING ACCORDING TO PLAN

IS THAT THERE NEVER WAS A PLAN.

As a little experiment let me ask you to quickly free associate to your ideal self. What are the qualities you would have—personal qualities, physical appearance, interpersonal relations with people, spiritual—if you were just as you wanted to be?

After you have made this list, go back over it and divide it into two parts: the ideal self which you believe is realistically attainable, and the ideal self which may not be realistically attainable. List those qualities that you think are attainable

____

____

and those that may not be attainable*

____

____

Spend some time thinking about your attainable ideal, your vision of who you would like to become, your real goals for yourself. Stop reading for a bit, close your eyes, and just enjoy the image of yourself as you'd like to be. Imagine yourself acting in ways you'd like to act, looking as you'd like to look, being who you'd ideally like to be.

BEHAVIORAL SELF-MANAGEMENT

In the book *I Never Promised You a Rose Garden*[13] a teenage girl suffers a schizophrenic episode and is sent to a mental institution. The girl lives in an ugly fantasy and cannot accept the world of reality. Her therapist at the institution is a very loving, kindly person who spends many hours trying to win the girl's confidence

*We need a balance between goals that are too high, and perhaps unrealistic, and goals that are not high enough. I believe our attainment may, to a certain extent, be limited only by our vision. Thus, even though we can't fly unaided, we should remember that it was through imagining the possibility of flight that the airplane was invented.

and trying to understand her inner reality of imagination and fantasy.

Finally, the girl is allowed to leave the institution on a trial basis, to live in the surrounding community. The other patients are excited about her leaving, for if she can succeed, they feel there is hope for them.

The girl arrives in the community, rents a room, and is full of fear and hope. However, soon she is lonely. A particularly poignant passage describes her joining a church choir in order to meet people. Standing next to strangers, singing, she feels alone and afraid. She doesn't know what to say to these people, or even how to begin a conversation with them.

She returns to the hospital. The other patients feel her defeat; they despair of ever again leading normal lives. When I read that passage I too feel helplessness and sadness. Yet, how could we have expected anything different?

Adolescence is a time during which most of us learn, albeit gropingly, important social skills: how to look at another person, how to initiate conversations—these are the skills of building friendships. How can we expect a person who has been isolated from society for several years to return to that society successfully without any practical preparation? The girl lived in a mental institution during those crucial adolescent years and did not have an opportunity to build relationships with peers. Of course she failed. She had never been taught the skills that would allow her to succeed. Understanding the frightening and menacing fantasy inside her mind was important. But it was not enough. She needed, in addition, to learn the *basic skills of normal human interactions.*

We have already discussed the first skill necessary for self-management—precise awareness through self-observation. Precise awareness is viewed as a necessary but not sufficient technique for obtaining self-control. Once individuals have observed their behavior, evaluated it, and set a goal, there are several additional strategies they may choose to use. These strategies may be broken down into three groupings: those that involve *environmental planning* (strategies which occur prior to the target behavior); those that involve *learning specific skills of the target behavior;* and those that involve *behavioral programming* (which have to do with what one does *after* the target behavior has occurred or has *failed* to occur).

Environmental Planning: Changing the Environment

Prearranging Antecedents and Consequences

One aspect of this technique involves *arranging the environment in such a way that it facilitates our acting as we want to act.* This environmental planning (stimulus control) occurs before the occurrence of the target behavior (i.e., the behavior that we are interested in changing or facilitating). Remember that we have a *physical* environment, a *social* environment, and an *internal* environment. All of these must be considered in our efforts to achieve our desired goals.*

In the East, an example of environmental planning may be found in the quiet, peaceful, simple furnishings of a meditation room (physical environment). This room is planned in such a way that extraneous distractions will be reduced, thus enabling the individual to focus more clearly on the task of meditation. Other examples of environmental planning include meditation with a group of people (social environment) in order to ensure daily practice (this is using social reinforcement to encourage the performance of certain actions). Similarly, in formal Zen meditation, the use of the *kwat*, a slap administered by the Master to a "nonconcentrating" student, represents a preplanned manipulation of the social environment (punishment) to reduce nonalert behavior

*Environmental planning goes counter to our popular cultural notions of willpower and self-management. For example, most of us would agree that a person who engages in an avoidance response—i.e., who avoids an environment or situation in which he would feel uncomfortable, or which he felt he couldn't handle—is showing a lack of willpower, a lack of self-control. It would seem that a person who truly had willpower would face the situation head-on.

Let me share an example that changed my view. When I was working with heroin addicts, my feeling was that because I was experienced in some of the most sophisticated self-control strategies in both Eastern and Western disciplines, I would be able to use heroin and not be overcome by it. As I worked more extensively with the addicts, however, I became aware that heroin was an incredibly powerful stimulus, and one I felt could control me, rather than my being able to use it as I pleased. I realized that I didn't have enough "willpower" to use heroin, and therefore made a decision to face my limitations and avoid a situation I didn't feel I could handle: using heroin. A similar view is expressed in the East, in which to avoid a powerful stimulus (e.g. water going around a rock) is seen as a convincing demonstration of self-control. Thus, self-control, or willpower may involve a variety of responses, one of which may be to avoid certain situations or environments which one does not feel competent to deal with.

and to make achievement of the meditative state more likely. Meditation itself may be seen as a type of internal environmental planning in that it may help one deal with subsequent fearful events with greater calmness.

In these examples, relevant environmental cues and social consequences have been planned in a way that will influence the occurrence of the target behavior.

A clinical example of environmental planning in the West may be drawn from the self-control strategies that have been developed to deal with obesity. Persons watching their weight are instructed to plan their home environment to encourage "slim eating" — e.g., using pictures of models who look healthy and thin; posting warnings on the dangers of obesity; arranging for there to be no high-calorie foods in the home; having low-calorie snacks in the front of the icebox.

Ziggy

Time Out

In the West, the technique of *time out* also involves environmental planning. We have probably all used "time-outs" informally—e.g., in the middle of an argument with a friend, we may leave the room (or be left!). Time out is a means of separating participants from a potentially explosive situation before that occasion occurs. This may entail telling an aggressive child that if he starts to hit a peer in school, he is going to be sent to a "timeout" room. This arrangement should be discussed *before* the actual problem occurs. This may be seen as a type of *contract*, and contracting is an important concept in behavioral self-management.

Contracting

A contract is *an agreement that is made with another person or with oneself* (a self-contract). Contracts facilitate self-directed change by creating positive consequences for reaching our goal and aversive consequences,* for noncompliance. Some contracts are informal. Most of us have made these informal, unwritten contracts, sometimes known as Grandma's Law (You may have dessert after you've eaten your spinach). Other contracts may be stated explicitly, even in writing.

It should be noted that contracts are only an aid in helping us make changes. As we will see in Chapter 4, they are not sufficient without a *motivation and commitment to change.* If there is no commitment to change, then the contract will be empty. For example, a contract made to "get along" better with one's peers is shallow if the person makes such an agreement and then continues to behave in the same old way, expecting the *others* to change their behavior. There needs to be a *spirit* of love and cooperation behind any contract that is made.

Once there is a motivation to change, some specific guidelines are helpful in making up contracts. Contracts should be fair,

*Bandura has suggested that self-regulative incentives improve performance not because they strengthen or extinguish a preceding response but because of their motivational function (i.e., anticipated satisfaction of desired accomplishments. (See Bandura, "Self-reinforcement: Theoretical and Methodological Considerations," *Behaviorism*, 1974, *4*, 133-155.)

honest, clear, reward small amounts of change, and involve the consent of all parties concerned.[14] Contracts should be made at a quiet time. They shouldn't be made right after an incident that has made you upset or angry. Wait until you have relaxed yourself and are feeling better; then see what it was that caused the problem and try to work out a contract that may prevent the undesirable behavior from happening again.

An example of a contract form you may wish to use is provided below. As this contract form illustrates, we can make contracts with other people, as well as with ourselves.

SELF-MANAGEMENT CONTRACT

Dates of contract: From ______________ to ______________

I ____________________________ agree to ____________________
(Note specific target behavior)

____

in the following situation(s) ______________________________________
(Note specific circumstances)

____

I plan to accomplish this by ______________________________________
(Note specific overt and covert environmental planning strategies and specific skills)

____

If I keep this contract, I shall be rewarded with ___________________________
(Note rewards to be provided by yourself or others)

____

(Signature) ________________________ (Date) ____________________

(Witness) ________________________ (Date) ____________________

Learning Specific Skills Involving the Target Behavior

Another important area in developing effective behavioral self-management strategies may involve the target behavior itself. For example, consider the target behavior of meditation. It should be clear by now that merely putting a person in a quiet environment doesn't ensure proper meditation. That person must know how to assume an appropriate posture, focus on breathing, and stop internal dialogue. Similarly, an overweight person needs to learn the skills that will make possible enjoyable, healthy eating: learning about proper diet, eating slowly, putting silverware down between bites, paying attention to the food's texture, smell, and taste, and so on. Likewise, the teenager in *I Never Promised You a Rose Garden* needed to learn the appropriate interpersonal skills in order to relate positively with others: initiating conversations, listening carefully, maintaining eye contact.

In the following section we discuss two of the more common self-management skills used in social learning theory: relaxation and systematic desensitization.

Relaxation

For many of us, an important behavioral self-management skill involves learning how to reduce anxiety, and manage stress and tension. A technique frequently used for this is progressive relaxation.[15] This involves systematically paying attention to each of our muscle groups. We are taught to flex and tighten various muscle groups in order to learn to recognize tension; then we are taught to let go, relax, and untense the muscle group. We are taught that just as we can make ourselves tense, so too we can learn to relax ourselves.

Each of us has certain places in our body that feel the effects of tension and stress more than others. By going through all the muscle groups we learn precisely how to pinpoint these areas. You may have noticed that by relaxing your throat, you can often stop your internal tension.

Below are listed a set of instructions for relaxing.[16] You may try the technique yourself, either by having a friend instruct you or by reading the material into a tape recorder, and then playing it back. The phrases in italics should not be read into the tape recorder. They are printed here so that after you have gone through the different muscle groups, you can return to a particular part of your body that feels tension and spend additional time relaxing that part.

Progressive Relaxation Exercises

Now is the time to relax. Find a nice comfortable position on a bed or on a floor mat and try to relax as much as you can right now. I am going to ask you to tighten certain muscles and study the sensations that come from these muscles while they're tense, and then notice what happens when you relax them and continue to relax them further and further.

Hands and Forearms. To start with, clench your right fist and try to keep all the other muscles in your body relaxed. Your forearm will be down flat (holding it up makes some tension in your upper arm). Study the feelings of tension in your forearm. Notice the location of the muscles and how they feel when they're tensed. [*Pause for tensing*]. . . . Relax now, all at once—don't ease off—let everything go all at once and then study the sensations in that muscle group as muscles relax further and further. [*Pause for relaxing*]. . . .

Now, of course, it goes more quickly if you can do it with both fists at once — so this time clench both fists. Once more study the sensations in these tense muscles — and as they begin to get a little tired locate them very clearly and specifically. [*Pause for tensing*]. . . . And again, let go all at once without easing off — relax. Now study the sensations as these muscles relax further and further. [*Pause for relaxing*]. . . .

Upper Arms. Now pull your forearms up against your upper arms as far as you can, keeping your forearms relaxed — you can tell they're relaxed when your wrists are limp. Fold them up right now and feel your biceps work and study the pattern of tension in your biceps — locate these muscles in your upper arms. [*Pause for tensing*]. . . . And relax. Let your arms flop and each time notice the contrast between how the muscles feel when they're tense and when they're relaxed. [*Pause for relaxing*]. . . .

Now straighten your arms out — completely straight — and try to turn your elbows inside out. Feel the muscles work up the back of your upper arms — study the feeling of tension in this muscle. [*Pause for tensing*]. . . . Relax now. [*Pause for relaxing*]. . . . And a final word about the thing that you do in order to relax the muscle — *enjoy* the *good feeling* as the tension gradually goes off more and more. [*Pause for relaxing*]. . . .

Now raise your arms out to the side. You have nothing to push against so it will take a little more time before the muscles get tired enough for you to feel the tension in them. These will be the muscles up across the tops of your upper arms and the muscles from the points of your shoulders up to the back of your neck. [*Pause for tensing*]. . . . And now relax and study the sensations as these muscles relax.[*Pause for relaxing*]. . . .

Forehead. Now raise your eyebrows and pull your scalp down to meet your eyebrows so that you can feel the tension in your forehead and up across the top of your skull. Study the pattern of tension. Don't worry if you can't feel your scalp — lots of people can't. [*Pause for tensing*]. . . . And relax now and just feel your forehead smoothing out and enjoy the good kind of creeping sensation as the muscles in your forehead and scalp relax. [*Pause for relaxing*]. . . .

Once more raise your eyebrows and feel the muscles work up there. [*Pause for tensing*]. . . . And relax. [*Pause for relaxing*]. . . .

This time instead of letting everything go, try to let go approximately half the tension in your forehead and try to keep it in a disciplined way at that level—stamping out the fluctuations so that the level remains constant. [*Pause*]. . . . Then let half of that go and once more try to keep it at that level without letting it vary upward or downward. [*Pause*]. . . . And half of that. [*Pause*]. . . . And half of that. Try to maintain just a tiny level of tension so that you can become aware of it when your forehead begins to tighten up just a little bit. [*Pause*]. . . . And relax now—let it all go and just enjoy the good feeling as your forehead relaxes and smooths out—gradually lets go and relaxes. [*Pause for relaxing*]. . . .

Now frown—pull your eyebrows together across the top of your nose—feel the muscles work there? Almost makes you feel angry, doesn't it? [*Pause for tensing*]. . . . Then relax. Let it go. [*Pause for relaxing*]. . . .

Eyes. Now close your eyes tightly—this will perhaps use a little bit of your frowning muscles. You can feel the circular muscles that go all around your eye and your eyelids and maybe a little of your muscle that wrinkles your nose is there. [*Pause for tensing*]. . . . Then relax—let all the tension go out and let your upper lids rest very gently on your lower lids. [*Pause for relaxing*]. . . .

Now as we continue through the rest of these muscles I want you to leave your eyes closed so that you'll be able to attend more easily to the sensations that are coming from your muscles without the interference of seeing things around you. If you find it uncomfortable to keep your eyes closed, open them for just a second and then close them again as soon as you can comfortably do it. Now, keeping your eyes closed, roll your eyes in a large circle and feel the muscles work as you move your eyes to the right—now notice those muscles that move your eyes downward—to the left—and up—and around—don't work them too hard because it's easy to strain your eyes. [*Pause for moving eyes in circle*]. . . . Then relax. Study the sensations as the tension goes out of these muscles that move your eyeballs about—think of looking at nothing and just let all those muscles go. [*Pause for relaxing*]. . . .

Mouth. Now act as if you were going to brush your upper teeth and retract your upper lip. You will find the two muscles that you use to do this—one that pulls up the middle of your upper lip and the other that pulls up the corners of your mouth—like when you smile. Now feel these muscles work. [*Pause for tensing*]. . . . And relax now—each time noticing what you do to relax and just observing for a moment the sensations those relaxed muscles give rise to. [*Pause for relaxing*]. . . .

Now pucker your mouth—feel the circular muscle around your mouth work. [*Pause for tensing*]. . . . And relax now. [*Pause for relaxing*]. . . .

Jaws. Clench your teeth—but try to leave your lips relaxed—clench your teeth and feel the muscles work there and in the corners of your jaw and on up to your temples. If you can't feel them in your temples, reach your finger up to your temple and feel them work there. Study the sensation of tension in these powerful muscles that close your jaw. [*Pause for tensing*]. . . . Relax now and just let your jaw hang slack and let all the tension go out of it. [*Pause for relaxing*]. . . .

Tongue. Now push your tongue forward against your teeth and feel the muscles work. Now pull your tongue back and feel the muscles work there. [*Pause for tensing*]. . . . And relax now—just let your tongue lie very passively in the front of your mouth. [*Pause for relaxing*]. . . .

Throat. Now push the back of your tongue upwards and feel your voice box move with it. Once more, if you have trouble feeling this, put your fingers on your Adams apple—feel it move—now push the back of your tongue down and feel your voice box go down and feel the tension go in the upper part of your throat. [*Pause for tensing*]. . . . And relax now. Let your tongue relax, as well as muscles that operate your tongue in the upper part of your throat. Pretend that you are going to clear your throat and feel your throat close. Feel it—hold it—study it—let go. Relax now. [*Pause for relaxing*]. . . .

Now swallow and observe what happens—notice the wave of relaxation that follows the wave of tension down your throat. Try swallowing now and note the wave of relaxation that follows it. And next, elaborate that wave of relaxation—just let your throat open up and relax. [*Pause for relaxing*]. . . . Now, swallow and stop in the middle with your throat contracted. Study the tension pattern. [*Pause*]. . . . Then relax it. Just enjoy the good feeling as your throat opens up and relaxes. [*Pause for relaxing*]. . . .

Now think of humming a high note. Feel the tensions in the muscles that tighten your vocal cords. [*Pause*]. . . . Relax now by singing the scales downward—feeling the changes in the level of tension in the muscles and finally ending up by picturing yourself forming a very low restful note as your vocal cords relax. [*Pause for relaxing*]. . . .

Shoulders. Now move the points of your shoulders forward and together. Feel the muscles work from the points of your shoulders down to your breastbone. These are your pectoral muscles. [*Pause for tensing*]. . . . Now relax a minute. [*Pause for relaxing*]. . . .

Now pull your shoulders back as if you were trying to touch the points of your shoulders behind your back. Feel the muscles work in *between* your shoulder blades and *around* your shoulder blades. [*Pause for tensing*]. . . . And relax now—and just feel the relaxation spreading all around your shoulders, all the muscles around your shoulder blades and upper back muscles and over the top of your chest—just let your shoulders droop and sag. [*Pause for relaxing*]. . . .

Neck. Now move your chin as you try touching your chin to your chest. Feel the tension [*Pause for tensing*]. . . . Now try to move your head to the right and to the left at the *same* time. Now, holding your neck stiffly, study the tension [*Pause for tensing*]. . . . And let all the muscles in your neck relax—just let them all go at once. Let them relax so deeply that if a breeze came along it would blow your head from one side to the other, almost as if you had no bones in your neck at all. Take no responsibility for the position of your head. Don't worry about its position—just let it be carried passively. [*Pause for relaxing*]. . . .

Back and Pelvis. Now, leaving your neck relaxed and working just from your shoulders down to your pelvis, arch your back gently—raise your back up. Arch it and feel the muscles work, the two great columns of muscles down your spine. [*Pause for tensing*]. . . . And relax. [*Pause for relaxing*]. . . .

Now rock a little bit—just rock your pelvis from side to side and feel a little more tension in one of these muscles and then in the other [*Pause for tensing*]. . . . Now relax and just lie still and feel yourself sinking deeper and deeper into the bed [floor] as your muscles let go and relax more and more. Each time notice what you do in order to relax the muscles so that you can use this later. [*Pause for relaxing*]. . . .

Buttocks. Now tighten your buttocks. [*Pause for tensing*]. . . . This should be easy to feel because this includes the largest muscle in you body along with a couple of others. Now relax and just sink back into the bed [floor]. [*Pause for relaxing*]. . . .

Thighs. Now tighten all the muscles in your thighs. In order to do this, tighten the muscles that would move your knees together and at the *same* time the muscles that would move your knees apart—and at the *same* time the muscles that would push down and would raise your thighs—and then, to top it off, think of crossing your right leg over your left, similarly your left leg over your right. Study the pattern of tension. [*Pause for tensing*]. . . . And relax now and just let all these muscles lengthen and smooth out—relax. Feel the muscles let go as they gradually lengthen and expand. [*Pause for relaxing*]. . . .

Lower Legs. Now point your toes downward so that they are in a direct line with your legs. Feel the muscles working in your calves—study the pattern of tension there. [*Pause for tensing*]. . . . And relax now. [*Pause for relaxing*]. . . .

Pull your toes toward you and feel your muscles work up your shin. [*Pause for tensing*]. . . . And relax now. [*Pause for relaxing*]. . . .

Feet. On the next one you have to be rather careful because it is easy to cramp these muscles. Try this with your toes. Curl your toes under—feel the muscles work up under your arch [*Pause for tensing*]. . . . And relax now. [*Pause for relaxing*]. . . .

Feel all your muscles smoothing out and relaxing so that you are completely relaxed now from the top of your head to the tip of your toes and that you continue to let all these muscles relax more and more. After being good and tight when you have tensed them, the muscles can continue to be more and more deeply relaxed for as long as 20 minutes.

Abdomen. Now, harden your abdominal muscles as if somebody were going to hit you in the stomach. [*Pause for tensing*]. . . . And relax. [*Pause for relaxing*]. . . .

Now harden your abdominal muscles again and study the pattern of tension—perhaps adding a little bit of an *attempt* to sit up. [*Pause for tensing*]. . . . And relax now. [*Pause for relaxing*]. . . .

Okay—once more—tighten these stomach muscles. This time pull your stomach in and tense [*Pause for tensing*]. . . . Now push it out—and in—and out—and relax. [*Pause for relaxing*]. . . .

Chest. Now, take about three-quarters of a deep breath, hold your breath and at the same time *try* to breathe in. Feel the muscles work—now, *try* to breathe out—feel the muscles work [*Pause for tensing*]. . . . And relax now. [*Pause for relaxing*]. . . . Now, as you did that perhaps you noticed that as you tried to breathe in you could feel your diaphragm flatten and then as you tried to breathe out you could feel it arch up. So let's try this once more—three-quarters of a deep breath—hold it—keeping your throat closed, *try* to breathe in some more. [*Pause*]. . . . Then *try* to breathe out [*Pause*]. . . . In . . . Out . . . In . . . Out . . . Feel your muscles work in your chest and diaphragm. They are powerful muscles which can help you to breathe correctly without running out of air.

Now, practice a different kind of breathing than usual. Breathe in—only leave your abdominal muscles relaxed while you raise your chest to breathe in. Using only your chest to breathe in, breathe in a little more deeply and a little more slowly than usual and then let everything go each time you reach the top of a breath. Breathe in deeply and slowly and then let it out. Breathe in slowly now by using your chest muscles. Hold it. . . . Let go. Again: breathe in slowly. . . . Hold it. . . . Let go. . . . This time when you reach the top of your breath, just let these muscles go for a few seconds *so that you don't have to do any work with any muscles in your body while you exhale. Let this be a signal to relax every other muscle in your body a little bit more and drift down gradually deeper and deeper* each time you breathe out. Again, breathe a little more slowly and a little more deeply than usual. . . . Hold it. . . . And then let go. Make no positive effort whatever when you are breathing out—just let the natural elasticity of your chest pour the air from your lungs. [*Pause for relaxing*]. . . . As you continue breathing, relax a little more slowly and a little bit more deeply, letting everything go, so that each time you breathe out it's like a sigh of relief.

Now, just continue relaxing like that for awhile now—deeper and deeper—without concentrating, because concentrating usually involves a little eyestrain. Attend to the sensations which are coming from your muscles. If any muscle has a little bit of residual tension left in it then you should be able to feel this tension—it will kind of "stick out" above the others. Lie quietly and passively and feel these sensations coming from your muscles along with the good feelings that come from your muscles as they relax further and further—perhaps finding one that sticks out a little bit. [*Pause for only three or four more breaths and sighs of relief*]. . . .

Now, relax from the tip of your toes to your head. Relax consciously, now your toes [3-5 second pause between parts of the body] . . . feet . . . ankles . . . calves . . . thighs . . . pelvis . . . stomach . . . chest . . . shoulders . . . arms . . . wrists . . . fingers. . . throat . . . neck . . . mouth . . . eyes . . . eyebrows. . . .

If you notice any little bit of residual tension, just try to find the source of that muscle and turn it off—don't try to relax by moving because you always have to shorten a muscle in order to move. It will take longer to relax the muscle if you move it. Just take the muscles where you find them and let them go down from there.

Now, in order to impress your overall feeling of relaxation, start counting backwards from 10 to 1. With each count, see if you can become a little bit more relaxed and perhaps get a little more of a drowsy, sleepy feeling. 10 . . . 9 . . . 8 . . . 7 . . . 6 . . . 5 . . . 4 . . . 3 . . . 2 . . . 1. . . . Now continue relaxing like that—deeper . . . and deeper. . . . Just let the chemicals of relaxation do you all the good they can. Relax for 10 to 20 minutes—or simply go to sleep. When you are ready to arouse yourself, gently move a hand, then an arm, a foot, then a leg. Open your eyes gradually. Treat yourself to a quiet, relaxed arousal!

Note: For people with physical problems, it may be advisable to consult your doctor regarding these exercises.

Systematic Desensitization

This is one of the more widely used behavioral techniques for dealing with fears and phobias.[17] Basically, the technique involves taking a fear or concern that we have, and imagining that fear while we are in a state of deep relaxation. The theory behind systematic desensitization is that if we are relaxed and comfortable, then the bad feelings that normally occur in association with a stressful or fearful event will begin to lessen, and eventually disappear.*

Below is a brief list of instructions that may be useful in helping us to desensitize ourselves to fearful or stressful situations.

*For alternative theoretical explanations of the effects of systematic desensitization, see Bandura, "Self-efficacy: Toward a Unifying Theory of Behavior Change," *Psychological Review*, 1977, *84*, 191-215.

Desensitization Instructions. As in almost any behavioral strategy, the first thing that is necessary is to define the area of concern. For the purposes of this exercise, think of two or three mild concerns or fears that you have and list them below:

1. ____

2. ____

3. ____

Sometimes, to help us pinpoint the nature and extent of our fears, it is helpful to use a "fear survey schedule."[18] This survey contains 105 items that are often sources of fear and anxiety. Illustrative items from this survey include such things as sharp objects, looking foolish, arguing with parents, meeting someone for the first time, making mistakes, being a leader, death, being with a member of the opposite sex, bats, sudden noises, expressing positive feelings, etc.

Once you have picked an area of concern, you can make a list of specific experiences (real or imagined) that relate to that fear. These items should range from the least fear-arousing situation (causing just a slight twinge of anxiety) to the most fear-arousing situation. It is usually worthwhile to come up with ten to twenty different events; these should be listed in increasing order of anxiousness. (Behaviorists call these "subjective units of disturbance"—SUDS.) An example of such a list, related to the fear of public speaking, is presented below; from least fear arousing to most fear arousing:

- I am called by a local school group to give a talk at the annual dinner a year from now.
- It is six months from the talk, and I get a letter in the mail confirming the engagement.
- Four months from the talk, I pass one of the members of the group on the street, and he tells me how much he is looking forward to my talk.

- I realize that the talk is two months away, and although that still gives me a lot of time to prepare, I begin to feel the pressure.
- I begin to make notes on the talk, and find it difficult to concentrate. I begin to wonder if I will have anything worthwhile to say.
- There are three weeks left before the talk. I've finished the first rough draft, and don't think it is any good. I get a mild choking sensation in my throat.
- There is only one week to go. I see an announcement in the school newsletter announcing my talk. I feel the time pressure closing in on me.
- The night before the talk—I'm reviewing my notes. I feel the butterflies in my stomach, and know I'm going to have trouble sleeping.
- It's 5 P.M. the evening of the talk, and I get in my car to drive to the dinner.
- I've just been introduced, and the audience is silent as I walk up to the podium. I spread my notes out.
- I'm in the middle of the speech. I look up at the audience and can't tell if they're listening or interested.
- When I look back down at my notes, I can't find my place. My mind goes blank. I stutter and stammer, and the audience begins to stir restlessly.

Once you have constructed a hierarchy of events, the next step is to relax yourself as per the instructions we have already given. Once you are relaxed, imagine the least fear-arousing item on the list (e.g., I am called by a local school group to give a talk to them at their annual dinner a year from now). If tension occurs, stop the scene and again relax yourself. Once you are relaxed, try to visualize the scene again. If there is still tension, stop the scene, and relax again. Once there is no tension in the presence of a specific scene, proceed to the next scene (e.g., It is six months from the talk and I get a letter in the mail confirming the engagement).

Continue in the above manner until you can visualize all scenes contained in the list with no anxiety. You may wish to practice this daily, for about 20 to 30 minutes. It should be noted that if you are dealing with a very severe fear or phobia, it may be important to seek professional help.

Behavioral Programming

In addition to environmental planning and skills relevant to the target behavior, self-management may involve behavioral programming.* This type of self-management concerns strategies related to what the individual does *following the occurrence of a target behavior.* These consequences may involve self-reward (verbal, imagined, material) or self-punishment (verbal, imagined, material). In other words, how we deal with ourselves if we successfully carry out our goals. Do we give ourselves a reward? What kind of reward? Is it a verbal pat on the back? Imagining the positive reactions of others? A visit to the concert we've wanted to attend? Or do we punish ourselves? Do we tell ourselves that we could have done still better, that we didn't try hard enough?

If we don't meet our goals, how do we deal with ourselves? Do we give punishment? What kind of punishment?

All of us maintain a constant internal dialogue, rewarding and punishing both ourselves and others. The way we reward ourselves, the way we talk to ourselves and others, is often rather random or counter-productive when viewed in terms of the goals we are actually trying to achieve.

We may punish ourselves after a good job for not doing better; we may likewise punish ourselves when we don't seem to be succeeding, rather than giving ourselves encouragement and hope. *Behavioral programming strategies teach us to make the*

*According to social learning theorists, there are three ways by which we learn: operant conditioning, classical conditioning, and modeling. In simplified form, the distinction between these three is as follows: Operant conditioning refers to the relationship between a behavior and its consequences (e.g., reinforcement or punishment). Classical conditioning (e.g., systematic desensitization) refers to the pairing or association of one stimulus with another. In the case of desensitization, the feared image is paired with relaxation so that eventually the feared stimulus loses its fear-arousing properties. Modeling refers to *learning by observing*: vicarious learning. This type of learning does not involve either reinforcement or pairing of stimuli. For a complete discussion of these distinctions, see Albert Bandura, *Social Learning Theory* (Englewood Cliffs, N.J.: Prentice-Hall, 1977); see also D. Whaley and R. Malott, *Elementary Principles of Behavior Modification* (Kalamazoo, Michigan: Behaviordalia, 1970).

"HEY! IS THIS ALL I GET FOR TELLIN' THE *TRUTH*?"

consequences of our actions more related to our own self-chosen goals. In this way we can "get on the same team with ourselves."

Let us now look at the behavioral programming techniques of reinforcement and punishment and see how they can best serve us.

Reinforcement and Punishment

In technical language, reinforcement and punishment refer to a stimulus (X) administered contingent upon a certain behavior (Y). Reinforcement stimulus (X) increases the likelihood that the behavior will occur again. In other words, if you do someone a favor (Y), and he thanks you (X), there is a higher likelihood that you will be inclined to do him a favor again. Punishment stimulus decreases the likelihood that the behavior will occur again. In other words, if you do someone a favor (Y) and she slugs you (X), there is a lower likelihood you would be inclined to do her a favor again. Let us now look at how reinforcement and punishment may be used to our advantage. We will discuss specific reinforcement, global reinforcement, specific criticism, and global criticism. We will talk primarily about social and self-reinforcement in terms of images and words. However, especially in our society, material self-reward is often used quite effectively too.

Specific Reinforcement

Reinforcement for specific behaviors would include such statements as:

- I feel proud of how much progress I am making in my self-change project.
- Thank you, John, for raking the leaves.
- You wrote that essay well, Jean.
- Thanks for helping me with the dishes, Sally.
- I sure did a good job in that counseling session.

This type of reinforcement, to be optimal, should follow certain guidelines. First, it should be clear *what behaviors are being reinforced.* Second, the *timing* of the reinforcement should be as soon after behavior as possible. Third, if a new behavior is being learned, reinforcement should be *liberal and frequent.* Further, since a new skill takes time and practice to learn, and perfection is rarely achieved the first time, reinforcement should occur for *small increments of improvements* (*successive approximations*).

Successive Approximations. Successive approximation involves setting a graduated series of subgoals, which are more easily reached than the major goals, and reinforcing ourselves upon attaining each increasingly difficult subgoal.

Godfrey gives himself encouragement for "touching" the

ball—which is a successive approximation to catching it. We, too, should be kind both to others *and to ourselves* for the attempts we make at new behaviors.

Global Reinforcement

Global reinforcement is noncontingent; it does not need to come after specific kinds of behavior—there is no specific reason for this type of reinforcement. Global reinforcement includes such statements as:

- You're a great son.
- You're a great daughter.
- I really love you.
- You're a good person.

Often we make the mistake of using global reinforcement for specific tasks: You're a good person because you just got a raise. Johnny, what a good boy you are for raking the leaves. The prob-

"THAT'S A GOOD GIRL!"

lem with global praise for a specific act is that a person may come to feel that his worth is dependent upon success. If this individual doesn't succeed, he may feel he can't be loved.

Global reinforcement should come at times unrelated to a specific task. This type of reinforcement can be called the "big cuddle": telling a child with a big hug that you love him; sharing warm feelings with a spouse; showing feelings of warmth and acceptance with ourselves.

Specific Criticism

Criticism for specific behaviors would include statements such as:

- Johnny, please quit running in the hall.
- Jimmy, I don't think you understand how to do these types of math problems. Let me explain.
- This soup tastes too salty, Jan.
- That backhand shot I just made was too low.

Giving a constructive criticism is not easy. First, it should be *specific*—dealing with the behaviors to be changed. Second, if possible, it should involve an *alternative.* To "Johnny, please don't run in the halls" we can add ". . . we can run when we get outside." (Running is not inappropriate in certain environments. If you take away one behavior—running—provide an alternative.) Third, ideally, criticism should be *nonthreatening.* One of the most effective ways to present a criticism was suggested by Lloyd Homme. He called it a sandwich (reinforcement/criticism/reinforcement).[19] Rather than "The soup tastes too salty, Jan," you might say (1) "Thanks for making dinner tonight. I sure appreciate it. The salad is terrific"; (2) "For my own taste, next time, I'd like a bit less salt in the soup"; or (3) "The vegetable casserole looks and smells exquisite, Jan."

Sometimes it may seem stilted to make a "full sandwich." A rule of thumb is to end with a compliment, not a criticism. ("The casserole sure smells good—but this soup is awfully salty").*

*A new behavior often feels contrived at first. Don't let that bother you. As long as your honest intent is to share your feelings and give constructive feedback, then a criticism in the "sandwich style" has the intent of being as gentle as possible.

"This year's sales incentive is tropical cruises blended with fear of job loss."

Specific Punishment. Criticism may also involve a type of punishment, as in the case of grades. We need to decide whether we are using criticism for feedback to bring about improvement in performance, or as a means of punishing poor performance. Punishment involves aversive consequences that occur after an undesired behavior. For example, a person who decides he wants to quit smoking may punish himself by giving a dollar to his most hated charity every time he smokes a cigarette. Or a person who wants to stop drinking may imagine himself starting to take a drink, then imagine an immediate feeling of nausea. This is called *using a covert (internal) image as punishment.* Or the individual who is trying to remove an unwanted thought may place that thought in his mind, and then yell STOP! This is operant punishment—referred to as *thought stopping* in the behavioral literature.

It is important that when punishment is used, it should be for a *specific behavior*, and not directed at the person (either others or ourself); the punishment should be *time-limited*, and *follow immediately upon the occurrence* of the undesirable behavior. A desirable alternative behavior should be formulated and its occurrence liberally enforced. When the above guidelines are followed, punishment techniques seem to be effective. However, it is unclear how effective they are for long-term change; and whether or not they involve any unhealthy side effects.

Global Criticism

I would suggest that this strategy is *never* useful. Examples of statements using global criticism might be "You're a bad boy," "She's an evil person," or "I'm really worthless." According to the social learning viewpoint, which stresses the situation specificity of behavior, global criticism is not accurate. Further, there's nothing a person learns from it that is of use.

The chart summarizes our discussion of punishment and reinforcement, suggesting the constructive use of each.*

	Specific Behaviors	*Global Traits*
reinforcement	yes	yes (big cuddle)
criticism/punishment	yes	no

Some Additional Thoughts on Reinforcement

It is perhaps commonplace to say that all of us wish to receive praise and reinforcement. Yet, even though we know it feels good to get praised, we are often very sparing in the kinds of praise that we give to others, and to ourselves. Keep in mind that praise can be verbal.

*In relation to this chart, it is interesting to think of the global personality traits used in the Diagnostic and Statistical Manual II (DSMII), a manual for professional mental-health workers to use in evaluating a person's mental health: e.g., neurotic, psychotic, manic-depressive, schizophrenic. For some of the implications of these labels, see the discussion of trait labeling in Chapter 5.

Praise and reinforcement can also be noverbal.

Think of a person that you're very close to. What do you say to him, or how do you let him know you are close to him? Think about that for a minute, and then jot down a couple of ways you have recently shown affection, either verbally

____

____

or nonverbally

____

____

In addition, it's sometimes hard for us to accept praise gracefully from others. For example, think of how you respond when someone praises you. Do you let that person know how good it makes you feel? Do you become self-conscious, and find it hard to accept the praise? Be aware of how you respond the next time you receive praise from another person.

Self-reinforcement: One Type of Internal Self-statement

Perhaps hardest of all is to give praise to ourselves. We are taught as children that to praise ourselves is narcissistic and egotistical. Thus, when we do praise ourselves out loud, we often get punished. When we criticize ourselves, we often get comforted—and told, "There, you're really pretty good—don't be so hard on yourself." We internalize those "rules," and we learn to talk to ourselves in critical ways, with very little praise. We do this because that mode of talking has paid off in the past.

Ask yourself this: How much do you like yourself? A little? Moderately? A lot? Now ask yourself this: when is the last time you've shown yourself that you like yourself? What's the last "treat" or the last pat on the back, the last reward you've given yourself? It's too easy to become our own worst critic. And yet, as the saying goes, if we aren't for us, who will be?

Let me ask you to make a list of the five things that you might say to yourself that would make you feel good. Include examples of both specific and global reinforcement.

1. ______________________________

2. ______________________________

3. ______________________________

4. ______________________________

5. ______________________________

Because we are so sparing in the kinds of positive things we say to ourselves, it is often difficult to list positive statements we make to ourselves. Therefore, I would like to push you a little bit on the above exercise. If you didn't list five positive things you can say to yourself, please stop and go back, and complete the exercise. Become aware of any resistance you may be feeling to doing this exercise.

After you have completed the list of positive statements that you can (or do) make to yourself, I'd like you to think about and list five things, or events, that make you feel good. One way of finding out what's reinforcing to you is to look for something you do frequently—this involves what Premack has referred to as a "high-probability behavior."[20] If, for example, you ask a child what he likes to do, he may say he doesn't know. However, if you watch him during free time, and note that he plays basketball a lot, you may infer that this is a high-probability behavior, and he finds it reinforcing.

If you are still having trouble listing five things that are reinforcing to you, you may wish to go through several magazines and cut out pictures or scenes that make you feel good. You may also wish to draw or paint scenes that give you a good feeling. Once you have done this, try to figure out what it is about that scene that you like. In other words, first identify a positive feeling in an intuitive holistic way; later, analyze precisely why it is a good feeling.

Another device that may be useful in helping us recall things or experiences that give us joy or other pleasurable feelings is called a "reinforcement survey schedule." This survey contains many different items, such as the following: eating (candy, fruits, nuts); solving problems (crossword puzzles; figuring out how something works); listening to music (classical, Western country, jazz, folk); animals (dogs, cats, horses, birds); watching sports; reading; dancing; playing sports; shopping; gardening; hiking; being praised (about appearance, about your work, about your hobbies, about your physical strengths, about your mind, about your moral strength); making somebody happy; babies; having people ask your advice; talking to friends; being close to an attractive person; making love; peace and quiet.

Take some time and think of five experiences, activities, events that you find very reinforcing, and list them below:

1. ______________________________

2. ______________________________

3. ______________________________

4. ______________________________

5. ______________________________

How often during a week do you do the things that make you feel good? How often do you say things to yourself that make you feel good? This may be an area in which you'd like to gather self-observation information and then try to increase.

Additional Uses of Internal Images and Self-statements

Most of us are almost always engaging in some sort of internal dialogue with ourselves. Often these dialogues are just gibberish, and not worth paying attention to. Sometimes the dialogues may be productive; other times, however, the dialogue may work against our own best interests.*

For example, when Eugenio Montare, an Italian poet, was given the Nobel prize for literature, he reacted to the news by shutting off his telephone and refusing to answer his door. The prize, he said, made his life "which was always unhappy, less unhappy."

Perhaps it is necessary for the struggling artist to have a world view of suffering and despair. Yet it seems apparent that there will be a relationship and perhaps even a self-fulfilling prophecy between the statements that Montare makes to himself and how he feels about himself and his life.

We have seen that the internal statements we make about ourselves and our behavior can serve as a type of reinforcement or punishment for that behavior. Likewise, how we picture ourselves

*One astute, anonymous observer of human nature has suggested the following continuum along which internal dialogue may occur: talks with God; talks with angels; talks to self; argues with self; loses argument with self.

and our actions—what *images* we have—can also influence what we do. These "internal events" can also have many additional uses.

Let us look at some of the ways in which our mind (what we say and what images we have of ourselves) and our body (what we do and how we act) interrelate. Let us look particularly at when this interaction serves our best interests, and when it doesn't.

In a behavioral approach, an effort is made to precisely pinpoint the nature and content of our thoughts, as well as their order in a sequence (i.e., do they represent antecedents to actions, actions themselves, or the consequences of actions?). Using this approach it is possible to determine the most constructive use of thoughts and images for our own particular goals. These covert images and statements may have many uses. Some involve helping us learn to perform behaviors better (*self-instructions, covert self-modeling* as rehearsal); some include behavioral programming (e.g., images or statements as consequences for actions—*self-reinforcement or self-punishment*); some involve learning to attribute to ourselves competency to direct our own lives (*positive self-attribution*); some involve setting a vision or image of ourselves (*covert self-modeling as goal setting*); some involve learning to obtain a perspective; some involve means of initiating actions (*antecedents to behavior*); some self-instructions help us interrupt maladaptive behavioral sequence; and some help us increase our motivation to succeed, and succeed well.

Let me give a few illustrations.

Covert Images and Self-statements as Behavioral Rehearsal. Internal statements and images may provide a practice, or rehearsal, for an actual behavior. (This is the same as a successive approximation to the actual overt behavior.) For example, research has suggested that practicing a dialogue to ask for a date facilitates actually performing the action.[21] Covert images may similarly be used to facilitate a psychomotor task. As Arnold Palmer has noted, one way to increase our ability to judge proper putting force is to imagine that we are rolling a ball toward the hole from where our putt lies. He suggests that the amount of force required to toss the ball up to the hole is the same as is needed to stroke it with a putter. Thus, he says, "If you can imagine how much force you need to toss the ball to the hole, you can readily transfer this image to your actual putting stroke."[22]

A study with student basketball players showed this relationship between imagery and action. A group of students were randomly divided into three groups; one group took a pre-test on the first day, practiced free throws for a certain amount of time, each day for 20 days, and took a post-test on day 20; the second group took a pre-test on the first day, and a post-test on day 20, with no practice in between; the third group took a pre-test on the first day, a post-test on day 20, and imagined throwing free throws during the days in between. If they missed a shot in their imagination, they would then imagine themselves correcting the mistake. Group one improved 24% between pre- and post-test; group two didn't improve at all; and group three improved 23%![23] Thus, imagery is a successive approximation to the actual act, a kind of rehearsal which may sometimes be as effective as actual behavioral practice.

Covert Images and Self-statements as a Means for Stress and Tension Reduction. Recent behavioral attempts to develop stress- and tension-reduction training packages have altered the traditional systematic desensitization paradigm in both theory and practice. As noted earlier, in classical systematic desensitization, relaxation preceded the fear-arousing imagery. In the new paradigm, the fear-arousing situation itself becomes a cue for relaxation.[24] This new procedure involves training in deep-muscle relaxation and then learning to notice anxiety by imagining the fear-arousing situation and maintaining that situation in the imagination. While maintaining the tension, the person practices controlling arousal by means of *muscular relaxation, covert self-modeling* (i.e., observing ourselves acting in a competent and successful fashion in the anxiety-arousing situation), and *self-instructions* to cope with the situation (e.g., "Relax," "I am in control," "I can handle the situation").

The practice of self-modeling and self-instruction may be considered both a type of goal setting (e.g., imagining how we would like to act in stressful situations) and a type of *rehearsal*, a means of reaching our goal.

You may wish to take just a moment and recall a situation in which you have felt anxious in the past, or one in which you anticipate feeling anxious in the future. Go through the situation in your mind, and let yourself experience the feelings that occur. Now, keeping the image in your mind, begin focusing on your breathing, giving yourself instructions to "let go, relax." Keep the image in your mind. Now, practice acting in that situation as you would like to act. It's *your* mind—you can have it imagine anything you want to do! Let it imagine you acting just the way you would like to. Let yourself play with different types of self-instructions and modeling that seem most appropriate for you.

Covert Self-statements as Attributions. When an event occurs, what do you say is the cause of that action? Does it make a difference whether the event that occurs is something good or something bad? What we say is the cause of the action is referred to by psychologists as "attribution."

Most attribution tests try to determine whether an individual attributes life events to outside causes beyond his control or to variables within his personal control. I would suggest that the variable of personal control needs to be defined even more precisely, in order to distinguish between personal control of negative events, and personal control of positive events. Let me illustrate the reason for this by giving excerpts of conversation with several patients I have seen. These are examples of attributions which, even though they are not in the patient's best interest, were said frequently.

- I'm an alcoholic because I can't control my life.
- I'm afraid to try anything, like writing, because I'm sure to fail.
- If I go to a party, people will think I'm awkward and ungraceful.
- I just don't know how to be a loving person. No wonder no one gets close to me. I drive them away.

Note that in each of the above examples the individuals *are* taking responsibility for their actions. However, these are *negative* actions and *negative* consequences for which they are taking responsibility. For these individuals, if an event goes positively, they do not take any personal credit. If it goes negatively, it is their fault. One patient noted that when he had a warm, intimate conversation with someone, and overcame his "shyness," this was because "the other person had a good personality"; or "I don't understand what happened"; or "something outside myself took over." Further, to this person the negative events seemed more real. Looking back on a day or a week and evaluating it, the good, positive things were perceived as a fluke and dismissed, while the bad things were seen as the "stuff of life, the real events." If individuals believe that they are in control of their own lives, and competent to direct their own actions, they will be more likely to act in a self-directed and purposeful manner. This belief can be influenced by the kind of verbal explanations they make to themselves.

It may be worthwhile to observe for a week the kinds of "attribution" statements you make. At the end of the week, you may wish to evaluate which statements appear to be in your own best interest, and which are not. You might also wish to make a list of positive self-attributions which you *do* make or which you would *like* to make to yourself. Keep this list accessible, and, if appropriate, practice instructing yourself to increase the frequency of these types of positive self-attributions.

SELF-CONTROL, FREE WILL, AND DETERMINISM: SOME CONCLUDING REMARKS

Skinner Is Right: We Don't Have Freedom

At the start of this chapter we saw different ways that our social, physical, and internal environments can influence our behavior. Skinner, among others, has pointed out that unless we realize the way we are influenced by the environment, we are not free. Let us take the overweight person as a case in point.

Although there may be a few people who are overweight because of a genetic condition, most of us are "naturally" overweight because of our environment. Most of us live in a culture of plenty—advertisements, restaurants, stocked cupboards. Because we are influenced by our environment we "naturally" feel hungry when confronted by these stimuli. For example, recently after a large Japanese dinner, my wife and I were walking by a pizza parlor.

"Umm," I said, "do you smell that pizza? I'm hungry."

My wife responded: "Are you hungry, or does the pizza smell good?"

Although she was right in her distinction, for most of us, when something smells good, it means we're hungry and should eat. When the clock says dinnertime, it means we're hungry. As long as we remain conditioned by external cues, and the culture is a culture of plenty, we will "naturally" be overweight.

The Existentialists Are Right: We Do Have Freedom

If we believe that we are determined by the environment, then what hope is there for us to exercise our free will and overcome the limits of the environment? There is a great deal of hope, and this hope is summarized in the line by Sir Francis Bacon: "Nature, to be commanded, must be obeyed."

In order to take control of our own lives, we must become aware of the ways we are influenced by our environment. In the "overweight" example, we need to become aware of the external stimuli that make us "want" to eat; and then we need to turn inward to hear the "real" internal signals (in this case, of hunger).

However, that is not enough. As long as we say we are naturally overweight, as long as we say "Oh, it's not my responsibility—it's my unconscious; it's genetic; it's the environment" we still are allowing ourselves to be passively determined.

We must also believe "as if" we have free choice, and affirm our ability to take responsibility for our own actions. At this point we will digress momentarily to say something about this "as if" concept. The psychological "as if" is similar to faith in religious terms. The difference may be that the new religion—science—has shown us that if we believe certain "as ifs" there will be certain consequences. Our new religious testimonials are merely the empirical research cited in the scientific journals. For example, if we believe a "doctor" is taking care of us, we often "spontaneously" recover, even though the "cure" is nothing more than a sugar pill.[25]

There are many different ways this "as if" comes up in this book. First, we need to believe "as if" we have free will. Until we believe that, we will continue to be passively determined. Second, during times of crisis, which is discussed in Chapter 3, we need to make an affirmation that our life is worth living, that our goals are worth choosing; and that I, as an individual, am worth taking time for. There is no way to empirically verify this affirmation. Kierkegaard called this the *leap of faith;* Sartre called it the *leap of choice.*

Third, as we discuss in Chapter 5, if we believe "as if" we are worthy and dignified people, we soon become that way. The beliefs, in a real sense, create the reality.

There are many people in the environment (in therapy, teaching, education, the legal system) who are in a position to influence us to take responsibility for our actions. Therapists, for example, may try to teach (or shape) a client to this belief by such statements as follows:

- I can't decide for you. You have to make the decision yourself.
- You realize that this is an important choice for you, and that by not deciding you are actually making a decision.
- You need to learn to act from choice, not compulsion.
- You can't blame the rules for making choices for you; it's your choice whether or not you decide to follow the rules.[26]
- Anxiety tensions are part of *your own doing*, and can be decreased if you identify the anxiety tension patterns and relax them.[27]
- Don't say "I can't" [choice outside oneself]; say "I won't" [choice within oneself].

The legal system likewise teaches individuals the importance of taking responsibility for their own actions. For example, in the Patty Hearst trial, in order to determine legal culpability, it was important for the jury to question whether or not physical duress or coercion overwhelmed "free will."

Thus we have the resolution of a paradox. The scientific literature suggests that initially we may be determined by environmental and biological influences (i.e., we are not free). However, significant others in our environment may help "determine" us to take responsibility for our own actions, and to take an active part in choosing our own destiny (i.e., we are free). In this latter capacity, the existential writers provide us an invaluable service. They hold us accountable for our actions—thus we are seen as responsible for our choices, and able to learn to choose.*

It is only when we can see how we are conditioned, see what consequences and cues shape our behavior, that we can begin to develop the personal standards by which we want to live and decide whether or not we want to continue to be shaped by these stimuli. As Erich Fromm pointed out, before a person can act according to his own conscience, he must have transcended the limits of the society into which he was born. Learning to see the kinds of cues and consequences that are expected of us and the cultural mores to which we are socialized is the first step in this "transcendence." For this reason, writers such as Jose Delgado urge that students be "taught awareness of their own mental and behavioral activity and shown how to use their intelligence, deciding which behavioral determinants to accept and which to reject.[28]

Thus, we have seen that the first step in behavioral self-management involves learning to see *the ways we are determined by the environment.* The second step involves believing "as if" we have free will and can *take responsibility for our own actions.* The third step is to *use certain techniques*, such as environmental planning and behavioral programming, *to increase our freedom.*

This concept of freedom needs to be seen along a continuum.† For example, we can see that being in jail or in a locked institution would limit the amount of physical freedom we have. Since social

*As we will see in Chapter 5, the paradox becomes even a bit more complex: (1) Skinner is right: we are determined by the environment; (2) The existentialists are right: we are every moment free to choose, and should act from choice, not compulsion; and (3) the Eastern disciplines are right: we need to let go of our concepts such as free will, choice, determinism; we need to cease always trying to feel in control of life, thereby letting go, yielding, and opening ourselves to experiencing the universe in a way that doesn't concern itself with causes.

†Just as freedom needs to be seen along a continuum, so do self-management, and willpower. In our culture, however, the belief is that people either have willpower or they don't: some people just seem to "have" more self-control and willpower than others. Social learning theorists believe that this willpower is not innate, but *learned.* Therefore, as more self-regulation skills are learned and practiced, we come to have more "willpower." Willpower is merely a descriptive label applied to a certain set of actions and thoughts. All of us can learn to have and perform these actions and thoughts.

learning theorists believe that there is a continuum of constraint, and that freedom is not an absolute concept, the individual is always being determined by the environment. Therefore, one aspect of "being free" involves *arranging the environment* so it will be possible for us to act in ways we "choose" as part of our vision.

Freedom also involves *perception of consequences.* When an individual confronts a situation, it is important to be able to not respond reflexively, but rather to pause and *perceive* several alternative actions. To do this, one has to be aware of antecedents which normally cause reflex responses, and to have the skills (e.g., social, physical, cognitive) to execute the perceived alternatives.

Also, our freedom may be limited by consequences. We may learn that certain behaviors are punished and certain behaviors are praised. Awareness of the consequences of our actions—how they may affect ourselves and others—is necessary so that we can "freely" choose our course of action, or to posit alternatives that help us achieve the consequences we want.

Antecedent	*Behavior*	*Consequences*
1. Recognition of stimuli that cause us to respond mechanically. 2. Actual physical environment—e.g., prison, etc.	1. Development of skills for a variety of behaviors. 2. Ability to perceive consequences of alternative actions. 3. Ability to recognize when behavior comes under stimulus control. 4. Ability to not allow ourselves to be bound by reflex responses to stimuli.	1. Ability to prearrange these to encourage certain "free" actions. 2. Recognition of how the consequences of our actions influence our behavior.

By learning about antecedents and consequences of our behavior, and by learning certain self-control skills, we are able to learn to "control the variables that alter [our] own behavior"[29] As Skinner noted, "We are all controlled by the world in which we live, and part of that world has been and will be constructed by men. The question is this: Are we to be controlled by accident, by tyrants, or by ourselves in effective cultural design."[30]

SUMMARY

In this chapter we discussed the advantages of ordinary awareness: they included such things as information processing, memory storage, reassurance, predictability, and systematic observation of our relationship to the environment to see how we are influenced by that environment.

Then we described the kind of precise awareness involved in behavioral self-observation strategies: discriminating and labeling a behavior; determining its antecedents and consequences; evaluating the results of our observations; and setting a goal, which involves determining whether one wants to increase the behavior, decrease the behavior, or learn a new behavior (i.e., new skills). This is quite different from the kind of awareness we described in step five of meditation, in which there is no goal setting and in which one lives in a present-centeredness—without discriminating, without labeling into categories, and without evaluating. The importance of goal setting was emphasized, both for daily achievement and for freely choosing a vision of who we want to become.

We noted that after we have observed the data, evaluated it, and set a goal, there are several additional self-management techniques we may use to reach that goal. These techniques comprise a variety of strategies that are individually tailored to the specific concern of the individual. These strategies may include environmental planning, which occurs *prior to* the behavior in question. This may entail prearranging antecedents (stimulus control) or prearranging consequences (e.g, time out; a contract). Other strategies may involve behavioral programming, concerning events and actions that occur *after* the target behavior has been accomplished. Specific self-management techniques were discussed, including reinforcement, punishment, contracting, thought stopping, relaxation, and systematic desensitization. Special attention was paid to the role of covert thoughts and images in self-management: as rehearsal, self-instructions, self-modeling, and for obtaining a detached observation.

The role of behavioral self-management techniques was discussed in relation to learning how to "get on our own team." These techniques teach us to become aware of how we are being influenced by our physical, social, and interpersonal environment;

of how we have developed self-defeating habits—of acting, of thinking, of emotional reflex responses, of negative attributions, of sparingly reinforcing ourselves. Self-management skills help us develop sensitivity to our internal selves—so we may hear the bird in our breast singing. They also teach us how to change our habits so that they are constructive and more self-fulfilling. We thereby learn not only to hear the bird in our breast sing, but we also learn the means to follow the melody of the song.

II

Zen Behaviorism: When the Zen Master Meets the Grand Conditioner

As we saw in Chapter 1, the Zen Master and the East teach us to be free—free *from* bondage to words, intellect, constructs, analysis, attachment to our "I"; and free *to* experience nature, others, ourselves. As we learned in Chapter 2, the Grand Conditioner and the West also teach us to be free—free *from* past conditioning patterns and habits; free *to* change our thoughts, actions, images; and free to choose a new way of acting and being in the world.

In this part of the book I would like to show ways in which the theory* and practice of the two schools—Zen Buddhism and social learning theory (behavior therapy)—may be combined. Because this has never before been attempted, and because we are going to be covering a great deal of material in a short space, I would like to offer an anagram of chapter headings which may be useful in guiding us through Chapters 3 through 7—CREATE. Although this anagram is admittedly a device, it is certainly a fitting word in terms of our discussion. Both Eastern and Western schools of thought are optimistic about our possibilities for personal growth; both acknowledge that people *do* change, that we can assume a greater degree of control and responsibility over our own lives, that we can re-*create* ourselves in terms of a new vision,

*We must make an important distinction between science and religion. Both operate on the basis of belief systems (theories about human nature). However, in science, empirical findings either confirm or deny the theory and cause the theory to be altered accordingly. In religion, the data does not alter the belief, and information that does not confirm merely serves to buttress the need for "stronger belief." This, of course, is merely a theory about how science is supposed to work.

and that we can gain a greater measure of personal freedom and dignity.

Yet both schools also acknowledge that most of us are not initially free, and that some kind of crisis, whether large or small, is often necessary to make us aware of how illusory our sense of freedom is. In Chapter 3 we discuss the nature of the Crisis and some of the events that may cause it. In Chapter 4 we show how the crisis provides an opportunity for taking Responsibility for, and for making an Evaluation of, our lifestyles and values. This evaluation and responsibility, in turn, give us the opportunity to develop a new awareness, and make an affirmation and commitment to a new alternative. In Chapter 5 we discuss this new Alternative: an integrated East–West vision. In Chapter 6 Techniques for achieving this new alternative are illustrated; and in Chapter 7, Education, we summarize the information covered in Part II, including step-by-step "how to" instructions for using this book as an owner's manual.

3
Crisis: Freedom as Illusion

WHAT IS FREEDOM?

Linus saved his head.

But he lost his freedom of choice.

Or did he?

Let me ask you to think of a creative risk, large or small, that you want to take—one that's a little bit frightening, one you may have been holding back from doing.

Most of us, if we think about it long enough, have some secret desire or ambition, some not-quite-ordinary dream or vision that we hesitate to carry out.

What holds us back?

Aren't we free?

What is this word "freedom," anyway? What does it mean to be free? Can we increase this freedom? Will we be happier if we do? Let's explore some memories we might have of being free. Take a moment, sit back, and recall a situation in the past in which you have felt free.

Imagine the situation: who was present, where you were. Try to recapture the feelings you associate with that freedom: feelings in your body, things you may be saying to yourself, images, etc. Then jot down some quick notes on this feeling of freedom in the spaces below. We'll come back to this again at the end of Part II, so make just a note or two. First, list situations in which you felt free (note where and who was present)—antecedents.

____

____

Then, list where you felt this freedom in your body and in your mind (e.g., physical cues, self-statements, etc.)—behavior.

____

____

Then, note the length of time the feeling(s) lasted (days, years, a few seconds)—behavior.

____

____

Finally, note what you did as a result of the feeling(s)—consequences.

____

____

Now think of times when you haven't felt free, when you have felt trapped, controlled. Again imagine one or two situations in which you experienced these feelings. List situations in which you have felt "unfree" (again, noting where and who was present).

____

____

Note the body and mind cues you experienced.

____

____

Note the length of time the feeling(s) lasted.

____

____

What did you do as a result of the feeling(s)?

____

____

Freedom is a strange concept. It's hard to tell if we have it or not. Sometimes we may think we're free; yet we are really being manipulated.* Let me give an example involving our dog. We trained our dog to "stay" by pointing a finger at her and saying "stay." At first we would give her a treat if she stayed only a few

*Sometimes, of course, along specified dimensions it is clear that certain individuals have relatively more freedom than others (see Bandura, *Social Learning Theory*, Chapter 6).

seconds. Then, through a series of successive approximations, we taught her to stay for longer periods. If she succeeded, we would say "Okay, come," and give her a piece of food.

One night we were leaving for the evening, and I wanted to put the dog inside the house. "Come," I said, but she wasn't interested in coming in and refused to budge. She was probably feeling proud of herself for being free enough to resist my orders. So I pointed my finger at her and said "You stay." She stayed. Then I said "Okay, you can come," and she did, right into the house.

The first "Come" was an order; the second one, "Okay, you can come," was intended (anthropomorphically!) to make the dog "feel" she had "free will," that she was "choosing" to come. Yet was she really choosing to come the second time? Or was it merely a conditioned response?

Well, we might say to ourselves, what can you expect from a dog. Certainly we human beings are too sophisticated to be manipulated* like that, right? Well, the literature seems to suggest otherwise. Conditioning can and does take place without awareness.[1]

Certainly all of us want to feel free.† All of us want to feel that we are in control of our lives and that we have at least some amount of involvement in shaping our destiny. If we feel we are losing control of a situation, we may become angry and defensive.‡

*When I use the term "manipulation," I refer to instances at either extreme of a continuum of influence. Manipulation occurs either when we are devious or dishonest about our intent to influence (the end of the continuum toward deviousness) or when we take advantage of another person's "one-down" situation (the end of the continuum toward coercion).

†We all have an initial reluctance to believe that we live in a deterministic world. For example, a client I was seeing complained of feeling that he was not very assertive. Through self-observation of when he acted assertively and when he did not, the client realized that his behavior changed depending on the circumstances and the people that were around him. This confirms what the research literature suggests about our behavior being situation specific (i.e., we act differently in different situations depending upon the circumstances; see Walter Mischel, *Personality and Assessment*, N.Y.: Wiley 1968). However, the patient noted that he was quite upset about the situation specificity of his behavior: "I don't like becoming aware that I act less assertively with some people than with others. It makes me feel less free, more controlled by others." We don't like to give up our illusion of freedom.

‡The importance of believing in our free will is probably nowhere more dramatically described than in Doestoevsky's *Underground Man*. The underground man stated that if he were faced with several alternatives, one of which was more attractive than the others, he would choose the more attractive alternative. However, if it could be predicted in advance which he would choose, he would choose a different alternative, simply as a display of his free

"Hey! I'm not through seducing you yet."

Many writers have stated that we are born free—free to choose our lifestyle, our values, and our mode of interaction. The existential writers have been the most eloquent in their praise of freedom, as well as the most searing in their admonitions that we

---

will. If this choice, too, could be predicted, he would pick none of the alternatives, and rather than lose his free will, would prefer to kill himself.[2]

It is interesting that we feel our free will is lessened if other people can predict our behavior; yet we like to believe we can predict our own behavior, *and* we like to feel we can predict other people's behavior.

are constantly choosing who we are, regardless of whether or not we are aware of choosing. These choices determine whom we become: our existence precedes our essence.

This vision of personal freedom is eloquent as a vision. However, although we believe in the importance, and even the necessity, of freedom *as an ideal*, an important question for us to face honestly is how free we are *in fact*.

This question of personal freedom is most crucial in terms of our own individual identity. How free are we to choose our identity, our vision of ourself, who we want to become? As Linus realized, we live in a world of consequences, and our choice is often determined by the environment around us—e.g., the realization of the consequences for our actions. Until we become aware that our lives are strongly influenced by the social, physical, and internal environments, we may be living under a false image of freedom: an illusion of freedom.

Naturalness—If It Feels Good, Why Change?

All individuals are socialized to the mores and customs of the culture. We learn what kinds of behavior to engage in in order to bring rewards and praise for ourselves, and what kinds of behavior to avoid in order to escape punishment. There is a large body of literature that discusses the role of different groups involved in this socialization process, including parents, peers, the educational system, the mass media. An individual learns to accept the social conventions that are taught, and eventually internalizes them. As long as we are comfortable in our ordinary routines, and life is going smoothly for us, we feel free, and there seems little reason to change.

This can also be illustrated by a story about our dog, Gudrin. We put up a small "child barrier" in the kitchen to keep Gudrin from going into the living room. We would tell her "No" whenever she tried to jump the barrier, and we would pet her when she would lie down next to it. She soon learned to fall asleep at the foot of the barrier. A few months later, we took the barrier down during a general housecleaning. Gudrin, however, never crossed into the living room, and continued to lie down to sleep in the same spot. That spot had become hers—it felt natural and secure.

Social learning theorists would suggest that we are like Gudrin in many ways. The habits we have—both positive and

"POLISH YOUR BUCKLES, KEEP YOUR BREECHES CLEAN ... TAKE A BATH EVERY WEEK WHETHER YA NEED IT OR NOT..."

negative—are often the result of many years of conditioning. We do them reflexively, without thinking. They feel "natural."

I recently saw a couple who complained that they had few friends and felt lonely. The husband was annoyed because he had to take all the initiative in calling people up for dinner, or a movie, or a general get-together. The wife said that she had never had to take the initiative in social interactions—that before she was married, men would always call her for a date. She noted that "it doesn't feel natural for me to do the calling," and added that she felt he was forcing her—making her feel "trapped and unfree."

From a social learning viewpoint, what we are trained (or conditioned, or socialized) to do feels natural, feels free. Those behaviors we don't get a chance to practice very often don't feel natural; rather they make us feel unfree, forced. However, the feeling of naturalness, the feeling of freedom about certain actions is not innate. Rather, it is a result of our prior learning. Because certain behaviors, certain likes and dislikes, now feel natural, we cling to them tenaciously as "ours." But we are merely clinging to an illusion of freedom; we are clinging to our past conditioning. Once we realize this, we have the choice to *un*learn negative self-defeating habit patterns, emotional reflex responses, and to learn new skills. With practice, the old habit patterns will disappear, will come to feel unnatural, and the new skills soon come to feel natural. The important point to emphasize is that, *unless we become aware of the process by which we are conditioned, we will continue to believe that our behavior is "natural,"* that we are "freely" choosing this "natural" way, and we will not ever be aware that we are merely choosing to return to old habit patterns that we were taught long ago.

THE CRISIS

Behavior before Awareness

The first development necessary in gaining awareness of our determinism is some sort of crisis or jolt. Skinner, for example, has suggested that awareness of ourselves and our behavior is not an automatic phenomenon, and that we only become aware when this awareness has a *survival value.*[3] In other words, *awareness of our behavior comes after the behavior has already occurred.* For example, it seems that at some point in almost everyone's life, there comes an event, or series of events, that jolts us out of our ordinary habit patterns of everyday living.

Often these "jolts" are small, and cause us only minor discomfort or awkwardness: e.g., telling a joke that doesn't get a

response; feeling slighted by an acquaintance; not getting a pay raise which one feels is deserved; losing something we value; not being able to decide between two alternatives. Usually we are able to dismiss these incidents as inconsequential, and quickly return to our ordinary routines.

However, sometimes the jolts are more painful, and may cause a great deal of confusion. These larger jolts—crises—may make us stand back from our ordinary routines—including our relationship to society, to other people, to ourself, and to a religious/spiritual dimension—and question them in a fundamental way. Let me suggest some types of events that may lead to this confusion.

Goals Which, Once Attained, No Longer Seem Meaningful

Every society holds out an image of the good life. In our society, the classical stereotype of the good life involves a middle-class family with two cars, money in the bank for the children's education, a home in the suburbs. Yet often, once these goals have been achieved, something seems to be missing.

Having moved along on the traditional reward structure of society from high school to college to professional or graduate school to job placements to promotions, an individual often arrives at what he has been told is happiness—and yet he does not feel it. The carrot for which he is striving, and for which society has taught him to strive, does not seem worth the price. This is illustrated in Hesse's *Siddhartha.*[4] Siddhartha spent several years learning the ways of business from Kawaswami and the ways of love from the beautiful goddess Kamala. He wore fine clothes, earned great wealth and property. Yet Siddhartha became "nauseated with himself, with his perfumed hair . . . with the soft flabby appearance of his skin."

> Slowly, like moisture entering the dying trunk of a tree, filling and rotting it, so did the world and inertia creep into Siddhartha's soul . . . the bright and clear inward voice, that had once awakened in him and had always guided him in his finest hours, had become silent.[5]

Leaving the world of business and pleasure, he walked to the river where, disgusted and tempted to drown himself, he fell

The Now Society

By WILLIAM HAMILTON

Steel, of course, has been my life. But sometimes I wish my life had been sitting with a pretty girl in a sunny cafe in Provence, drinking Beaujolais.

asleep. That night, he dreamt that the songbird, which Kamala kept in a golden cage, had died. Thus, attaining the material goals of society may leave a sense of emptiness, a feeling that the bird in the breast has not been heard and that, in the process of attainment, some important part of us has died.

Not Being Able to Obtain the Rewards Held Out by Society

An individual is taught to work hard to achieve certain goals, and our cultural mores suggest that there will be certain rewards for hard work. In America today, however, there is no longer necessarily a direct correlation between hard work, educational training, and achievement of success. There are no clear-cut paths, no certainties. The Horatio Alger myth is breaking down. Not only have the traditional societal "carrots" been held out increasingly later in life, but the rewards themselves have become more difficult to obtain, because of increased competition and the existence of fewer interesting, prestigious, and secure positions. After this hard work, if the rewards are not forthcoming, a person may be jolted into stepping back and questioning the cultural mores into which he has been socialized.

Interpersonal Loss

Another event that often constitutes a crisis is the loss of a loved one. By shaking us loose from our conventional perspective, such an event often makes us realize that some of the goals we have been striving for may not be so important in the end.

We have already discussed the fact that we are conscious of impending death and yet unable to do anything about its inevitability. When Adam and Eve were in the garden, and ate from the apple, they were punished for their increased awareness of the knowledge of good and evil, not only by feelings of embarrassment and modesty but also by being forced to confront their finitude and mutual death. "You were dust and to dust you shall return" (Genesis 3:19). Biblical poets from the psalmists to the writer of Ecclesiastes have cried in anguish at man's condemnation to death. The protagonist in Camus' play *Caligula* says, "men die and they are not happy." Cessation of earthly existence is a fact; we cannot change it. No matter how much research is done in nutrition and medicine, no matter what goals we choose for our life, whether we are good, evil, or amoral, the rain falls and we die.* The poets' shouts seem to echo uselessly in a deaf, indifferent universe; God is a God of silence. Because of increased awareness, we realize we are condemned to death. Some existentialists, such as Heidegger, feel that only the dread of death, the lonely *Angst* that results from awareness of our own nothingness, can inspire us to truly create our destiny. A particularly poignant example illustrating our human frailty occurred in a *Playboy* interview with Dustin Hoffman:

*In social learning theory terms, the problem is that death is an inevitable consequence of life. It is interesting to note that many Western and Eastern religions attempt to make death either a positive or an aversive consequence (i.c., concepts of heaven, hell, rebirth, *karma*). Proponents of Judaism and Zen admit that we don't know what occurs after death. The only rebirth they speak of occurs *during* life (see Chapter 4).

Hoffman: I was an attendant, which meant that I went to work every morning at six-thirty or seven and worked all day, eight or nine hours, cleaning up the patients' mess, their excrement, playing Scrabble, cards, ping-pong with them; taking them to hydrotherapy, to workshops, to dances, playing volleyball. I played piano for some of them, like the doctor.

The doctor had been a brilliant pathologist at the hospital, but he had had two or three strokes and had been reduced to less than a child. He had to be fed, changed. His wife was a doctor, too, and every day she would come to visit him at lunchtime. You could see they'd had a terrific marriage. She'd always ask, "Did he eat? How's his appetite?" She never gave up hope. He could talk only in gibberish, like baby talk. "Gegadabadoo?" he'd say. And I'd say back to him, "Vegavegava." And he'd laugh.

But, anyway, I'd play the piano for him. He loved the song "*Goodnight Irene.*" He could almost sing it: "Goo-nigh, Irene, goo." And one day he was sitting on the sofa, singing, and suddenly the door opened and he stopped. It was his wife. And he stood up—he'd never done that before—and rushed toward her, shuffling as best he could, and they met midway in the room, like in a movie. He was crying. I'd never seen him cry before. Crying buckets. And she asked, "What is it?" And he looked at her and there was a moment of such lucidity in his face. And he said, "I can't, I can't, I can't." And I broke down. I quit soon after that. I couldn't do it any more. But I'll never forget that scene. You put it in a movie and nobody would believe it. I might put it in a movie, though, at that. He's dead now, and to be able to make him live again, even in a film, would be nice.[6]

The Mystery

There are those who have an awareness crisis that has no apparent cause. Many who have confronted these feelings have described them in mystical, religious, or existential terms. In Jean-Paul Sartre's novel *Nausea* the protagonist Roquentin is haunted by an overwhelming awareness that he knows nothing about life. Even the things that do exist for him, such as stones and trees and self, seem to exist without any reason. When this mood is on him Roquentin calls it *nausea.* William James had earlier called it the *ontological sickness*, in which monotonous days come and go, cities look alike, and nothing happens that means anything.

Thus, there are many events which may cause us to be jolted

from our ordinary activities. The reaction to these events may range from a mild confusion to awkwardness to a painful existential anxiety about our relationship with the universe, and how, in a fundamental sense, we fit into the scheme of things.

The Effects of a Crisis on Our Self-concept

Nowhere are the effects of this crisis—or jolting—more acutely felt than in our concept of ourselves. As long as we feel we are on the "railroad track of existence," the signals are clear and our self-esteem is based upon predictable indicators of success. However, if our sense of self is built upon external criteria, then it may be quite fragile. We may continually look for a reaffirmation of that self, both from others

Oh, I suppose it doesn't really mean anything — but someone tried to put me on "hold" today.

and from the material possessions that we have around us.

Jack and I are checking all our status symbols.

We may see everything directed at us, threatening our sense of self, and use many types of crutches to build up self-confidence.

As long as our sense of worth is dependent on external criteria—social praise, number of possessions—we will constantly be threatened with losing it. Therefore we may become possessive of our accumulations, competitive over our job positions. The focus may be on building our own sense of identity rather than on sharing ourselves with others.

If our sense of self is dependent upon others, we may be overly swayed by their perceptions, as in the case of the Asch experiment, or willing to unquestioningly follow the orders of authority, as illustrated in the Milgram experiment.* (Refer back to Chapter 2, "The Power of the Environment, Social Environment.")

We may hide behind a self-created image, a *persona* in Jungian terms, a mask that we create and which we present to others. Part of this *persona* may involve basing our identity not on who we are as people, but on our role in society. As long as our sense of identity and positive self-esteem are based only on our work, there will inevitably be a time when we will face a crisis, either through forced or voluntary retirement.

What happens to our sense of self when we are "jolted"?

We may feel, as Heidegger noted, a "non-essence" within ourselves.[7] We may become confused about our identity, unsure of who we are. As Alice put it in *Alice in Wonderland*,

> Let me think: was I the same when I got up this morning? I almost think I can remember feeling a little different. But if I'm not the same, the next question is, "Who in the world am I?" Ah, that's the great puzzle.

When external standards break down, and we are left with the feelings of emptiness and nothingness, where do we turn to answer the question of "Who in the world am I?" How do we deal with this time of crisis? What are its implications?

*In the Milgram experiment, individuals followed the orders of a "scientist" even when these orders involved the (seeming) punishment by electrical shock of other individuals. Milgram told his subjects he needed their help in training individuals (who were really the experimenter's confederates) to perfect performances, and that each time the confederate made a mistake, they should be shocked (up to a presumed 450 volt level). Although the confederates shouted for the subjects to stop the shocking, and although the subjects themselves became disturbed at what they were doing, the majority of the subjects continued to administer the shocks. (S. Milgram. Behavioral Study of Obedience. *Journal of Abnormal and Social Psychology*, 1963 (67) 371–378.)

The Chinese word for crisis consists of two characters. The first character may be translated as "danger," the second as "opportunity." The facing of fundamental questions about our current lifestyle, the realization of the ways in which we have been conditioned and socialized, a feeling of loss of traditional support systems, and the confusion over what comes next may be a frightening experience, a time literally filled with mental and emotional "danger."

However, a crisis* may also be a time of hope, for we have an opportunity to take responsibility for our lives, to evaluate how we have been conditioned and how we would like to live. We also have the opportunity to develop a new awareness, and to choose and affirm a way of creating ourselves anew. In Chapter 4 we turn to a discussion of these opportunities.

SUMMARY

In this chapter we suggested that we are *not* born free. Rather, we have learned certain ways of acting, certain preferences, and we *believe* that we are freely choosing these preferences. In reality, however, it appears that these choices are merely the result of our prior conditioning. We live in an illusion of freedom. We will continue to live in an illusion of freedom until a crisis jolts us out

*The Chinese word *wei-ji* has no exact English equivalent. "Crisis" may have too many connotations of a deficit, a problem. However, the "turning point" implied in *wei-ji* may also occur at times of growth and positive change.

of our ordinary habit patterns. Several different types of "crisis" were suggested, ranging from feeling that past goals are no longer meaningful, not being able to obtain society's goals, interpersonal loss, to a sense of the religious and spiritual mystery of existence. When this crisis occurs, it is most acutely felt in our self-concept, and we may be forced to ask fundamental questions about who we are as individuals. This crisis, in addition to being a time of danger and confusion, may also be a time of opportunity: an opportunity to see how we have been conditioned, and to choose a new vision of how we would like to live.

4

Responsibility & Evaluation: Toward a New Awareness & an Affirmation

When one is unenlightened,
the snows of Mt. Fuji are the snows
of Mt. Fuji, and the water
of Tassajara is the water
of Tassajara.

When one seeks enlightenment,
the snows of Mt. Fuji are not the snows
of Mt. Fuji, and the water
of Tassajara is not the water
of Tassajara.

DEVELOPING A NEW AWARENESS (AWARENESS BEFORE BEHAVIOR)

The Problem: Things Are as They Seem

The poem beginning this chapter provides us with a landmark, a guidepost on our path.[1] If we look at the first stanza, we note that all appears normal, yet we are considered "unenlightened." This is because, as we pointed out in Chapter 3, the way we initially "see" is the result of our conditioning. As long as we unquestioningly maintain the daily routines into which we have been socialized, we are responding primarily as conditioned human beings, and our mode of seeing is blinded by our preconceptions about reality.

Writers on the psychology of consciousness, such as Charles Tart,[2] note that our ordinary awareness of the world, though it feels natural, is merely a projection of a reality that is conditioned by the culture. Each of us sees the world through tinted glasses, with the result that we have preconceptions that can act like blinders. The way of the East suggests that techniques like meditation are necessary in order to develop an awareness of our preconceptions, and eventually as a way to remove them entirely. As Naranjo and Ornstein put it: "Meditation is a persistent effort to detect and become free from all conditioning, compulsive functioning of mind and body, habitual emotional responses. . . .[3]

Social learning theorists also note how fickle our senses are, and how easy it is for us to make mistakes when we observe our own behavior. Further, they stress how difficult it is for us to develop "outsight," which involves perceiving the relationship between our behavior and the way it affects and is affected by the environment.[4] This is why they suggest the need for *controlled self-observation.*

Through the practice of meditation, as described in Chapter 1, and through systematic self-observation, as described in Chapter 2, we may become more sensitive to and more aware of our conditioning. This awareness helps us realize how many "reflex choices" we make each day.

This sensitivity to and awareness of all our actions is one of the main goals in Zen, as illustrated by the following story entitled "Every-Minute Zen":

> Nan-in was visited by Tenno, who, having passed his apprenticeship, had become a teacher. The day happened to be rainy, so Tenno wore wooden clogs and carried an umbrella. After greeting him, Nan-in remarked, "I suppose you left your wooden clogs in the vestibule. I want to know if your umbrella is on the left or the right side of the clogs."
>
> Tenno, confused, had no instant answer. He realized that he was unable to carry his Zen every minute. He became Nan-in's pupil, and he studied six more years to accomplish his every-minute-Zen.[5]

It is quite difficult, however, to remain aware of each moment. This was pointed out by Dostoevsky through his character the General in *The Idiot.* The general tells Myshkin of the time ten years before when he had stood in front of a firing squad. Knowing he had only five minutes to live, he decided to make the best use of his time, so he spent two minutes thinking of his friends and relatives and two minutes reviewing the past highlights of his life. In the last minute he thought of all the wasted moments and decided that if only he could have a reprieve, he would be aware of every second of his life, never missing a second.

When Myshkin asked him if he had been able to follow through on this vow, the General replied, "No, it is not possible."[6]

Unless we make a strong commitment to develop a new

awareness and sensitivity, it will be easy for us to fall back into old ways, and to once again feel that our old ways are "natural." The development of this new awareness has several advantages, for it allows us to learn to see more choice points, both large and small. We will learn to perceive these choice points when we are deciding on a career, or a spouse, or times when we respond reflexively, or when we get angry over trivia, as well as times when we get caught in double-bind situations. Let met give a few illustrations of different types of choice points.

Interpersonal and Professional Choices

There are many different types of choice points. Some of them may involve quite large decisions—e.g., regarding a career, a spouse, whether or not to have children, and other such broad value and life style decisions. Important choices have to be made on matters such as these, and it is instructive for us to quickly think back over our lives and honestly assess how many of our choices were made carefully, how many were made *for* us, and how many "just occurred."

Emotional Choice Points: Freedom to Choose Our Reactions

Choice points are not always apparent. We may find ourselves confronted by a situation in which there seem to be no alternatives. An example, on a far more horrendous scale than most of us will ever have to face, is given by Victor Frankl, who was held prisoner in a Nazi concentration camp.[7] He had no choice about being imprisoned. However, he did have a choice in terms of his attitude toward that imprisonment. Confronted by an ugly and degrading environment, some people gave up and died; some, like Frankl, made a conscious choice not to be overwhelmed by the environment and found a new will to survive.

It is important for us to realize that even if we have no alternatives in the external environment, we do have alternatives in the internal environment: they involve the way we respond to the situation. For example, let me ask you to look at the two monkeys in the illustration. What do you think is off to the right of the picture? What are they looking at?

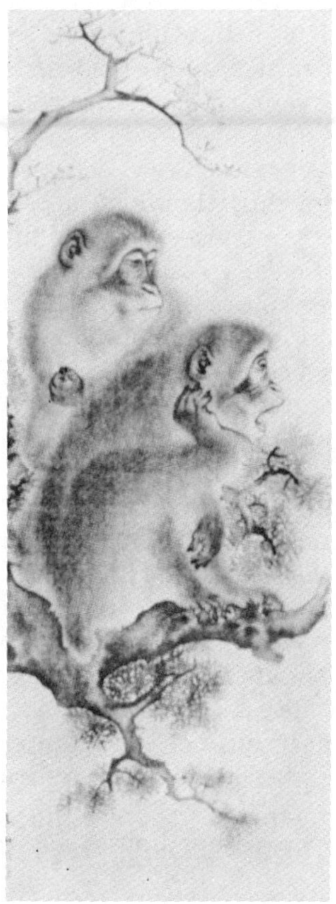

We don't really know what is out there, but we do know that both monkeys are having a reaction to it. The monkey in the foreground is upset and hysterical. At first glance, it may look as though the monkey in the background is indifferent; however, if we look at this monkey more closely, we see that the left hand is making a strong gesture, suggesting a centeredness and a preparedness.

I use this picture to suggest that there will almost always be, in varying degrees, something "out there in the world" that will be upsetting and stressful. There will always be troubles and imperfections in the world. The picture illustrates that, even though upsetting external events exist, *we have some degree of control in terms of choosing how we respond to the stress.*

Double-bind Situations

Double-bind situations are those in which a person receives two simultaneous, contradictory messages of equal importance. Double-bind situations seem particularly controlling because they appear to allow the individual no course of action. No matter what you do, you are wrong. Therefore, seemingly you have been deprived of your freedom to act in a competent, effective manner.

The following anecdote illustrates a double-bind situation I experienced recently. I was carrying bricks from our driveway to an area thirty yards away where I intended to put in a brick patio. The bricks weighed about five pounds each, and at first I carried five or six per load. Soon, I tried to increase that amount, and finally, after much juggling, I managed to stick eight under one arm. I stood up and turned to walk to the patio. A car honked, and a young couple, who were househunting, asked me, "Do you know anything about the house for sale across the street?"

"Yes," I said, "they are asking for bids."

"Oh, do you know at what price the bids are starting?"

"No, I don't," I said, feeling a pain in my arm, and beginning to walk away.

"Have there been any other houses for sale in this area recently?"

"No," I said curtly, feeling more pain from the weight of the bricks.

"What is the closing date for the bids to be in?"

"Don't know," I growled.

"Do you know where the realty office is?"

"No," I said, turning and walking away.

"Thanks for your help. Oh, by the way. . . ."

I threw the bricks down, feeling a throbbing in my arm, and annoyed with myself for being unfriendly. Only in retrospect did I become aware that I had allowed myself to remain in the double-bind situation: holding heavy bricks which I wanted to take to the patio while at the same time wanting to be friendly to some people asking for help. Rather than doing *neither* well, I could have (1) set the bricks down on the brick pile and talked to the couple; (2) told them to wait a minute, I'd like to talk, but first I wanted to carry the bricks into the yard; or (3) walked over and given them the bricks to hold while we talked. Thus, we see that there may be alternative ways of acting even in double-bind situations.

Before we can make a decision, we have to be finely tuned in to situations (such as the double-bind situation above) in which we have the opportunity to decide. The brick incident may be relatively small and unimportant; but it represents a crucial first stop in choosing how we want to act: *awareness that there is, at every moment, an opportunity for choice.*

DEVELOPING AN AFFIRMATION

The Problem: Things Are Not as They Seem

As we suggested in Chapter 3, it is only when we face a crisis and are jolted out of our ordinary conditioned habit patterns that we have the opportunity for personal freedom, the opportunity to stand back and question our lifestyle, values, and conditioning; the opportunity for a new way of "seeing."

But as the second stanza of the poem at the beginning of this chapter suggests, the crisis, the seeking of enlightenment, is not necessarily easy or pleasant. There is a confusion, a "danger"; things are not as they seem. For some, this period of confusion shakes their entire "ground of being." Camus, for example, describes his confrontation with the meaninglessness of the universe, and states that the only important philosophical question for a human being is that of suicide: "judging whether life is or is not worth living. . . ."[8] Confronted with a confusing, meaningless universe, Camus chooses and affirms life. He affirms the search for meaning, at the same time realizing that the search itself may be no more meaningful than Sisyphus pushing the rock up the hill, only to have it roll down again.

To some degree, when we are attempting to make changes in our lives—whether big or small—we are all faced with the same question: Is it worth it? What is the payoff, the reward, the reinforcement? In other words, what is our motivation?* During the time of crisis, it is necessary for us to make an affirmation that the search, or the change, *is* worth it. We need to commit ourselves to our choices, whether they involve the passionate choosing of life itself, as in the case of Camus, or other important choices of family and professional commitments, or lifestyle changes. To make an affirmation, to be willing to commit to and take responsibility for a new way of acting, is an extremely difficult task. In many ways, our old habit patterns are comfortable. We have spent many years developing them. When we initially try to act in new ways, we are like a young child taking tentative first steps. We feel awkward and self-conscious. We wonder if it's worth the extra effort. Why not continue to crawl? Why risk the chance of failure?

These are valid questions, and must be faced as part of our decision-making process, as part of our affirmation. A further difficult problem is the one of where to look for alternatives. We know the old ways. We don't know the new. What's on the other side of the confusion? Is there a third stanza to the poem?

Let us turn to an exploration of the decision-making process, including a discussion of the need for finding alternatives, the fear that is involved in choosing and taking responsibility for an alter-

*I would like to make a distinction, which is not often made in our everyday language, between motivation and willpower. I define motivation as the desire and the determination to do something, and willpower as the skills to carry through with the desire. Motivation involves the important first step of deciding that something is worth doing, that a contract is worth fulfilling, that the reward for certain actions are worth the effort involved. Before we make any kind of contract with ourselves or with others, we have to have made a decision that we are willing to risk having the contract work. Then, once we are willing to undertake a self-change project, we need the skills to carry through with the project, the willpower. Certainly, there is an interrelationship between motivation and willpower. For example, once you begin a project, if you break the project down into small units (successive approximation) and reward yourself liberally for each section completed, you will begin to feel more desire and determination to succeed.[9]

native, the importance of affirming and getting behind our decision 100 percent.

The Decision-making Process

Search for New Alternatives

Once we learn that our vision of freedom, or free will, has heretofore been illusory, we are in a position to begin to search for alternatives, to stand back and make a decision—to make freedom a reality. In choosing a vision, we may look for alternatives to our modes of ordinary awareness, alternatives to our career choices, alternatives to our habitual emotional responses, and/or alternatives to our current values, lifestyle, and ethics. Looking at certain alternatives may involve a fundamental questioning of ourselves. It may cause us to assess the ways in which we have been influenced by social variables (e.g., reinforcement, money, prestige). We see and understand the ways in which our vision of the world has heretofore been conditioned by patterns of ordinary awareness. We also come to realize the way in which all these variables have thus far fit into our decision-making process.

Initially, we may decide that everything we've always stood for is wrong, and find ourselves merely reacting against the society's socialization process in the proverbial adolescent rebellion. Rather than choosing new alternatives and modes of acting, we may simply fall into a pattern of choosing only to rebel against that which is. As Neitzsche noted, "Youth's soul turns on itself, tears itself to pieces, takes revenge for its long self-delusion. Ten years later, one comprehends that this, too, was still youth."[10]

We may realize that some of the old ways, though only part of the truth, did have some merit to them after all. Yet, when there are two or more alternatives, how do we know if we are making the right decision? How do we know what is the right way to re-create ourselves, so we don't make the same mistakes? What are the criteria that can be used in making a choice?

Fear and Trembling[11]

It is not easy to make a decision. The existentialist Jean-Paul Sartre has stressed that we are literally condemned to freedom, and that if we haven't felt the anguish over decision making, then we have never truly made a choice. We need to realize that ultimately, in an existential sense, there are no right or wrong answers; there are no criteria other than those of our own choosing; there are no ultimate guidelines by which to live our life, except those which we choose to make ultimate. As Dostoevsky believed, if God doesn't exist, everything is permitted. There is nothing to cling to, no values, no commands. We are alone without excuses.[12] *And*, we must take responsibility for our choices.

Evaluating Alternatives and Making a Choice

Amidst the uncertainty, we are still faced with the need to make choices. There are certain skills involved in the decision-making process. These skills may not lessen the fear and trembling about actually making a decision, but they do provide guidelines for helping us feel we've done as thorough a job as possible, and they may, in certain types of decisions, help optimize the possibility for a successful outcome.

The first step in decision making, as we have seen, involves *seeking information about different alternatives.* Once such information has been gathered, there is a need for *careful evaluation* in which the consequences of the different alternatives are considered. Here we are faced with the question of how much evaluation is beneficial. We would agree that there is a danger of too much evaluation and too little action. Hamlet is a classic example of the difficulty of decision making—he was constantly evaluating whether or not to act, how to act, and thereby lived in a cerebral world without ever moving forward on any of his plans.

There are two old proverbs: "Look before you leap," in which an individual is advised to evaluate before he moves forward toward his goals, and "He who hesitates is lost," in which evaluation and thinking preclude effective action. Let me suggest that we look for a delicate balance between these two proverbs. In our decision-making efforts, having gathered relevant information about the alternatives, having evaluated as much as possible the consequences of alternatives, we must then realize that we cannot ever operate with complete security about a decision; we must *risk a choice.*

Getting Behind Ourselves 100 Percent

Once we have made a choice, we need to *affirm it, and to get behind it 100 percent.* This isn't as easy as it sounds. Very few decisions between two alternatives are clear-cut. Usually there are pros and cons to any choice. Evaluating positive and negative consequences is necessary while we are deciding. Let's take a trivial example. Your spouse has asked you to go to a movie tonight. You want to please your spouse and go (alternative 1), and yet you're really tired and would like to stay home this evening (alternative 2). You weigh the consequences: e.g., if you go, you may feel tired and not enjoy the movie as much; if you stay home, you'll be disappointing your spouse. There is no clear "right" answer.

However, once you've evaluated and made a choice, you need to take responsibility for the choice and get behind that choice 100 percent. If you go, go and have fun, with no complaints, without saying, "But I didn't really want to." If you stay home, stay home 100 percent, and don't lose sleep feeling guilty. As the Master said:

We now see that in re-creating ourselves, we need to involve ourselves in a conscious decision-making process in which we existentially choose to affirm and take responsibility for our commitment to whatever decision we make, whether it is large or small. If we accept the existential view that we are always "choosing," then we would assume that our choices would always be in our own best interest (that is, have positive consequences for us). If we choose something that is not in our best interest, there would have to be a reason, such as (a) we don't have the skills to choose otherwise; (b) we are not aware of alternatives; or (c) we are getting something positive, in some way, out of the choice (even if there are simultaneously undesirable consequences).

It seems that we only choose to change when we believe that the positive consequences for change (e.g., *negative reinforcement*—the removal of an aversive stimulus—or *positive reinforcement*) outweigh the fear of risk, the extra effort, and whatever advantages we already get from the old way of acting. At every moment, we have the opportunity to decide whether or not our choices are really in our own best interest.

To help us in the affirmation and commitment to choices in our own best interest, we may *seek models of excellence* (whether living or dead) whom we admire, who affirmed life, and who led lives we would like to emulate. We can *stress to ourselves the positive aspects of our affirmation*—that is, call up images and statements of support and encouragement, knowing in advance there will be difficult times. We may *look to a future image* of ourselves acting in new ways, and pay attention to the advantages of our "new way of acting," our "new self." We may also use specific methods such as *thought-stopping techniques* to counter negative, unproductive, "sabotaging" thoughts. ("The Development of Thought-Stopping Techniques" is discussed in detail in Chapter 6, under "Combining Eastern and Western Techniques: Case Examples," in "Case One.")

At this point, it may be worthwhile to take a moment to write about your own personal motivation,* and to note what's

*As a way of pinpointing aspects of your "ideal self" that you may wish to commit yourself to working toward, you can look back to your list of "Realistic Goals" in the section "The Element of Choice in Personal Freedom: Choosing Our Vision" in Chapter 2. You may also wish to look at "What is Freedom?" in Chapter 3 to help in determining times you have and times you haven't felt free.

in it for you to affirm and commit to creating yourself. Ask yourself:

What is the present condition? What happens if no change is made?

____

____

What positive benefits and advantages can be gained by changing? What are the incentives to succeed?

____

____

What are the difficult times that you see ahead if you do decide to change? What excuses might you make to sabotage your own efforts? (e.g., it doesn't feel natural to change. I can't change. It's too hard. I have no willpower, etc.)

____

____

Regardless of what we choose, it seems that the most important thing is not so much the content of the choice, but the affirmation involved in the act of choosing. As the existentialists have stressed, *an individual, by choosing, creates him/herself.*

Thus, after all the analysis and evaluation of our alternatives, we also need to learn to let go of analysis, and risk the choice. We need to switch from the mode of ordinary awareness to the mode of the altered state. In so doing, we may let go of our evaluations, obtain a new perspective, and watch ourselves play our "as if" roles as "mere mortals on the stage of life." As we work to make changes in our life, to create our new "self," we become actors in personal dramas unencumbered by theories of personality, able to see our lives with a sense of humor, to laugh at ourselves, because we can see both our reason *and* our unreason with detachment. However, at the same time we sense the humor, we also attempt to live our lives as openly, authentically, and fully as is humanly possible. We choose existentially to be the kind of actor we want to play, based on our visions of people and models, living or dead, real or fictional, that we believe led lives we would like to emulate.

So now, having assumed responsibility, having affirmed our commitment to create ourselves, and having embarked on a serious quest with a twinkle in our eye, let's turn to one possible model of an integrated vision: a path of heart.

SUMMARY

In this chapter we discussed ways in which a new awareness could be developed by using both meditative and behavioral self-observation strategies. It was emphasized that in order to make conscious choices, we have to become aware of the myriad of choice points that we potentially face each day. Some examples, such as interpersonal and professional choice points, emotional choice points, and double-bind situations were given. This chapter also emphasized the importance of making an affirmation and commitment to choosing a new vision. Finally, the decision-making process was explored, including the search for new alternatives, fear and trembling, evaluating alternatives, and getting behind ourselves 100 percent.

5

A New Alternative: The Path of Heart

Does this path have a heart? If it does, the path is good; if it doesn't, it is of no use. Both paths lead nowhere; but one has a heart, the other doesn't. One makes for a joyful journey; as long as you follow it, you are one with it. The other will make you curse your life. One makes you strong; the other weakens you.

> Anything is one of a million paths. . . . Therefore you must always keep in mind that a path is only a path; if you feel you should not follow it, you must not stay with it under any conditions. To have such clarity you must lead a disciplined life. Only then will you know that any path is only a path, and there is no affront, to oneself or to others, in dropping it if that is what your heart tells you to do. But your decision to keep on the path or to leave it must be free of fear or ambition. I warn you. Look at every path closely and deliberately. Try it as many times as you think necessary. This question is one that only a very old man asks. My benefactor told me about it once when I was young, and my blood was too vigorous for me to understand it. Now I do understand it. I will tell you what it is: Does this path have a heart? All paths are the same: they lead nowhere. They are paths going through the bush, or into the bush. In my own life I could say I have traversed long, long paths, but I am not anywhere. My benefactor's question has meaning now. Does this path have a heart? If it does, the path is good; if it doesn't it is of no use. Both paths lead nowhere; but one has a heart, the other doesn't. One makes for a joyful journey; as long as you follow it, you are one with it. The other will make you curse your life. One makes you strong; the other weakens you.[1]

In a real sense, the crisis discussed in Chapter 3 may be like a death—the death of an old lifestyle. In Hesse's book *Siddhartha*, the protagonist goes through many symbolic deaths *during* his lifetime. He dies when he leaves his father to live with the ascetics; he dies when he leaves the ascetics to search on his own; he dies when he leaves the city, and the ways of the businessman Kawaswami and the ways of the goddess of sensual pleasure, Kamala.

Yet each time Siddhartha dies, each time there is a death of an old lifestyle, there is an opportunity for re-choosing himself, an affirmation of a new lifestyle. Siddhartha literally has the opportunity to be reborn within the context of life.

As was suggested in Chapter 4, we too have the opportunity for choosing a new life, a new vision of ourselves. In this chapter we will examine the ways in which the Eastern and the Western visions of the human potential may be integrated.

We begin the creation of this integrated vision—this path of heart—at a time of confusion. As in the second stanza of the poem that began Chapter 4, things are not as they should be. We are literally searching for a third stanza, a new alternative.

Let us now turn to a discussion of the Zen and the social learning theory concepts of the "self" and see how these two views may be combined to help us formulate a new alternative.

THE SEARCH FOR THE "REAL ME"

We may laugh at Irwin's belief that Uncle Vilo may be found in close proximity to the location of Gaylord's "real me." But what is the "real me"? All of us have said, or heard someone say, "He's not acting like himself," "I didn't feel true to myself when I did that," "She's doing that for others, not because she really wants to," "Relax, be yourself." All these statements suggest the existence of a real me, a "real self," which is often covered by a facade. As noted in Chapter 4, the Jungians have called this facade the *persona.*[2] Carl Rogers has referred to it in terms of *not acting congruently with oneself.*[3] David Reisman referred to this phenomenon as *other-directedness:* that is, having one's direction in life determined by people and events outside oneself.[4] Many of us, like Ira below, have a fear of exposing this real me to the outside world:

Ira is distinguishing between "a side of me" and the "real me." Although intuitively we understand what Ira and Gaylord in the above cartoons mean by "a side of me" and the "real me," most of us would have difficulty explaining this precisely in words. Although we believe in the existence of a "real me," many of us would have difficulty saying where to turn in order to look for it, and would not be certain we could recognize it, even if we could find it. In the following material we will discuss both the Eastern and Western approaches to finding this "real me."

Removing Preconceptions and Trait Descriptions

Removing Preconceptions

As we noted in Chapter 3, as long as we are trapped in our conception of ourselves, we don't allow ourselves the freedom to experiment outside the bounds of this conception. Removing preconceptions gives us the freedom to see who we are in the here and now, and also gives us the freedom to begin to choose (or re-choose) a vision of ourselves—who we would like to become.

A parable from the tea master, Nan-in, is instructive in illustrating this point:

> Nan-in, a Japanese tea master during the Meiji era, received a university professor who came to inquire about Zen. Nan-in served tea. He poured the visitor's cup full, and then kept on pouring. The professor watched the overflow until he could restrain himself no longer: "It is overfull, no more will go in."
>
> "Like this cup," Nan-in responded, "you are full of your own opinions and speculations. How can I show you Zen unless you first empty your cup?"[5]

Just as the professor couldn't see Zen until he removed his preconceptions, so too, we can't begin to find our real me's until we remove our own preconceptions.

Yet it is extremely difficult to perceive our own preconceptions because we are not aware that we have any. To help in learning to see your own preconceptions, let me ask you to do three quick exercises. First, think of the worst person you are actually acquainted with and see occasionally. Quickly think of the two worst characteristics of this person, and write them below. Don't think too hard—write down the first two that come to mind.

1. ______________________________

2. ______________________________

Now, just as quickly, think of and write down two of your own positive characteristics.

1. ______________________________

2. ______________________________

Finally, write down two of your negative characteristics.

1. ____

2. ____

Please do the above exercises before proceeding, because we will refer back to them.

Trait Descriptions

In psychological terms, *a trait is a verbal label that is used to describe an individual's behavior across a variety of situations:* e.g., "He's a hyperactive child," "John is a sensitive man," "Jeannie is an aggressive woman," "Zed is a self-actualized human being." Psychologists (e.g., Allport, Cattell, Jung) study traits in order to determine whether individuals have consistent patterns of behavior, whether all people have certain basic traits, and whether certain traits are healthier than others. Normally these traits are thought to be innate (Freud's *aggression*, ego psychologists' *self-actualization*), although some theorists (e.g., Allport) talk of *acquired traits.*

All of us, whether psychologists or not, use trait terms when describing ourselves and others. See, for example, the words you used to describe your worst enemy and yourself above. It is very difficult not to use trait descriptions. For example, try describing a mutual acquaintance without referring to personal traits.

Psychologists attempt to be more scientific and objective in their assessment of traits by using a variety of diagnostic tests and instruments. The assumption is made that, when a person has a particular trait, this trait appears "across situations." For example, an "aggressive" person is someone who is aggressive with parents, spouse, siblings, peers—at home, at school, and in the office. The "hyperactive" child is hyperactive in all situations with many different types of people.

However, although psychologists claim to be objective in assessing traits, research is showing that the characteristics people "assess" in others are more related to the way they themselves see the world than to the actual behavior of the individual(s) involved. This seems to be true for laypeople as well as psychologists. For example, research results indicate that once stimuli are grouped, the perceiver tends to retain the category even in the face of contradictory evidence. He pays less attention to new evidence and focuses on confirming information.[6] In one study it was found that psychotherapists categorized patients in the initial two to four hours, and that this categorization was enduring after twenty-four sessions. Additional information that didn't confirm the initial conceptualization was ignored.[7] A very important study showing the way traits are (mis)used was done by David Rosenhan of Stanford University.[8] In this study eight "normal" individuals had themselves admitted to different psychiatric hospitals. They gained entrance by telling the admission officers that they heard voices (of the same sex), saying "empty, thud, hollow." Beyond alleging the symptoms and changing their names, vocations, and employment, no other changes in life history, personal relationships, etc. were made. Immediately upon gaining admission to the hospital, the pseudo-patients were given diagnostic labels. Seven were classified as schizophrenic and one was classified as manic-depressive. During the course of their hospital stay, the "pseudo-patients" were given nearly 2,100 different pills, ranging from tranquilizers to anti-depressants. As Rosenhan noted, this range of medication is itself remarkable, since the "pseudo-patients" presented identical symptoms. All the "pseudo-patients" took copious notes during their stays, and this was identified by the staff as "compulsive writing behavior."

A psychiatrist pointed to a group of patients standing in line a half-hour before lunchtime, and noted that such behavior was characteristic of the oral-acquisitive nature of the syndrome. "It seemed not to occur to him that there were very few things to anticipate in a psychiatric hospital besides eating."[9]

When the "pseudo-patients" were finally discharged from the hospital, they were diagnosed as being "in remission." In other words, the hospital staff felt that even though the person was no longer disturbed enough to remain in the hospital, he was still a "schizophrenic" and his illness was likely to recur.

The relationship between behavior and trait descriptions illustrated by this study may be described as follows:

Behavior before Diagnosis	*Diagnostic Label Assessment*	*Behavior after Diagnosis*	*Interpretation of Behavior after Diagnosis*
claims of internal voices heard	schizophrenic	writing; waiting in line to eat	compulsive, oral-acquisitive

The behavior before diagnosis was seen as a symptom; the label "schizophrenic" was diagnosed as the disease causing the symptom, and subsequent behaviors were re-interpreted by the staff in ways that were consistent with the diagnostic label given to the patient.

Skinner has called this line of reasoning a *middle way station.*[10] The middle way station refers to the step of interpreting a person's behavior due to a state of mind (anxious person; oral-acquisitive nature) rather than to the situation (important interview; nothing to look forward to in a hospital but meals). For example, let's imagine that an individual is about to go for a very important job interview. We observe this person and notice how anxious and tense he is (behavior before diagnosis). We *describe* that person's behavior by saying "He's an anxious person." In so doing, we give that person a trait (anxiety) which, in addition to describing his behavior, we assume also *explains* and *predicts* his behavior.

Behavior before Diagnosis/Label	*Label*	*Assumption*
Person acting anxious before interview	Anxious person	Anxiety is that person's state of mind and he will act that way across situations; if he doesn't appear anxious, he is only "in remission"

Social learning theorists, such as Mischel, point out that it is more useful to limit our discussion to a person's *behaviors*, the situations that provoke them, and their ramifications, rather than to the labels we attach to those behaviors. In that way, we are able to remove some of the limitations of ordinary awareness, and allow ourselves to remain more open to the total range of an individual's skills and capabilities. As Mischel noted after reviewing the literature on personality traits, "Traits are categories of the observor to describe behavior, and not necessarily the property of the observed behavior itself."[11]

Just as we apply trait descriptions to other people, we also apply them to ourselves. These trait descriptions make up our "self-concept." Social learning theorists are among those who hold that these self-descriptions do not explain behavior, and therefore, as Skinner stresses, are nothing but an "explanatory fiction."

This social learning theory view is similar to the existential view, which likewise rejects trait labels (essence) and focuses on a person's behavior (existence).[12] It is also similar to the Zen view, as we saw in Chapter 1. For example, throughout the Zen literature there are stories, *koans* and *mondos*, which point out the limitations of words to describe experience and, in the case of our current discussion, the limits of words in describing people.

> *Student:* Master, whenever appeal is made to words, there is a taint. What is the truth of the highest order?
>
> *Master:* Whenever appeal is made to words, there is a taint.[13]

The Zen way suggests that trait descriptions remove us further from the reality of experience and behavior, thereby removing us from the truth of the "highest order." As related to Rosenhan's study, Zen believers realize that we come to see people in terms of trait descriptions rather than as they "really are." Therefore, the Zen way suggests that we need to learn to remove labels or stop labeling in order to see people in all their humanness. As we discussed in Chapter 1, this involves seeing the flower the five hundredth time as we saw it the first time: that is, to see the flower with all the freshness of a new experience, unencumbered by words and labels. In psychological terms, the Zen way suggests that people learn to see without forming trait descriptions, and to observe nature, self, and other people without using categorization and trait labeling.

Thus, both Zen and social learning theorists agree that traits are, at best, not useful; and, at worst, they can be quite harmful. However, traits are very much a part of our language, our way of thinking, and are not easy to give up.

It might be worthwhile to try this experiment to give yourself a bit more freedom to see yourself. Take one of the two negative traits which you wrote down about yourself. For example, let's consider a label "hyperanxiety." Now take one of the data charts from the second chapter, and follow the steps of self-observation. First, define what you mean by "hyperanxiety." Then observe this behavior for a few days. Note particularly if you are hyperanxious twenty-four hours a day. If not, are there certain times of the day when you are more anxious than at other times? Are there certain people around whom you are more anxious? Are there certain physical places in which you are more anxious or less anxious? Are there certain situations (e.g., large party, alone with a friend) which cause more anxiety than others?

Observe this trait of yours for a couple of days. I think you will begin to find that, to a certain extent, a trait description is meaningless. There are many, many variations in the way a trait manifests itself each day, depending on the circumstances. Give yourself the freedom to see how you *really* act, rather than simply your conceptualization of how you act.

Now let's try another experiment. Go back to the two words you used to describe your worst enemy. Let's say they were "uncaring" and "selfish." Rather than use these words as trait labels—"he's an uncaring and selfish person"—let's try to rephrase them in terms of behavior: "He *acted* selfishly and uncaringly toward me in the following situations." This involves much more than making a semantic distinction for, in fact, we now give our enemy the freedom to be *who he really is.* We may find that this person also can be generous and caring toward other people. He may even be caring toward us at times. As long as we maintain trait labels, we blind ourselves to the very real nuances of behavior. We also blind ourselves to the possibility of change. Traits are seen as long-enduring, part of a person's "real me." They nearly preclude the possibility of an individual's learning new ways of acting. However, as social learning theorists stress, just as our behavior is learned, it can be unlearned and relearned. We can act in different ways if we so choose, and if we give ourself the freedom to *not* be bound by trait descriptions.

Thus, we can see that Zen, existentialist, and social learning theorists suggest that the concept of "self" is a fiction. We begin to know more about our "real me's" not by conceptualizing ourselves, but by *acting*, *experiencing*, and *observing* our behaviors as they really are.

Finding Out What's Left
Once We Remove Preconceptions

The Zen View of the Real Me: The Artist of Life

According to the Zen view, once we remove our preconceptions, we will see our true self, and this "real me" is positive, unifying, and innately good. In D. T. Suzuki's words, every human being is "so constituted by nature that he can become an artist of life,"[14] and "Zen, in its essence, is the art of seeing into the nature of one's being—giving free play to all the creative and benevolent impulses inherently lying in our heart."[15] This basic, good, and real self is quite different from Freud's warring, aggressive id; rather, it is similar to the Jungian integrated, *individuated self*[16]; to Buckes' *cosmic consciousness*[17]; to Rogers', Maslow's, and Goldstein's *self-actualizing ego.*[18]

However, within the Zen framework, if we conceptualize these potentials in terms of positive traits, we are distorting reality. Traits, even positive traits, are but *descriptions* of reality, and not reality itself. Thus, in Zen, the "real me" is often referred to as "no-self" or "egolessness" or the Tao: that which is beyond words.

But what are some of the qualities of this Zen "no-self"? How will we recognize it when we find it? If the real me in Zen is not describable in words; and if even certain aspects of the discovery of this real me cannot be described, is there any information that can help guide us in our search? Or are we to be left empty-handed?

There are certain guideposts that may be helpful in the search for the real me. However, guideposts must be thought of in Zen terms as the finger pointing to the moon: once the moon has been seen, the finger is no longer necessary.

The guideposts we will use here consist of a parable and an analogy.

Finding The Real Me: A Parable

Strivata stood in front of the oak panel door, waiting for Naciketas to come with the key. Strivata waited anxiously at first, looking quickly over both shoulders for Naciketas' arrival. Several minutes passed, and still there was no sign of Naciketas. Realizing the anxiety within, Strivata decided to sit at the base of the door, wait patiently, and meditate on the intricate carvings which extended in coiled fashion from the upper right-hand corner. Naciketas approached from behind, and his shadow climbed over Strivata's and ascended the door.

"I am glad you have come," said Strivata. "There is no way for me to enter without the key."

Naciketas laughed.

"Do not laugh," Strivata responded angrily. "The sun is setting, I am becoming cold, and I have waited long for you."

"I thought you would return before me, so I left the door unlatched," Naciketas replied.

Strivata entered the unlocked door. The sun went down, casting all in dark shadows. Yet, even before the fire was built, Strivata saw more clearly.

There are several points worth noticing in this parable. For example, notice that the door (symbolizing Strivata's true self) was unlocked and Strivata could have opened it without help; the "key" (to enter the door, to enter the self) was within all the time. However, although Strivata needed no teacher to open the door, to find his "real self," it seemed that a teacher was, in fact, needed, if only to point out no teacher was needed. Once Strivata realized this lesson, even though the room was becoming dark, he "saw more clearly."

Finding The Real Me: An Analogy

The second guidepost we will use is the analogy of a mirror representing the Zen concept of the real me. There are four qualities of the mirror which are applicable.

1. Quality of Emptiness. When a mirror is clean and free from dust, dirt, and stains, it is empty. In psychological terms, when our minds are empty (that is, free of verbal statements and images), there is an absence of preconceptions, strivings, and thoughts. Since, as was pointed out earlier, preconceptions influence the way we interpret ordinary reality, the "emptiness" of the mind allows us to see "what is" without the ordinary cognitive chatter and constructs.

According to the Zen way we are born with this wisdom of emptiness, and are thus able to interact fully and "clearly" with whatever is around. Thus, in the words of the *Prajna Paramita Sutra*, "the emptiness [of the mirror] is actually [its] fullness." Our mirror–like nature becomes "stained" by words, labels, strivings, ambitions, and soon reality becomes distorted to meet one's preconceptions of it. Therefore, one aspect of finding the real me is to return to a state of emptiness by wiping the preconceptions from the face of the mirror.

2. Quality of Acceptance. The second quality of a mirror might be referred to as acceptance, or nonevaluation. The mirror accepts everything into itself without making any distinctions or judgments (wisdom of equalness). Any object put in front of the mirror—a big ball, a red cat, a poor person, a rich person—is reflected by the mirror without distinction. The mirror does not comment on whatever is around it: it merely accepts it into itself.

In psychological terms, the mirror reflects in a manner what Carl Rogers would call *nonjudgmental*; what social learning theorists would call *without evaluation.*[19] A person who has this "mirror nature" would be able, in Paul Tillich's words, to "accept that you are accepted."[20]

3. Quality of Accurate Discrimination. The third quality of a clean mirror is that it is able to differentiate and discriminate: for example, large from small, green from red, a happy face from a sad face. This has been referred to as the *wisdom of accurate reflection.* Thus, at the same time the mirror accepts everything into itself (quality of nonevaluation) it is also able to tell the difference between the objects that it is reflecting (quality of discrimination). In other words, our true selves, according to Zen, are both able to see and accept everything into themselves equally, while at the same time making discriminations about different objects.

4. Quality of Nonattachment. Finally, the clean mirror may be characterized by the wisdom of nonclinging or nonattachment. When an object is put in front of a mirror, the mirror reflects that object instantly without any distortion or projection (quality of nondiscrimination). Further, as soon as the object is taken away, the mirror is able to "yield" or let go of the subject. Thus, the real me, according to Zen, fully and completely interacts with whatever is in front of it, and yet does so in a nonpossessive, nonclinging manner.

Naranjo and Ornstein have elaborated on the concept of consciousness as a mirror as follows:

> The mirror allows every input to enter equally, reflects each equally, and cannot be tuned to receive a special kind of input. It does not add anything to the input and does not turn off receptivity to stimuli. It does not focus on any particular aspect of input and retune back and forth but continuously admits all inputs equally. . . .[21]

Thus we see that our true nature, according to Zen belief, is like the empty mirror: it interacts fully with the environment, accepts all into itself without evaluation; is able to discriminate; and is yielding and nonpossessive. As Shinru Suzuki Roshi noted, "The perfect man employs his mind as a mirror: it grasps nothing, it receives but does not keep."[22]

Implications of the Zen View

As we have seen, the Zen way posits that the mirrorlike nature of our *self* is innately good and positive. Further, this real self is within all of us, if only we are willing to see it. There are three important implications of this view of personality. First, the individual who is searching for the "real me" is able to *trust himself* in the very act of searching. Believing that our inner nature is good, we are "content to let behavior bring out a self which cannot be fully conceptualized. One trusts this self enough to suspend conscious reflective control over it."[23] This allows us not only to trust ourself more but also to be more open, willing to see the spark of goodness within ourselves, and therefore able to be more open and sensitive to other people.

Secondly, this Zen view of the self implies a possible *causal relationship between the individual and his/her subsequent actions.* That is, if we believe in ourself, we are more likely to engage in taking risks, try new paths, let ourselves be free to act creatively, and listen to and trust our body signals regarding physical and emotional health and healing.

Finally, this Zen view of the person has important implications for the therapist and educator. If these professionals believe and trust in the innate ability and goodness of the individual, they will be more likely to allow their students/clients *room for personal exploration and latitude for acting creatively.* For example, within the ego psychology model of therapy practiced by Carl Rogers, the client is treated as a person competent to direct his/her own actions. Likewise, a physician "healer" of psychosomatic complaints who believes in innate abilities will be more likely to encourage the patient to take an active role in healing him/herself.

Thus, the relationship between mind and body, between our view of ourself and our subsequent behavior, and between the educator/therapist's view of the individual and his/her subsequent style of healing and teaching are all areas that may be affected by the Zen view of the "real me."

ZUTS, ALORS!

VOT'S ZIS? A FRENCH SPY ON BOARD?!
UH-OH..

HEY, ZONK— COME UP A SECOND!
TAKE HER TO ZE SURFACE, HANS!
JAWOHL, MEIN KAPITAN!

WHAT'S GOING ON DOWN THERE?— WHO ARE YOU PLAYING NOW?
WHAT DO YOU MEAN, WHO AM I PLAYING? I'M JUST BEING ME!

UM.. I KNOW, BUT...
HOW MANY TIMES DO I HAVE TO TELL YOU—ROLES ARE NATURAL! WE ARE THAT ROLE WHICH WE ARE THE MOST COMFORTABLE PLAYING!

UNIVERSAL PRESS SYNDICATE © 1975 G. B. Trudeau
YOU, FOR INSTANCE, PLAY THE ROLE OF THE WELL-MEANING, MODERATE EVERYMAN. NOTHING WRONG WITH THAT—GO WITH IT!
8-3

AND YOU?
I HAVE CHOSEN TO PLAY THE ROLE OF A WORLD WAR II GERMAN SUBMARINE.

THAT MUST BE A TOUGHIE.
WELL, YES— I'M ONLY JUST BEGINNING TO FULLY ACCEPT IT.
GBTrudeau

CHOOSING THE "REAL ME"

The Zen concept of self emphasizes that our "real me" is within us already, and will unfold naturally once we clear away our preconceptions. As we have seen, social learning theorists agree that we need to clear away the preconceptions (trait labels); however, they suggest that there is no innate essence within us. Rather, like existentialists, they emphasize the role of *choice*, stressing that the kinds of choices we make help determine our real selves. Existentialists such as Brentano and Husserl,[24] have talked of *Verstellung*—intentionality—and its importance in determining who we in fact become. Action and choice are essential to the vision of the self. According to the social learning theory model and existential view, the real me is what I *choose* to do.

In the last frame of the Doonesbury cartoon (opposite), Zonk points out the difficulties of choosing a new role. Zonk notes, however (in the fourth frame), that this new role is *not* just *playing* at a role, it is in fact *being* me.

How does this model of choosing a "real me" relate to the Zen view that the real self is already within us? According to Eastern philosophy, we will naturally unfold in a "self-actualizing" manner, and that evolution moves toward what de Chardin[25] described as an "omega point of consciousness." Social learning theorists emphasize the *interaction between individuals and their environment*[26] ; and, since they believe that evolution is random, they stress the need to learn techniques by which we can take more control over our own behavior.

In the social learning theory/existential model, we have to decide what role we want for ourselves, and then use certain techniques (described in Chapter 2) such as self-management skills, in order to attain that role. In the Zen model, we also use certain techniques (described in Chapter 1). The primary difference, however, is that the East believes the techniques only help us recover what is already there, whereas the West believes that we become what we choose to become.

Perhaps Western personality theory and research will never empirically prove whether the true Zen Master merely uncovers what is already there, or learns, through diligent practice, to make himself into a truly exceptional person. Perhaps the question itself is unanswerable, just as is the question of whether or not Michelangelo's sculptures were in fact encased in the rough marble, waiting to be freed by him. What is important is that Michelangelo believed "as if" the sculptures were waiting to be freed, that he had a vision of what the sculpture would look like, and that he had the necessary skills and techniques to reach his vision.

If we believe the Zen model is worth attaining, and if we attempt to act "as if"[27] we have Zen's real me within us, and "as if" other people are also "divine beings" who should be respected, this will influence our behavior toward ourselves and others. Acting as if we are this way may turn into a positive self-fulfilling prophecy, so that we become what we believe we are. As the Japanese scientist Tomio Hirai noted, "although the start of the study [personality theory] is different in East and West, the results are the same."[28]

INTEGRATING THE EAST-WEST VISION TO FIND THE PATH OF HEART

Some people turn to the East for the spiritual values that seem so lacking in an increasingly materialistic and impersonal society. Others turn to the East for the relaxation and tranquility provided by self-regulation techniques such as meditation and yoga.[29]

Yet we live in the ways of the world. And much of the Eastern philosophy, though it sounds appealing, doesn't quite seem to make sense within the context of our Western socialization. In the West, we are taught to stand up for ourselves, to be assertive. Yet the East says to yield.

In the West, we are taught that it is important to have a strong, healthy self-concept, yet the East says we should be egoless.

In the West, we are taught to be productive, to plan for the future, to set goals, to accomplish tasks; yet the East says to let go, enjoy the here and now, remain calm and centered in the present moment.

In the West, we are taught the importance of commitment and relationship, yet the East says we should be nonattached and indifferent.

The chart that follows gives a complete listing of all the concepts to be discussed in this chapter, how they differ from East to West, and their negative and positive ramifications. In this section I would like to deal with some of these contradictions; by the end of the chapter, you will know how they can be integrated and how, paradoxically, such an integrated Eastern and Western vision may provide a model of the "path of heart."

Productivity (Becoming) and Centeredness (Being)

A few years ago I gave a workshop on meditation to high-risk coronary disease-prone business executives. I had them free-associate to the qualities of a "good businessperson." Their responses included the following words:

- aggressive
- motivated
- ambitious
- hard-working
- productive

I then had them free-associate regarding qualities they felt meditation had, and they responded with the following words:

- passive
- quiet
- tranquil
- unconcerned

I asked them to compare the two lists, and asked why they were here—wouldn't becoming a good meditator preclude their being a good businessperson?

EAST

Concept	*Negative Aspects*	*Positive Aspects*
Egolessness	don't believe in oneself; passive; not willing to make decisions and choose a direction; not taking responsibility for one's actions; overdependence on others: lose oneself in trying to please them	ability to take risks more fully without fear of being judged by others; ability to experience oneself in a variety of situations without self-concept being threatened; ability to be with other people without gameplaying and without being threatened by them; ability to adapt to a wide variety of situations; ability to be nonself-conscious, and therefore more open to others; ability to engage in a variety of actions without attachment to rewards for actions
Naturalness, spontaneity; centeredness	not able to set goals for oneself; living only in the moment; no planning or future direction; lack of vigor	willing to trust oneself, to let go, trusting intuition; openness to experience, creativity; relaxation, peace of mind, living in moment, seeing action in inaction
Yielding	mushiness, lack of standards, flaccid, giving up; not willing to stand up for oneself	flexibility, ability to let go, gentleness, softness, accepting helplessness; openness to others' ideas and inputs
Nonattachment (acceptance)	noncaring, numbness; withdrawn, no feelings	nonpossessive, able to see more clearly and objectively; broad perspective; nonjudgmental
Consciousness (altered states)	nonfocused; goalless; useless in the ways of the world	living in moment; nongoal-oriented; noncognitive openness to others, to nature, to experience

WEST

Concept	*Negative Aspects*	*Positive Aspects*
Strong ego	development of mask to hide behind; fear of letting "true self" show; fear of fallibility, of being incompetent; trying to impress others to build a sense of self-worth; seeing others as a threat to identity; needing status/possessions to bolster identity; less willing to listen to others, less caring about others' opinions	personal sense of identity; sense of uniqueness; feelings of self-control (attribution theory); positive feelings about oneself, and willing to work hard to keep those positive feelings; feeling of competence, and willing to act on that feeling
Self-control, productivity	not living in the moment; constantly goal setting, evaluating, categorizing; overly aroused, maladaptive interpersonally, and from health standpoint, type A behavior	skills to set goals, evaluate one's progress; willingness to strive for personal vigor, excellence, perfection
Assertiveness	nonyielding, pushy, bully	willingness to stand up for one's rights; firm in one's beliefs; trusting of one's judgments
Attachment (caring love)	fear of losing others, objects, oneself (death); possessiveness; resentment	cares strongly about certain ideas, people; willing to commit oneself for those one is attached to
Consciousness (ordinary awareness)	ignores certain inputs; insensitive to delicate stimuli; words take place of experience	precise awareness; thinking, labeling, evaluating, goal setting; makes order out of sensory inputs

Productive individuals are those who can set goals and accomplish tasks. In terms of our discussion of attribution theory, such people believe they are in control of their own lives; they make things happen; they don't feel themselves passively determined by their environment. They accept new challenges, take risks, and strive for excellence.

So far so good. Certainly all of us who have lived in the West would not disagree with the utility of these qualities.

However, there are some potential drawbacks to these qualities. From a health standpoint, this type of behavior may lead to heart attacks, ulcers, migraine headaches, and psychosomatic problems. From an interpersonal standpoint, it may be difficult for competitive and ambitious people to get close to others to be able to share and work cooperatively. And finally, from a personal standpoint, it may be difficult for this type of person to enjoy the quietness of a moment, for fear of wasting time and not conquering a new problem.

Again, most of us in the West would agree that these are real or potential drawbacks to the productive, fast-paced life. Yet we would also have some reservations about the consequences of giving up our ambitiousness and goal-orientedness for an Eastern mode emphasizing yielding, egolessness, and letting go. Let me see if I can state some of the concerns that may be going through our minds. First, we would be afraid that our productivity might decrease, and that the quality of our work would be less excellent. There is a common belief in our society that we need to have a certain amount of tension and anxiety to perform optimally. Heidegger,[30] for example, felt that the anxiety of facing death caused us to deal with life more honestly and fully. It is thought useful for athletes to have butterflies in their stomachs to give them a "keen edge." Dancer-actress Donna McKechnie, star of *Chorus Line*, said when she was asked how she prepared for the show after more than a year in the same role, "I'm terrified each time. It's a condition I create for myself—it's a life or death situation. I'm auditioning each time—in order to keep my performance fresh."[31] A similar view was reported in a national news magazine:

> Newsmen and newspapers, goes one rather convincing theory, should stay out of the limelight, should remain a little insecure and run scared to do their best.

Thus, the first concern would be that yielding could cause a loss of a certain self-centered drive, an ambition that leads to personal achievement.

A second and related concern about yielding is that it may cause us to be seen by others (or by ourselves) as passive, powerless, helpless, and ineffectual. We may fear losing all sense of pride and self-esteem, and becoming so noncaring, so calm and relaxed, that nothing bothers us, and we become unmotivated, listless, apathetic.

"Your tranquilizers must be working, Doc. Now I don't give a hang if I ever pay you."

We may fear that yielding and egolessness will become an excuse, a copout that keeps us from facing our responsibilities, for not standing up for our beliefs and asserting our rights.* We may fall

*This may be a real concern, as evidenced by the Milgram experiment in which individuals followed the orders of a "scientist" even when those orders involved the (seeming) punishment of another individual. This "yielding to authority" is a serious problem. However, it may be *only* when we realize how susceptible we actually are to external influence that we can develop personal standards that would prevent this from occurring (see footnote in this chapter and Chapter 7, footnote 2; see also S. Milgram discussion, Chapter 3, footnote in section entitled "The Effects of a Crisis on Our Self-concept."

prey to and be crushed by others. As former Olympic miler Glen Cunningham expressed it:

> It would be a shame to get rid of anthems and the ceremonies, as some people suggest. God created nations. The "One World" idea is baloney. I tell my kids, "You stand for something or fall for anything."[32]

We have now laid out our concerns about yielding and letting go. We have also seen some very real problems that may occur if we are overly productive and ambitious. Let's now look at a vision which suggests we can learn to perform optimally, be productive in the ways of the world, and at the same time, have the ability to yield, let go, and maintain a centeredness, a tranquility, and a peacefulness in our actions.

Who sees inaction in action
and action in inaction
He is enlightened among men
He does all actions, disciplined.[33]

Inaction in Action

The *Gita's* person of wisdom realizes that activity is not only legitimate, but necessary. As the Zen Master Po-Chang wrote in 814 A.D., "A day of no working is a day of no eating." The *Gita* acknowledges that we need to set goals and strive for excellence and perfection. However, we need to learn to do these actions with the calmness and acceptance of inaction. Thus, the wise person acts, he seeks to make changes in the world, but he remains centered and unattached to the results of the actions.

Actions do not stain me
Because I have no yearning for the
fruits of action.[34]

In social learning terms, the man of wisdom has learned to do behaviors without a need for reinforcement, peer approval, or rewards. He does not strive to enhance his self-image, to gain prestige for himself. In this way Zen "substitutes an atmosphere of relaxation, serenity, and simplicity for the tensions created by our strivings to become, to possess, and to dominate."[35]

An example of this combination of centeredness and productivity is poetically illustrated in the book *Siddhartha*. The businessman for whom Siddhartha worked, Kawaswami, was astounded at Siddhartha's attitude: Siddhartha "always seems to be playing at business, it never makes an impression on him, it never masters him, he never fears failure, he is never worried about a loss. . . ."

Yet at the same time Siddhartha seemed unattached to his goals, he was also very productive. He explained this to the goddess of sensual pleasures, Kamala:

> Listen, Kamala, when you throw a stone into water, it finds the quickest way to the bottom of the water. It is the same when Siddhartha has an aim, a goal. Siddhartha does nothing, he waits, he thinks, he fasts, but he goes through the affairs of the world like the stone through the water, without doing anything, without bestirring himself. He is drawn and lets himself fall. He is drawn by his goal, for he does not allow anything to enter his mind which opposes his goal. That is what Siddhartha learned from the Samanas [ascetics]. It is what fools call magic and what they think is caused by demons. Everyman can perform magic; everyman can reach his goal, if he can think, wait, fast.[36]

Thus, Siddhartha was suggesting that centeredness—thinking, waiting, fasting—gave him a singlemindedness that allowed him to achieve goals more quickly, to be more productive. If we look back at the picture of the monkeys in the last chapter, we see that the monkey in the foreground is quite anxious, whereas the monkey in the background is not. I would suggest that, no matter what the particular situation is that these two monkeys are observing, the monkey in the background will deal more effectively with it. He appears ready to act. For all of us there will always be stress situations each day; the important variable is how we react. An attitude of calm, centered equanimity gives us an advantage in dealing with such situations, and helps us waste less energy and be more productive.

In summary, therefore, it seems we can learn to act without

anxiety, and can learn to be productive while remaining centered and calm. As the old Samurai saying puts it, we can be

Swift as the wind
Quiet as a forest
Fierce as fire and
Immovable as a mountain.

Action in Inaction

The *Gita* suggests that just as individuals can learn to be productive while staying calm and centered (inaction in action), they likewise can learn to discover great beauty and productivity in seemingly doing nothing (action in inaction).

In stillness, man discovers unexpected activity. At one level, doing nothing means becoming aware of the basic, most fundamental actions of the body. For example, even as the individual sits perfectly quiet, the heart still beats, the lungs still breathe. Without these actions, no other action is possible. To be aware of breath and heartbeat is therefore to be aware of the beauty and wonder of two fundamental actions of existence. And as we sit quietly and listen to our hearts beating, firmly and steadily, we know that one day we are going to die, and it is beyond our power to stop our death. Through the calmness of inaction we may learn a kind of acceptance. Herrigel has described this state of action in inaction as one "in which nothing definite is thought, planned, striven for, desired, or expected; which aims in no particular direction and yet knows itself capable alike of the possible and impossible, so unswerving is its power—this state, which is at bottom purposeless and egoless, was called by the master truly 'spiritual.'"[37]

This doing nothing, as Erich Fromm noted, may be seen as a type of creativity, even though no visible "things" are produced. For example, it may be suggested that a true Zen Master writes a poem—wordlessly—when (s)he watches the sunrise. Creativity may be a method of perceiving even though no actions have occurred.

To learn to see action in inaction allows us to cease striving for future goals, and to live in the moment, to see the beauty in the here and now, to have a present-centeredness. Life becomes its own end. As D. T. Suzuki observed,

> The Chinese love life as it is lived, and do not wish to turn it into a means of accomplishing something else. They like work for its own sake. The machine, on the other hand, hurries on to finish the work and reach the objective for which it is made. The work or labor in itself has no value except as means.[38]

Integrating Action in Inaction and Inaction in Action

The combination of action in inaction and inaction in action was vividly illustrated for me while taking yoga training from the Chinese master from Tibet. He was teaching hatha yoga postures. Before we began, there was a brief meditation in which we practiced "centering" ourselves (action in inaction). We then proceeded to do an exercise (inaction in action). At the end of an exercise, he would have us lie down and "surrender" (a return to action in inaction). I was quite stiff at first, and decided to practice hard because I was anxious to show the teacher my limberness and proficiency.

One day, during a particularly complex posture, the Master walked by me as I sighed, took a deep breath, groaned, and twisted my limbs into the correct posture. I looked up, ready for his smile of praise. There was none. Although the teacher spoke almost no English, he looked at me, said "Too fast," and walked on. I fell over. I lay on the floor, quietly breathing, and thinking over his words. When I opened my eyes, the teacher was looking at me, smiling: "Good surrender."

The goal of hatha yoga is not to be able to do a complex, twisted contortion of the body, but rather to perform the exercise with calmness and acceptance (inaction in action). The individual should not be inflexible in his goal setting, therefore he is able to stop his actions at any moment and return to the supine position (action in inaction). If equanimity and balance are sacrificed to accomplish a specific posture, although the posture may be reached, the exercise has lost its purpose.

Zen acknowledges that man wants to know his limits, and that once he has achieved basic sustenance, he will search beyond, to learn who he can further become. However, this learning must begin with the basic action of inaction, so that the learner doesn't become like Icarus, soaring beyond on wax wings without a base (action without inaction).

Let me illustrate this with the following toe-touching exercise. Before actually trying the exercise, read through the instructions. Then you may wish to return and practice.

1. Before beginning the exercise, practice a brief breath meditation. Pay attention to the action of your breathing, even as you sit motionless.

2. After meditating, sit with legs straight, arms hanging at your side (a). Put your fingers around your toes, breathe in, and bend forward, keeping your legs straight (b). Try to touch your head to your knees and your elbows to the ground (c). Then return to position (a) while exhaling.

3. Surrender: lie down, close your eyes and let go. Note: in this exercise the goal is *not* to touch your knees to your head or your elbows to the ground. The goal is to learn awareness of your limbs—how far they can stretch—without losing balance and equanimity. The action must be done slowly and methodically, for to do it too fast is to pull a muscle or bruise a joint. The exercise teaches you to do actions with calmness. After completion of the exercise (inaction in action) one surrenders by returning to a lying-down position (action in inaction).

If during the exercise you feel yourself getting frustrated because your limbs don't stretch as far or as much as you want them to, don't continue to push and struggle harder. *Stop and surrender.* Keep the calmness and acceptance of inaction. Lie on the floor and surrender. Breathe slowly several times.

Thus, while we continue to grow and stretch ourselves, we also maintain our balance and tranquility. We learn to set goals, to try to achieve perfection, and we also learn how to yield and surrender.* Each day the individual tests his limits, tries to go a

*Meditation and yoga would seem to provide a useful combination of *setting goals and acting* (exploring new directions) and *not acting* (reducing stimulation). As Hebb Berlyne suggested, if a person's routine is boring, lifeless, then he/she does not function optimally. However, if there is too much stimulation, the individual likewise may function poorly, being overwhelmed and distracted. (D. Hebb, The Motivating Effects of Exteroceptive Stimulation. *American Psychologist,* 1958, 13, 109-113. D. Berlyne, Conflict and Arousal, *Scientific American, 15* (1966) 82-88.

Another interesting point about yoga is made by Laurence E. Morehouse, a physiologist at the State University of Iowa and currently professor of exercise physiology and director of the human performance laboratory at UCLA. He suggests that exercising three times a day for ten minutes at a time is sufficient to keep anyone in excellent shape. He suggests also that the first exercise is the most important and then the second, and that the last is least important. He notes that more exercise and harder work does not result in greater improvement. One gets the biggest response from the first ten minutes and the increment of improvement after ten minutes is not too great. Perspiring is not necessary for effective exercise.

bit beyond, and then surrenders to the supine position. In this way perfection is seen as a playful game of becoming which has no relevance to ego or fame. We are able to act productively in the ways of the world without losing our equanimity, and without being consumed by the need to reach a goal. Thus, we become disciplined: in trying to set goals, to make changes in our lives, to perfect ourselves; and also in learning to let go, yield, and flow with the moment—a "good surrender."

EGOLESSNESS AND STRONG SENSE OF SELF

Turning from External to Internal Reinforcement*

Initially our reinforcement or praise comes from other people. How we feel about ourselves depends how others feel about us. However, at some point, our search for approval from others may become a problem, and we may need to turn inward and find out what our own standards are, what we believe in, how we want to act.

If we compare the slow, methodical quality of a yoga exercise with the type of exercise—e.g., quick push-ups and sit-ups—taught in most Western physical education classes, we see that this is an especially interesting hypothesis.

*To clear up any possible semantic problems, let me state the distinction I am making here between external and internal reinforcement. *External reinforcement* refers to praise we receive from others (e.g., an A for a good class paper). As noted, we "internalize" the standards we are taught, and soon we "feel good" when we get an A. What I mean by *internal standards* can be illustrated in the following way: (1) we realize and evaluate *how* we have been taught to feel good—e.g., an A for a paper; (2) we look for alternatives—e.g., perhaps the content of the paper should also interest me; (3) we choose our own critieria and standards of excellence—e.g., I want to still perform excellently, but I should define for myself what an A is; I should choose for myself the areas in which I feel it is worth performing well.

These new standards will be the result of a combination of our past conditioning and current models (whether living or dead) whom we admire. The difference, however, is that now we are choosing how we would like ourselves to be conditioned (the path of heart), rather than continuing to respond passively to prior training. Thus, by seeing how we are determined, by learning to perceive increased alternatives, by learning the skills of decision making and self-management, we increase our personal freedom, and move from external reinforcement to internal standards of reinforcement.

A particularly vivid example of this is illustrated by a client I saw who was addicted to heroin. As part of therapy, we spent several sessions practicing meditation. At the end of one of the sessions, he told me: "In the last couple weeks I notice that I don't need people and can be alone . . . and I can also be with people and enjoy them . . . this is different than I used to be; always before I needed lots of people around me . . . drifted from group to group." He said that meditation seemed to give him what he called an "inner self-confidence." For this particular person, there was a great deal of peer pressure to use heroin. Only when he had time to himself, only when he could gain a sense of "inner self-reliance," was he able to choose more freely how he wanted to behave.

Almost all Western psychotherapeutic systems[39] stress that this switch from external to internal reinforcement is one of their primary goals. A person who can be reinforcing to himself can set his own standards, will show less reliance on group mores, and will be more able to determine and fashion his own system of morality. He will be less swayed by group pressure, and not as likely to accede to it; and he will probably be less likely to do things just because of societal expectations—shoulds and oughts. Finally, writers such as Erich Fromm have suggested that it is only when we have a sense of personal identity that we are able to enter into a true long-term love relationship.[40] As Gibran noted in *The Prophet*,

And the oak and the cypress grow
Not in each other's shadows.[41]

Going Beyond Self-reinforcement

Initially we need to turn from an other-directed search for approval to an inner-directed search. Yet there may be disadvantages to self-reinforcement. First, if we focus too much on ourselves, we may become narcissistic, self-aggrandizing, without a willingness to share or give to others. Second, we may believe that we have all the answers, and thus close ourselves off from the advice of others. We may become unreceptive, pompous, unfeeling of others. There are several writers in both the Eastern and Western tradition who believe it is to our advantage to go *beyond* self-reinforcement, and to no longer need either the reinforcement of others or ourselves. As Abraham Maslow, in the *Psychology of Being* noted, "The greatest attainment of identity, autonomy, selfhood is itself simultaneously a transcending of itself, a going beyond and above selfhood. The person can then become relatively egoless."[42] The Maitri Upanishad stated that "he who has seen this highest self becomes selfless"; and in the New Testament, Jesus says, "He who loses himself will find himself."

Let us look at what some of the advantages of this "egoless" state might be. First, if we see our "self" as an illusion, we will be less concerned about seeking social reinforcement, possessions, and self-aggrandizement. Therefore, as Erich Fromm noted, we will be able to "drop our ego, give up greed, and cease chasing after the preservation and aggrandizement of the ego, to be and to experience ourselves in the act of being, not in having, preserving, coveting, using.[43] We will be able to live and experience without the need for being praised, positively evaluated, and labeled and singled out as unique. As Karen Horney suggested in *Neurosis and Human Growth*, ambition and striving because of pride "prevents the potential of the real self from developing."[44]

Egoless individuals, in social learning terms, would be less concerned with receiving external reinforcement and would feel positive enough about themselves across situations that they would no longer need to reinforce themselves. Thus, such a person's mind would not be filled with positive self-statements; nor would this person be searching for positive statements from others. The mind would be "free" to be like a mirror, to be open and receptive to the world around and within. The egoless person has no "hidden agenda" of trying to win points, play games; no need to put others down. This may make the person not only more open to others, but concomitantly, less self-conscious. That is, there would be less need for the egoless individual to reflect upon himself, to evaluate and be preoccupied with himself. He (or she) would have learned to value himself, and could therefore let go and trust his actions. In social learning terms, the egoless person has desensitized himself to himself (removed affective connotations of his image of himself), and can thus act fully and spontaneously, without inhibition and fear of looking awkward.*

"You know what my ambition is? To one day be conspicuous by my absence."

Second, an egoless individual would be free to engage in a variety of behaviors and tasks. Since there is no self, and since in the words of the *Bhagavad Gita*, the person of wisdom is not attached to the fruits of his action (i.e., not looking for reinforcement for task performance), he can perform all actions or no

*This ability to act without "self" consciousness or a focus on "I" is strongly emphasized in the Eastern martial arts. In swordplay, for example, the swordsman must do away with thoughts of winning the contest or displaying his skill in technique. [See Takano Shigeyoshi, "Essay on the Psychology of Swordplay," in N. W. Ross, *The World of Zen* (NY: Random House, 1960), p. 293.] He must maintain the mental attitude called *muga*—an attitude characterized by absence of the feeling "I am doing it." Alan Watts has observed that this "noninterfering attitude of mind constitutes the most vital element in the art of fencing as well as in Zen" [quoted from his *The Spirit of Zen* (New York: Grove Press, 1958), p. 108].

actions. This should expand the repertoire of behaviors an individual is willing to engage in, as well as his or her willingness to take risks in new, unexplored fields; to dare for creative synthesis; to attempt to chart new areas; and, in Nietsche's words, to "live dangerously."

Finally, if as Carl Rogers noted, the person who has a flexible self-image can assimilate many experiences into awareness without feeling threatened, the person who is relatively egoless—who has no self-image, the ego of non-ego, the mirror—would be freest, and be able to assimilate the most experience.

The quality of egolessness may be especially important in the rapidly changing "future shock" society. Since the concept of a self is an illusion, as long as we attempt to have a high sense of self in a fluctuating society, our "self-esteem will be subject to alterations in models, available satisfactions, environmental demands, and other features associated with our rapid culture change."[45]

The so-called egoless person, not having to worry about enhancing his "self" through the societal role he performs or the possessions he accumulates, has the flexibility to adapt to a wide variety of situations. He is able to act without fear, for he is not worried about whether his actions will be judged by others. Further, as Claudio Naranjo noted, the nonattachment that comes with egolessness is the source of the healthy person's ability to stand on his own, not mistaking his identity for that of an owner of things or a performer of a certain role. "It is also the source of the basic independence from others which is, in turn, the prerequisite for true relationships."[46]

Finally, the egoless person realizes the limits of believing we can take control of our own lives. As we have stressed, on the one hand it is important for us to believe "as if" we can take responsibility for and control of our actions (i.e., make self-attributions). However, we may fall into the trap of believing too strongly in our own fiction. We can't in fact control everything in our lives. We are, in many ways, small, delicate, fragile creatures. There are many events we are helpless to change. If we live only in a paradigm of "my will be done," we will never learn the ability to let go, to yield, to surrender ourselves, to accept helplessness, to gain what may be called a transpersonal or spiritual awareness. The spiritual teachers don't say, "my will be done," but "thy will be done."

YIELDING, ASSERTIVENESS, SELF-CONTROL AND SPONTANEITY

Yielding and Assertiveness

All right, you win. But you must admit I intimidated you!

Yielding is not an easy skill for those of us brought up in the Western competitive mode. Yet competition and assertiveness, which are not necessary for basic sustenance, and often represent unchanneled, overlearned aggression, often over trivial ego games, no longer serve the productive survival function they once did, and may be destructive.

Although there is no question that it is important for individuals to learn to stand up for themselves, to assert their rights, it may also be important for people (both males and females) to

"Listen, I gotta go. There's a guy waiting to use the phone."

know how to yield, to be soft and compassionate. Further, it may be important to have a broad enough perspective on life to realize that one doesn't have to assert oneself over trivial points. Once we have decided what are the issues of importance in our lives, we can then "let go" and be unconcerned about more trivial matters.

As a way of introducing the advantages of yielding, let me tell you a story about the supposed origins of the martial art, jujitsu. According to legend, the art of jujitsu originated during a cold winter in China. Several people were watching the snow fall on two trees in the middle of a wide field. The larger tree stood firm and rigid as the snow piled up on its limbs. Finally, the accumulated snow became so heavy that its branches could no longer bear the weight, and they cracked. The smaller, less rigid tree also accumulated snow on its branches. However, its branches were limber enough to bend toward the ground, casting the snow off, and returning to their original position. Thus the smaller, more flexible branches lasted throughout the winter; the tree that yielded survived.

This yielding (*wu-wei*) was characterized by Lao-tse as the "watercourse way." If we watch water flow down a stream toward a rock, we note that the water divides and goes around the rock. It yields to the rock's presence. Yet, although the water yields, it survives in the long term, and it is the rock that is worn away. Lao-tse's watercourse way is much the same evolutionary self-protection measure as the chameleon changing its colors so it cannot be recognized.

Secondly, the ability to yield should help us to let go of goals that are too high or too rigid, and to "flow" with circumstances over which we have no control.

"I'M BRIGHTENIN' THE CORNER WHERE I **AM**!"

This "letting go" may give us a greater conceptual flexibility, not only in terms of changing our goals, but in finding alternative and creative ways to attain them—a *cognitive flexibility.*

An interesting example of yielding occurred when we first went to visit my parents with our new daughter. My father rushed up to see Shauna, and said, "Oh, let me see her throw her arms around me." Rather than throw her arms around him, she recoiled in fright and began crying. Instead of becoming upset at this, he said, "Terrific, I really wanted to hear her cry and it sounds beautiful." What he had done was to flow with her crying rather than feel sad that he was rejected, or get angry at her for rejecting him.

Another example of conceptual flexibility produced by yielding was beautifully illustrated by Reed Martin in his book on legal and ethical issues in behavior modification.[47] He told the story of some prisoners who were taunting their guards. This made the guards angry and caused them to provoke the prisoners, who then further taunted the guards. How would you have broken this cycle? In this case, the psychologist consultant, rather than punish the prisoners for their provocations, taught the guards to not be bothered by the prisoners' remarks (i.e., he *desensitized* the guards).

Both of these vignettes illustrate principles similar to the techniques of yielding in *aikido*, a Japanese martial art. In aikido ("way of harmony"), rather than confront someone head-on, one perceives where the other's energy is, and merely tries to flow with it. As in the case of jujitsu and the snow on the trees, this yielding can often be a power technique.* Thus, the yielding way of water may often provide the most powerful means of reaching goals.

Further, the yielding way may teach us to appreciate the moment more, to learn that there is often more satisfaction in expectation, in the process, than in the actual attainment of the goal. For example, both the Tantric literature of India and the "sensate focus" of Masters and Johnson's sex therapy techniques emphasize yielding, letting go, and flowing with the sensuality of the moment, rather than focusing on the goal of achieving orgasm.

Thus we can see that there may be several advantages to yielding: it has survival value; it provides the ability to *not* get irritated over trivia; provides the ability to be soft and compassionate; allows us to avoid becoming trapped by goals; enables us to find alternative paths to our goals; and makes us capable of enjoying the process of reaching our goals.

*The principle of "yielding" is illustrated in a communication skill called *paraphrasing* (a skill often used in client-centered therapy). When someone is upset at you for something, rather than become defensive or make a counterattack, you can instead take their statement, acknowledge it, and paraphrase it back to them: e.g., "It seems you're upset at me because I did X." Once they acknowledge that you hear them, you are both then placed in a position to deal more calmly with the issue.

Yielding and Self-control

Many of us, if we were to free-associate to the term "self-control," would conjure up images that are rigid, mechanical, unspontaneous, unplayful, robotlike, overly controlled. And if we were to compare self-control skills to yielding skills, we would, more than likely, conceptualize them as polar opposites. I would like to suggest, however, that self-control and yielding may be two sides of the same coin. This idea became clear to me during a meditation training session with a student. I was having the student meditate on a mirror. After the session she commented, with frustration,

> I felt myself just about to give up control, and fall into the mirror, *but I didn't have enough self-control to let go. . . .*

The letting-go can be a conscious choice. It doesn't happen automatically, but needs to be learned. The learning involves an ability to take risks, give up control. For a lot of us, this is quite frightening. It takes a great deal of self-control to give up this control. Thus, *conscious yielding may be seen as the ultimate self-control.* It is this yielding, I believe, which is integrally related to the concept of egolessness; to an ability to share oneself with others; to work cooperatively and to relax and be centered.

Without control, there is no freedom.

Self-Control and Spontaneity (Naturalness)

A related issue involves the relationship between self-control and spontaneity. For example, the main prerequisite for self-control is awareness of how we are conditioned. In this way, we can "uncondition" ourselves, and not be compelled to act by nonconscious reflex. The term "reflex" needs to be thought of in its broadest sense—ranging from a knee-jerk response, to salivating when we smell or see good food, to the expectation that we will obtain praise for doing "what we ought to do."

When we have the awareness and self-control to no longer be bound by reflex, when we have *unconditioned* ourselves to ego games, then we have the freedom to be spontaneous. As Alan Watts observed, it is at this time that "the mind reaches the highest point of alacrity, ready to direct its attention anywhere it is needed. . . . There is something immovable within [the mind] which [at the same time], moves along spontaneously with things presenting themselves before it. The mirror of wisdom reflects them instantaneously one after another, keeping itself intact and undisturbed."[48]

Thus, one may argue that awareness is necessary so that we can learn how we are conditioned. Then self-control and practice are necessary so that we can learn to keep from acting with reflex responses. Self-discipline is further necessary so that we can let go of our "selves": that is, so we can risk not being in control, trusting ourselves. For example, as mentioned earlier, to meditate effectively, we have to be willing to give up voluntary control of our breathing. In other words, to breathe spontaneously—that is, with awareness and without voluntary control—we need to develop a self-control to *relinquish* control. This does not mean acting nonconsciously; rather, the goal is to breathe effortlessly and to maintain total awareness of the process of breathing. In meditation, the individual is no longer breathing: rather, *breathing is.* Further, the individual *knows* that breathing is. Such breathing may be called spontaneous. In this way it may be possible to reconcile the apparent contradiction between self-discipline, immovable wisdom, and spontaneity. The meditator, self-disciplined and exceedingly aware of himself, simultaneously is able to breathe fully in the moment with the spontaneity and nonconscious naturalness of a small child.

Does trying to maintain at every moment an awareness of our ongoing actions, trying to be controlled every moment in our behavior, keep us from "letting go" and flowing? Does self-control become a kind of rigidity? Terms like "immovable wisdom," "detached observation," "self-discipline," and "self-control" suggest a stiffness and withdrawing that would make spontaneous action cumbersome, if not impossible. How can this be reconciled with the story of the Zen Master who, when asked by the monk about the secret of Zen, shouted "Kwat" and hit the monk with a stick? Is there a difference between spontaneity and control or is it merely a semantic distinction?

What is the meaning of spontaneity? First, there is an implication of an immediacy of action without the encumbering interference of self-conscious thought. However, this immediacy of action is the exact opposite of a conditioned reflex which, though it occurs immediately, occurs without choice on the part of the individual. Spontaneity seems to be a behavioral response so well-learned that it no longer requires conscious cognitive mediation; the nature of the response, however, is not narrow like a conditioned reflex, but subject to various alternatives. Further, perhaps reflecting the Zen emphasis on living in the moment, the response appears to have no regard for consequences. In the *Bhagavad Gita*, a disciplined man is spoken of as one who has not a hair's breadth between his will and his action: He speaks exactly what he wants to say, he stops eating at the moment he is no longer hungry. His every action or nonaction is an intentional doing, wholly within his control. He has learned the ways through which he was conditioned and therefore never responds by mechanical conditioned reflex. Rather, at every moment he *chooses* whether or not he wishes to respond. This seems to suggest a balance of spontaneity and self-control.

Some Final Thoughts

> Naciketas, the seeker after knowledge, came rushing up to the Master, who was sitting quietly meditating. "Master," he shouted, out of breath and quite anxious, "let me see you be spontaneous." Whereupon the master bowed politely and said "I am."

There is an old adage that power perfected becomes grace; in our terms, self-control perfected becomes spontaneity. This may be seen in the delicate flower arranging of Japanese *ikebana*, in the graceful and swift finger movements of violinist Yehudi Menuhin. The delicacy and grace come only through (1) practice, diligence, and awareness on a daily consistent basis; and (2) ability to believe in oneself so that it is possible to let go, and trust the effects of our practice without holding back—to let the results of our practice flow forth naturally.

But self-control becomes rigidity and nonspontaneity unless we learn to also "let go" and yield. On the other hand, yielding can become passivity, noncaring, a giving up. Therefore, we need to learn the skills both for taking control of our lives and for giving up and yielding: skills for building a strong ego and for being egoless; skills for learning to set goals, to live intentionally, and then ability to let go and not be bound and limited by our own vision. We need a combination of trusting our instincts (i.e., past learning) and continuing to practice new skills and behaviors so that we don't become rigid.

An example of this relationship between self-control (strong ego) and yielding (egolessness) was illustrated by the development of our daughter Jena's legs. At first, Jena's legs were soft and undeveloped. She could not stand (analogue of weak self-concept, undisciplined, chaotic, passive life). Soon, however, she learned to stand. Her legs became firm and powerful and supported her weight (analogue of strong ego, willpower). However, she then went through a stage in which once she stood up, she was unable to seat herself from that position (rigidity, unyielding). The firm legs were useful (to stand up) but their rigidity kept them from yielding and letting her sit. Only later did the skill of yielding come, as her legs bent at the knees, and she could finally sit down by herself (egolessness, letting go). Thus, letting go on one side of self-control may be passive, a giving up. Letting go on the other side of self-control (i.e., with self-control skills, a conscious decision) is both necessary and useful.

LIVING IN THE MOMENT: INTEGRATING ORDINARY AWARENESS AND THE ALTERED STATE

All of us have experienced the problem of intruding thoughts and images which seem to distract us from the task at hand. We may be trying to relate to our family, yet thinking of business problems. We may be talking to a friend, yet thinking of the lawn that needs to be mowed, or a drop in the stockmarket. We may be trying to concentrate on a specific task, yet thinking of going sailing, or the date we have on the coming weekend. For example, how many times have you interrupted yourself singing a jingle you didn't know you were singing, caught yourself chattering to yourself without listening, or going to do one thing, becoming sidetracked, and ending up involved in something entirely different?

An example of holding thoughts in our head is illustrated in the following Zen parable "Muddy Road":

> Tanzan and Ekido were once traveling together down a muddy road. A heavy rain was still falling.
>
> Coming around a bend they met a lovely girl in a silk kimono and sash, unable to cross the intersection.
>
> "Come on, girl," said Tanzan at once. Lifting her in his arms he carried her over the mud, and set her down on the other side of the intersection.
>
> Ekido did not speak again until that night when they reached a lodging temple. Then he no longer could restrain himself. "We monks don't go near females," he told Tanzan, "especially not young and lovely ones. It is dangerous. Why did you do that?"
>
> "I left the girl there," said Tanzan. "Are you still carrying her?"[49]

Ekido was involved in internal ruminations and evaluations. Like Ekido, when we become preoccupied in a world of internal thoughts and analysis, we may be less receptive to the realities of the ongoing moment. According to Zen belief, as long as we are analyzing reality, we are not living it; therefore, we need to move beyond thinking about experience to the immediacy of direct experience. As Alan Watts has noted, "To think over what is past, to wonder what is about to come, or to analyze the effect upon oneself is to interrupt the symphony and lose the reality."[50]

In Chapter 1, we described how, in the fifth step of meditation, we learn to develop a present-centeredness, without goals, without evaluation. We would all agree that this fifth step of meditation involves living in the moment. Similarly, in Buddhist informal meditation, as described by Rahula, we are also living in the moment. In yoga, this type of self-observation is practiced as if one were a "witness": one tries to notice exactly what one is doing—to invest ordinary activities with attention. The witness does not judge or initiate action, he simply observes. In the words of Frederick Spiegelberg, "Meditation deals with the daily task of the meditator. The street cleaner has to take his task of sweeping as the starting point for meditation. So, likewise, must the potter take his task of producing clay utensils on the potter's wheel. . . . One may do what he will so long as he is clearly aware of what he is doing. . . ."[51]

However, from here on in, it gets more complex. For example, let's look at a story used in the Zen literature to illustrate living in the moment:

> A man was fleeing, pursued by a tiger. He came to the edge of a precipice, the tiger right behind. In desperation he climbed over the edge down a long vine. Above him the tiger roared. Below him lay a thousand-foot drop into raging rapids. Further, two mice, one white and one black, had begun gnawing through the vine. Suddenly, the man noticed a luscious strawberry growing just within reach. Holding onto the vine with one hand, with the other he plucked the strawberry. How delicious it tasted.[52]

At first glance, it seems to meet the criteria: here, amidst death on all sides, he enjoys the strawberry in the here and now. Yet, note how the man lives in the moment. He *decides*, amidst all the other stimuli, to pick the strawberry. He *focuses* on the strawberry. He *evaluates* how it tastes. Couldn't he also have focused on the tiger or the mice and evaluated how it would feel to be devoured or the feel of the air as he fell toward the rapids below? Couldn't he even have focused on the texture of the gnawed vine he was clinging to? He chose, instead, to focus on a positive external object: a strawberry. Thus, although living in the moment may involve nonevaluation (as in meditation), it may also involve focusing, evaluation, decision making, and covert statements (e.g., "Well, it looks like this is the end—stay calm—is there a last bit of pleasure possible? Ah, a strawberry! Why not!"). Thus, the man, through selectively focusing his attention, chooses his reality for the moment.

All of us are constantly choosing our realities of the moment, whether we realize it or not. As we saw in Chapter 4, research on ordinary awareness suggests that often our choices are not conscious, but are determined by our previous learning, and by the stimuli at hand. Most of the time we are ignoring a multitude of stimuli around us. Sometimes we ignore things that we really should focus on. For example, *Playboy* notes:

> We understand that bird-watching was classified as a "hazardous" hobby by the British medical magazine *Practitioner*, after an enthusiastic ornithologist—intent on watching a bird—was eaten by a crocodile that he failed to notice.[53]

Yet, if we spend our entire life looking for the crocodiles, we may never see the delicate beauty of the bird.

How do we decide what to focus on? How do we decide whether to evaluate, or not evaluate what we focus on?

Let us turn to a discussion of the advantages and disadvantages of different types of awareness. We will look at two areas: What we focus on (internal versus external focusing) and how we focus (with evaluation, without evaluation).

What We Focus On

External Focus: Advantages

Sometimes there is an advantage in focusing externally so that one doesn't turn inward too much, become too self-conscious, or worry excessively about one's own problems. In certain cases therefore, external focusing, with a concomitant decrease in internal ruminations, may be very appropriate. An example of this may be seen in one of the sexual therapy techniques used by Masters and Johnson. They instruct the couple in what is termed "sensate focus." Each partner zeroes in on what gives the *other person* pleasure. Thus, there is less internal reflection or self-evaluation on one's own competence (e.g., Am I performing correctly? Am I adequate to the situation?) Focusing on the other seems to take the pressure off the individual and aids his/her performance.

Another advantage to external focusing is that it facilitates avoidance of aversive stimuli. For example, Kanfer and Goldfoot noted that a person, with his hand submerged in cold water, could withstand pain longer by focusing on external stimuli.[54]

Similarly, there is a certain healthiness in not being excessively preoccupied with focus on ourselves. The story is told of Noel Coward going to the Tomorrow Club, an exclusive club of famous literary personalities. He wore full evening regalia, and, when he entered the club. realized that everyone else was dressed very casually. As the eminent heads turned toward him, he said, "Now I don't want anyone to be embarrassed. . . ."[55]

External Focus: Disadvantages

On the other hand, Freudians, social learning theorists, and existentialists have pointed out the *dangers* of external focus.* Existentialists describe the way we may often hide behind things—food, others, daily activities—to keep from facing important questions about our place in the world, a sense of ultimate loneliness, and fear of our own death. Freudians discuss the use of dynamic projection in which we may focus on something external to avoid having to focus internally on what is bothering us. For example, we may focus on how lonely other people appear in an attempt to keep from facing our own loneliness. Similarly, if we are feeling insecure and unsure of ourselves, we may focus on how the clothes we wear appear shabby, as opposed to feeling our own "shabbiness." The short-term advantage of this external focus is that it is not as painful to describe our clothes as shabby as it is to admit feelings of pain and lack of esteem about ourselves. The problem, however, is that there are many stimuli associated with the "self." Therefore, if we don't deal directly with our problems, we will be constantly searching for external focuses. This leaves a large gap in our everyday ability to be as open and responsive to as many situations as possible.

What we need to determine is whether or not there are times when it might be appropriate to divert our attention from a particular object or thought and to focus either internally or externally. Is cognitive avoidance of something *necessarily* an appropri-

*Psychodynamic theorists refer to avoiding important issues in our lives as *repression.* Repression occurs when an individual is unwilling to face certain events and thus places them in the unconscious. Social learning theorists refer to such a process as *cognitive avoidance.* As in Freudian theory, cognitive avoidance refers to ignoring or avoiding a particular response. Skinner has noticed that cognitive avoidance is "extremely powerful" because it is negatively reinforced (i.e., aversive stimuli are removed. B. F. Skinner, *Science and Human Behavior* [New York: Macmillan, 1953]).

ate escape or avoiding device? How can we learn to choose what is most appropriate to focus on, so that on the one hand we don't avoid reality (as Charlie Brown's father did in the cartoon in Chapter 1) and yet on the other hand, we don't dwell excessively on the negative, thereby denying ourselves the pleasure of enjoying a luscious strawberry?

Internal Focus: Advantages

We have noted that if we only focus on ourselves, we may ignore others. However, there are some situations in which it is helpful to put the focus of attention on ourselves, especially in our interaction with others.*

> *Internal Focus* (I-Statement): I'm having trouble understanding you.
> *External Focus:* You're not being clear.
>
> *Internal Focus:* I feel hurt when you do that.
> *External Focus:* You're inconsiderate to do that.

In the above examples, making I-statements takes responsibility for a problem rather than laying blame on another.

Internal Focus: Disadvantages

If our focus is primarily internal—egocentric—we may be less able to relate to and be concerned with the problems of others. Further, we live in the world. To focus exclusively on ourselves

*Other advantages of internal focusing—such as being aware of our body signals, becoming more aware of our thoughts, etc.—have already been dealt with in Chapters 1, 2, and 4.

may not be beneficial in a survival sense. We may ignore or miss certain important cues in the environment—a thunderstorm, a red light—because of excessive self-preoccupation. In addition, such preoccupation with ourselves may be seen by others as a type of narcissism, which decreases their desire to be around us.

HERMAN

"That's a relief. I thought I'd gone deaf!"

How We Focus: The Nature of the Evaluation

Just as we may select whether we would like to focus internally or externally, we may also choose *how* we would like to focus. We have pointed out that the type of focusing in behavioral self-observation strategies involves evaluation, analysis, goal setting, determining antecedents and consequences, whereas the type of focusing in meditative technique does not involve any of these processes. What effects do different types of focusing have on experiencing? As we saw earlier, altered and mystical states of consciousness, different types of meditative strategies, and ordinary awareness are different in only two respects: *what* one focuses on, and *how* one focuses. In this focus with or without evaluation; with a pinpointing of attention on one subject; with a selective awareness of certain aspects of an object; with an "unfocused" awareness? The way we focus will influence what is perceived, how it is perceived, and thus will affect the nature of the experience.

Let us now turn to specific examples illustrating how the nature of our evaluation may effect our behavior. We will consider four different areas: positive evaluation, nonevaluation, negative evaluation, and negative thoughts.

Positive Evaluation. Imagine for a moment that you are riding a bicycle up a steep hill. As you are riding, there are several things you may be saying to yourself. You may be making a *positive evaluation* about (1) your progress: "I'm making steady progress up this hill," (2) your physical health: "I'm sure feeling good and in good shape," and (3) your goal: "I'm getting close to the top—I'm almost there." All of these statements may serve as self-reinforcement, and thereby increase the likelihood of a "second wind," a renewed effort, and the possibility that you will continue to bike up the hill, have pleasant feelings about yourself, and reach the top.

Positive evaluation is the simple technique of saying positive things about what we are doing and who we are. It is a useful technique because it increases self-confidence and improves our self-image. However, it may have drawbacks as well.

Let's take another example: Imagine yourself using a screwdriver to turn a screw into the wall. As you focus completely on the task and notice that the screw begins to turn, you may say to yourself, "Ah, it's beginning to work." Two things may happen: first, you may feel more confident, get renewed energy, and continue to turn very appropriately. However, something else may happen: the screwdriver may slip. This may happen for two reasons: (1) you may let up and relax, because you think you're succeeding, and/or (2) your attention may shift from the task at hand to yourself: "I'm doing well." Thus, in some cases, it may be that we perform better in a task if we continue to focus on the task, without any kind of evaluation.

Nonevaluation. The advantages of nonevaluation have been discussed at length by Eastern writers, particularly with regard to martial arts such as fencing and archery. It is suggested by these writers that any kind of evaluation, even positive evaluation, diverts attention from the task at hand. Therefore, an individual is told to try to become "egoless": i.e., without focus on himself, and without any type of self-evaluation—not even positive. This has also been discussed by Western writers in books such as Galloway's *Inner Game of Tennis* and Adam Smith's *Powers of Mind.*

Let us return to our biking example. It is possible, when riding the bike up the hill, not to evaluate, but simply to ride. One may perform this nonevaluation by a meditative focus on a specific object (e.g., a pinpointed visual focus on the road in front of one's tire) or by an opening-up informal meditation: (e.g., a nonspecific, all-senses-attentive focus).

Negative Evaluation. Imagine biking up the same hill, but this time saying to yourself, "Ugh, what a long way to go!" This statement may have several possible consequences: (1) it may make you say, "Oh, come on, let's try harder," or (2) it may make you feel tired, so that you get off the bike and walk it up the hill, or (3) you may give up, turn around, and go home.

In our screwdriver example, we may evaluate that the screw is quite tight and we are not having much success. As a result of that evaluation, we may say, "It is important for me to focus harder—this is a tough task." This may improve the subsequent performance. However, it is also possible that our attention may shift from external negative evaluation (a tight screw, a steep hill) to internal negative evaluation (I'm not competent, I can't do this task well). In the latter case, the negative evaluation is nonproductive and a negative thought.

Negative Thoughts. Negative thoughts occur when we make a negative evaluation, but don't change our behavior as a result of this evaluation. The following is one example of a negative thought: You and a friend decide to go to a movie. On the way to the movie, you say, "You know, going to a movie really doesn't sound like very much fun, but let's go anyway." Similarly, in our biking example, you may make a negative evaluation: "Ugh, what a long way to go," and yet continue to bike up the hill, groaning and complaining. More than likely, a negative thought would cause your progress to be slower, cause you to feel more tired and to have fewer pleasant associations about the ride. Negative thoughts are, by their very definition, worthless. They put you, or whomever you're with in a no-win situation.

Focusing on the Past and the Future

Living in the moment may involve using imagery and focusing with one's mind to either project future goals for oneself, or, perhaps, relive past experiences.

"I DON'T DRINK TO FORGET. THE PAST. I DRINK TO FORGET THE FUTURE."

Past Focus: Constructive or Destructive?

We can review the past in a nonconstructive way. We may call up unpleasant memories about which we feel bad, and yet about which we are helpless to make any changes. However, it is possible to review past accomplishments and past experiences in a constructive way. For example, we may call up pleasant experiences such as shared memories. Reviewing past accomplishments may show us how much progress we've made toward our goals. Reviewing past mistakes may give us important feedback so we don't make the same errors again.

Future Focus: Constructive or Destructive?

If we think about the future and merely worry uselessly about it, then we are engaging in worthless negative thinking. However, it is possible to review the future in a constructive way: planning, evaluating, making careful choices. Further, we may observe our desired self in the future to see how we would like to become. This focusing on a future desired self may be reinforcing and make us feel good, particularly if we think our present actions will help lead to that future desired self. Further, the future desired self may provide a model and vision of what we would like to become, and thereby help us change our present behavior in order to facilitate reaching that goal.

Some Final Thoughts on Living in the Moment

We have talked about living in the moment as focusing completely on the here and now. But we have also suggested that there may be several ways of focusing on the here and now, each with advantages and disadvantages. Depending on the goal of our "living in the moment," sometimes Western strategies, involving evaluations, attributions, images, and selective awareness may be more effective; sometimes Eastern strategies, involving nonevaluation and either a pinpointed or opening-up awareness, may be more effective. For example, there are times when positive evaluations may be quite effective (covert self-statements as self-reinforcement), times when they may not be so effective (as when they take our attention from a task). For certain tasks, it seems that nonevaluation may be the most effective focusing strategy. Here is a chart that may be helpful in pinpointing the specific strategies, their advantages and disadvantages:

Where We Focus	*Advantages*	*Disadvantages*
external	survival, reducing inputs, keeping from self-ruminating, avoiding pain, giving attention to others	avoiding important self problems, limited view and "repression," "cognitive avoidance"
internal	awareness of internal cares, hearing body signals, taking responsibility for actions	excessive self-rumination, avoidance of others
past	constructive: learning from mistakes, seeing past accomplishments, getting perspective on progress	destructive: useless dwelling and self-castigation
future	constructive: goal setting, planning	destructive: useless worrying without taking any action

How We Focus	*Advantages*	*Disadvantages*
nonevaluation	allows us to direct total attention to task	does not provide opportunity for feedback
positive evaluation	may serve as reinforcement, encouragement	may divert attention from task
negative evaluation	gives feedback, may be cue for looking for alternative response	if no action is taken, becomes a useless, negative thought

Negative evaluations may be helpful as a means of giving us feedback about our performance. However, these evaluations should be precise, specific, and related to the task. They should not be self-referential, and they should not be statements we can't act on—i.e., negative thoughts.

Further, we may focus on the past and the future as one way of living in the here and now. Focusing on the past and future removes our attention from the environment at hand, and takes us into our internal environment. This focusing can either be advantageous and enjoyable, or unpleasant and worthless. When we do focus on the past or future, we should be conscious of having made a decision to do so, and should make it a constructive experience. Further, we should try to ensure that we don't dwell excessively in the past or future at the expense of the present situation. For example, even though some delay of gratification (delaying present wants for future goals) is necessary, it would be a mistake to continually postpone present enjoyment for the sake of attaining some future goal. We perform an enormous number of behaviors during a day. It is to our advantage to become more aware of *what* we focus on throughout the day, and *how* we focus. In this way we can learn the best technique, or combination of techniques, depending upon the nature of what we are doing. As the dialogue between the monk and master suggests, we may learn much truth from living in the moment (especially those of us who can recall a time when we did not realize we had eaten until we found our plates empty):

Monk: Do you ever make an effort to get disciplined in the truth?
Master: Yes, I do. When I am hungry, I eat; when I am tired, I sleep.
Monk: This is what everybody does.
Master: No.
Monk: Why not?
Master: Because when they eat, they do not eat; they are thinking of various other things, thereby allowing themselves to be disturbed.[56]

DETACHED OBSERVATION (NONATTACHMENT) AND CARING LOVE

But if in your fear you would seek only
love's peace and love's pleasure,
then it is better for you that
you cover your nakedness and pass out
of love's threshing floor
into the seasonless void,
where you shall laugh
but not all your laughter, and weep
but not all your tears.[57]

Many of us can probably recall experiences in which we felt overwhelmed by an event, or events. At those times, we may have felt too sensitive, too fragile to cope and may have tried to pull ourselves back, to gain a perspective, to become "re-centered." On the other hand, many of us may have felt the numbness, the total withdrawal and detachment by which we build an island of protection around ourselves.

Is there a middle ground? Can we learn to maintain the emotional involvement that Gibran talks about, *and* maintain a perspective, keeping ourselves "centered"?

The following story entitled "Is That So?," raises this question:

> The Zen Master Hakuin was praised by his neighbors as one living a pure life.
>
> A beautiful Japanese girl whose parents owned a food store lived near him. Suddenly, without any warning, her parents discovered she was with child.
>
> This made her parents angry. She would not confess who the man was but, after much harassment, named Hakuin.
>
> In great anger, the parents went to the Master. "Is that so?" was all he would say.
>
> After the child was born it was brought to Hakuin. By this time, he had lost his reputation, which did not trouble him, but he took very good care of the child. He obtained milk from his neighbors and everything else the little one needed.
>
> A year later the girl-mother could stand it no longer. She told her parents the truth—that the real father of the child was the young man who worked in the fish market.
>
> The mother and father of the girl at once went to Hakuin to ask his forgiveness, to apologize at length, and to get the child back again.
>
> Hakuin was willing. In yielding the child all he said was, "Is that so?"[58]

Can Hakuin really love the child *and* give the child up so easily, or is he really acting from numbness and noncaring? In order to try to answer that question, it is necessary to further examine detached observation. This discussion will illustrate how Eastern concepts such as nonattachment, nonpossessiveness, indifference, and acceptance can be related to caring love.

Detached Observation: Its Uses

As we saw in Chapter 1, the East places an important emphasis on being able to obtain a perspective on our actions: an "immovable wisdom; a spectator resting in ourselves." Western writers have noted the importance of a similar kind of detached observation. Allport, for example, notes that the healthy person (religious individual) is one who "exercises his capacity for self-objectification, viewing with detachment his reason and unreason, seeing the limitations of both. He holds in perspective both his self-image and his ideal self-image."[59] This self-objectification, Allport added, includes a touch of humor,[60] the ability to laugh at ourselves.

Most Western psychotherapeutic schools also attempt to teach the client or patient a type of detached self-observation. It is felt that when we learn to see ourselves "objectively," we are able to look more honestly at ourselves to see both our strengths and our weaknesses.[61] In Rogerian therapy, for example, the therapist, by accurately reflecting the client to himself in a nonjudgmental way, teaches that person to "see his own attitudes, confusions, ambivalences, and perceptions accurately expressed by another but stripped away of the complications of emotion."[62] Sigmund Freud noted the importance of "this detached observation" in his work with Breuer, *Studies On Hysteria.* Freud stated that to help the patient overcome resistance, the therapist must help the patient assume an objectivity to his own dilemma, "a crystal ball attitude by the patient toward himself."[63] In this way, Freud noted, the patient learned to see that he had nothing to fear by revealing his true memories and "his customary defenses are shown to be unnecessary." In social learning theory, this detached observation may be effected by *systematic desensitization* (see Chapter 2), a process which Ferster and Staats have suggested is the functional equivalent of the dynamic and client-centered relationship process.[64] In effect, systematic desensitization allows the aversive stimulus to become less threatening, so that it can simply be observed, without any emotional overlay. And, as Jacobsen noted in relation to progressive relaxation,[65] by learning to see objectively the difference between our problems and our emotional reactions to our problems, we are in a position to deal much more constructively with the problems themselves. Thus, one aspect of detached observation is the *removal or cessation of emotional overlay*. This observation allows us to view ourself as an event "out there," as if we were merely part of the environment.

Detached Observation as a Continuum

At one end of the continuum of detached observation is behavioral self-observation. In behavioral self-observation, when an individual is asked to observe a specific set of experiences (e.g., weight) there is likely to be a high degree of emotional, critical evaluation associated with the observation. An example further along on the continuum is illustrated by the following cartoon:

Oh, I know you *like* me — but if you *loved* me, this would be in slow motion with lots of backlighting.

In this cartoon, the man observes himself running on the beach. As he implies, if this observation coincides with previous expectations, models, and visions of what love is—"if there is the appropriate backlighting"—then one knows it is love; otherwise it is only liking. However, even though his observation is "more" detached than our normal ordinary awareness, it still exists along a continuum, and has many elements of normal self-observation with the accompanying critical self-evaluation.

Abraham Maslow has described the process of "more detached self-observation as a type of transcendence": "The ability to transcend [in psychotherapy] parallels the process of experiencing and of self-observing one's self-experiences in a kind of critical or editorial or detached and removed way so that one can criticize it, approve or disapprove of it and assume control."[66] An even more detached observation than Maslow describes would involve having the person observe how he reacts to the *process* of self-observation. Consider, for example, this patient who had a history of violent behavior. After several weeks of meditation and self-observation of "angry behavior" he told me, "One evening I got God-damned pissed when my roommate began to play the electric guitar late at night. But then I "listened" to my pissedness, listened to the guitar and laughed. Then I fell asleep."

Roger Walsh has illustrated this process of increasing detached observation, acceptance, and humor: "The more complete this acceptance, the more effective it was in deflating this negativity. If, for example, I became anxious about something and then got angry that I was scared, and then got depressed that here I was again getting angry at being scared, then it became apparent that it was necessary to accept all the layers of this emotional onion and effectively say that it was okay to be depressed, that I'm angry at being scared. As soon as the outer onion ring was accepted, then the inner ones also collapsed with it."[67] Each stimulus becomes a cue to stand back further and observe, and accept. As the critical evaluations decrease in intensity, there is more acceptance. Further, this detached observation may help us to cope better in daily living by keeping things in perspective. As we acquire perspective, we realize life is filled with ups and downs, positive and negative events. By observing the variety of these events, we realize the cyclical nature of emotions, and may thus learn to maintain a distance, to become less dependent and less in flux with each individual situation. This may also teach us an ability to tolerate ambiguity better, as we flow with the ups and downs, learning a patience and calmness in dealing with and observing each new event.

As we move along the continuum, not only does the nature of the observation change (less self-critical evaluation) but the content becomes less narrow (e.g., observing weight, positive self-statements) and more encompassing (observing one's self and all one's behavior).

Later on in the continuum, detached observation seems to involve merely *observing, without any editorial comment.* This is often most effectively done with images, and without words. As Staats and other social learning theorists have pointed out, the words we use have been conditioned to have certain positive or negative meanings.[68] Therefore, the very act of labeling when we self-observe or self-evaluate causes, to a certain extent, some affective connotation of the event.

Oh, our first argument! I'm going to get the camera!

Through detached observation, we learn to become *less attached to any of our actions,* or the fruits of our actions, *less needing of social reinforcement.* A Western means of achieving nonattachment may be by having so many different "irons in the fire," so many people around, so many jobs, that no one action takes on too much importance. The Eastern way would be to remain nonattached to the fruits of *any* of one's actions, like the mirror—merely to perform the actions and observe the performance.

The highest state of detached observation—the immovable wisdom described in Chapter 1—seems to come when an individual has focused on himself for so long, and has received so much self- and other reinforcement, that he overcomes the need to focus on himself. This may be referred to as a kind of "self-saturation," a desensitization of one's self to the self. At first, even though we may be observing ourselves objectively without emotion, we would probably be most likely, given a variety of stimuli, to focus on the "self." However, soon we may *habituate* to the self: it truly loses its affective value, and becomes just another object. At this end of the continuum, we enter the realm of *egolessness*, where an individual no longer has a stumbling self-conscious reaction to himself and events because, paradoxically, he is so "self"-conscious. In other words, he knows himself so well that he no longer need worry about knowing himself, there is no longer any strong affect associated with the "self." Through meditation and other techniques we have discussed, we may learn this type of detached observation—to be detached even from our "selves."

One final point needs to be made about this detached observation continuum. As we have seen, detached observation involves the absence of self-evaluation and self-judgment; therefore, according to Zen, it in no way interferes with spontaneity: e.g., "beyond assertion and denial show me the truth of Zen. Quick, quick, or thirty blows for you."[69] Life is the ongoing present, and according to Zen belief we should respond directly, spontaneously, and without conscious mentation and evaluation.

Integrating Nonattachment and Caring Love

But there is evaluation in Zen. For example, the evaluation that we are evaluating too much, or that we have not been aware enough both occur, as in the story "Every Minute Zen" (see the section on "Developing a New Awareness" in Chapter 4.) However, at the same time there is evaluation, there is also a *simultaneous detached observation of that evaluation.* This is the important point, for the detached observation influences the nature of the evaluativeness by allowing it to be seen dispassionately and accepted nonjudgmentally. Finally, in terms of self-reinforcement, it seems that initially the "Master-to-be" covertly prides himself in his/her self-awareness and self-discipline. Although attachment to one's nonattachment still "stains the mirror," this seems a stage through which we must go before being able to truly be free of attachment and the need for reinforcement, either from others or from our selves. It would seem that this attachment to reinforcement *would also be observed:* e.g., perhaps the Master would say "Oh, see how silly I am, still enjoying an occasional pat on the back."

Now, let us return to the story of Hakuin. Given the above model of detached observation, it is possible to see that Hakuin really cared intensely about the child. He took good care of the child, and obtained everything it needed. Yet, though Hakuin loved the child, he was able to yield and not to be possessive.

Thus, we see that we can be nonattached and at the same time intimately involved. This nonattachment is different from numbness. It is not a closing off. Rather, it is an acceptance — similar to the way that the mirror accepts all into itself.

The Hindu word from the *Gita* which is translated as *indifference* (*aksano*) means nondifferentiation: seeing all as the same. The mirror accepts all: it accepts red/green, pain/pleasure as one; yet it likewise can differentiate between and participate in both. I once had an astrology reading which illustrated this point: "On the personal side, emotions may rise and fall, so maintain equilibrium and poise." If equilibrium and poise are translated as centeredness, nonattachment, acceptance, then we see that one can remain indifferent and participate fully in the rising and falling of emotions.

The story is told of a Zen Master who came back to the monastery to find the place strewn with the bodies of his colleagues and students who had been slain by bandits. He sat down and meditated for a long period; then, at the end of meditation, he cried.

Rather than numb the pain
of parting, he sat straight
with an elfish smile

According to the model suggested here, nonattachment may help us to be more open and receptive, more willing to feel and express our emotions. For example, Ornstein and Naranjo suggest that when we desire something, we tune out other stimuli that are not related to that want. Therefore, the "practice of psychological nonattachment can be considered an additional way to remove the normal restrictions on inputs. If there are no desires there is less of a bias at any one moment to tune in perception, our awareness of the external environment becomes less restricted, less of an interaction, and more like a mirror."[70]

Further, in terms of task efficiency, it is often better to be nonattached. A veterinarian operating on a dog, for example, is more effective if he doesn't have a squeamish emotional reaction, but rather sees the dog's pain, and then concernedly and calmly performs the necessary techniques.

In summary, we see that attachment is useful in getting us to take care of that in which we are invested (find reinforcing). The danger of attachment, however, is a possessiveness, an unwillingness to let go. A poetic example of the pain of attachment is illustrated by Siddhartha and his son. The son left his father to go into the woods. Siddhartha was distraught at losing his son and ran after him. He said to himself that his son was still young and needed his protection. In truth, he was hurt at losing possession of his son.

As in the case of Siddhartha, our attachment may keep others from experiencing their own personal freedom; it may also keep us from experiencing ours—we become bound up in possessing and fear of losing, rather than experiencing and living. By learning detached observation, we realize that although we may choose to increase our caring love, choose to decrease our anger over trivia, we ultimately need to see the importance of being nonattached to, and accepting all.

Nonattachment plus caring love allows us the advantage of experiencing the stream of life to the fullest, without the disadvantage of clinging to that which cannot be held.

SUMMARY

In this chapter, we saw that finding the path of heart by combining the East–West vision involves a delicate balance among several different abilities, including the abilities to

- Stay centered, relaxed, rested without being passive; to maintain a keen edge, stay alert, to be without useless tension and competitiveness
- Balance our own self-interest with an awareness and sensitivity to the rights and needs of others
- Be rigorous, goal-oriented, instrumental, and productive; and also to remain present-centered, nonstriving, receptive (action in inaction and inaction in action)
- Accept ourselves as we are, without guilt, without putting ourselves down; and, at the same time be able to work on changing ourselves, creating, growing toward our ideal vision
- Stand up for ourselves, maintain a sense of uniqueness while also being able to yield, to be gentle, to flow with events.
- Use words and analysis when they can be productive and poetic; and to *not* use words when they hide and distort reality

- Choose how we want to live, to have the self-control to achieve our goals; and also the spontaneity to let go of goals, the flexibility to choose new goals, and the creativity to *perceive* both new goals and alternative means to those goals

Thus, the model of health suggests the integration of productivity and centeredness; a strong ego and egolessness; assertiveness and yielding; self-control and yielding; self-control and spontaneity; and nonattachment and caring love.

6
Techniques: Following the Path of Heart

If you have the wisdom to perceive
a truth but not the manhood
to keep it, you will lose it again,
even though you have discovered it.

~Confucius

I commend you Siddhartha,
for you have once again heard
the bird in your breast sing,
and followed it.

~Siddhartha

I'm sure many of us have had the experience of having a sudden insight, a moment of understanding, only to have that insight slowly fade away amidst daily habits and routines. As Confucius noted, the wisdom to perceive a truth (developing a new awareness; perceiving a new alternative) is necessary. But insight is not enough. We also need to be able to *keep* that truth (the commitment, the affirmation, the skills to follow through). As Siddhartha suggests, we need both the skills to hear the bird in our breast sing and the skills to follow it.

The goal of this book has been to develop both skills. In the first chapter we presented an overview of the different Eastern techniques and goals: the way of the Zen Master. In the second chapter we presented an overview of the Western techniques and goals of health: the way of the Grand Conditioner. In the third, fourth, and fifth chapters we described how Eastern and Western skills could be combined to develop a new awareness and how Eastern and Western visions could be combined to provide a new alternative, a path of heart.

In this chapter, we turn our attention to the specific ways in which different Eastern and Western techniques may be combined to reach and follow our path of heart.

Where to Begin

Each of us has our own hurts, loneliness, joys. Each of us has our own goals and visions. The bird in each of our breasts is unique, with its own distinctive melody. Our first step is to try to get in touch with this, to choose what we would like to commit to—to find our personal vision, our own particular melody. The area you choose to work on may be related to your ideal self (as conceptualized in Chapter 2); or you may wish to work on some area suggested in the integrated vision in Chapter 4. The format of this book is just as useful for working on reducing weight, stopping smoking, becoming more affectionate with a spouse, as it is for working on committing to an intense spiritual and personal journey. The vision can be anything, large or small, as long as it is important to you.

A Word of Caution

A word of caution may be in order here. All the areas of the vision may seem exciting to work toward, just as all aspects of your ideal self may seem worth attaining. However, my suggestion is that you not try to work on several areas of concern at the same time, but rather pick one area that seems most appropriate, and focus specifically on that area. Otherwise, there is a likelihood that you will try to do everything—try to cover too much too quickly, and feel frustrated in each part of the task. (You may wish, at this point, to refer to the frustration and difficulty involved in making a decision in Chapter 4.

A second word of caution is that self-change is not an instant process, much as we would like it to be. Most habits or patterns of living and acting have developed over a long period of time. Acting in a new way may at first be quite difficult. Therefore, we have to be willing to commit to and affirm our willingness to work toward our own self-chosen goals. In thinking about making such an affirmation, it may be worthwhile to return to Chapter 4, where you were asked to look into your own motivation and commitment.

. . . And a Word of Hope

The assumption made in both the Eastern and Western schools of thought is that *these skills can be learned. People do change.* We *can* make progress toward attaining our vision.

COMBINING EASTERN AND WESTERN TECHNIQUES: CASE EXAMPLES

What I would like to do in this section is to show, through case examples, how the Eastern and Western techniques may be combined. At the end of each case, I give a general framework that you the reader may use if the technique seems applicable to your area of concern.

Case One: Overcoming Low Self-esteem

The client was referred because of a long history of what she called "low self-esteem." She was an Englishwoman in her middle 40's who stated that she often felt on the verge of becoming an alcoholic because of her "binge drinking." She described how she would spend long periods of time in a day thinking about acting, but not acting. Every time she decided to do something, she would pull back, from fear of failure. This extended to large behaviors—like job hunting, or going out to meet new people—to smaller, seemingly trivial behaviors—like brushing her teeth, or taking a shower.

After a certain period of time, she would become upset at her lack of accomplishment, her passivity, and feel a need to perform a great action to make up for lost time. She would then go on a drinking spree, and try to live out an unrealistic fantasy. For example, she once actually flew to London to present a plan on television to save the world.

This woman noted that she never gave herself the opportunity to feel or experience any pleasure. She was afraid of feeling guilty for "wasting" her time in this manner instead of accomplishing something really "worthwhile." She also said that she felt she could only be loved or valued as worthwhile if she could accomplish a large, significant task. Therefore, she spent most of her time putting herself down, telling herself she was worthless, incapable of being loved. She was obviously a very sensitive person who felt a lot of pain at being caught between wanting to perform a significant action and feeling she couldn't do anything at all.

One of the cooperative tasks we worked out during the course of therapy was to try to help her get more in touch with what we called the "reasonable voice" within her. This reasonable voice didn't constantly put her down; this reasonable voice told her she was worthwhile just as she was; it tried to help her structure her time so she could begin to accomplish some of her goals. This reasonable voice gave her permission to relax, let go, and experience the pleasure of the here and now; and it gave her guidance on how to practice interpersonal approach skills with other people, both male and female.

Our task was to increase the frequency of statements from the reasonable voice, and to decrease, or eliminate statements of the unreasonable voice: shoulds, oughts, putdowns, etc. She was taught breath meditation, as outlined in Chapter 1. She was told to watch her thoughts, and whenever the unreasonable voice was heard, to just let it go, and continue focusing on breathing. She was similarly instructed to watch her thoughts during the day, and whenever the unreasonable voice appeared, to just let it flow away.

However, we didn't want to let the *reasonable* voice flow away. We wanted to increase its frequency. Therefore, following the Premack Principle, we hypothesized that we could increase the frequency of the low-probability behavior (reasonable statements) by making them occur just before a high-probability behavior. Since smoking was a high-probability behavior,[1] the client was asked to put reasonable statements on 3 × 5 index cards and attach these to her cigarette carton. Before she smoked a cigarette (high-probability behavior) she was instructed to read and enjoy one of the note cards (low-probability behavior). During the six months of treatment, the client found a job (her first in five years); she began to date men, including one with whom she had "the most meaningful relationship I have ever had," and which gave her hope that she could in fact learn to relate to men.

Below are the statements that she compiled as statements from her "reasonable voice."

On validating her "core self" and self-acceptance she listed:

- It's OK to do small things without feeling I'm a small person.
- I am accepting myself more and more as I am, as I feel.

- I am getting better-looking every day because the way I look is subjective.
- I don't have to prove that I'm OK. I *am* OK because I exist.
- Every day in every way I am getting better and better, more OK.
- I am more and more aware of, willing and able to be my own best friend.
- I don't have to become a star to accept myself or get acceptance from others.
- Look, I don't have to set the world on fire. I can gradually listen to the inner voice. I can listen to the reasonable voice, not the one that's always telling me *should*, putting me down.
- More and more I seek, and believe that I am OK after all.
- More and more I'm exposing myself as I *am* instead of as what I'd like to be seen as.

On planning and structuring her time in the here and now to accomplish future goals, she listed:

- I don't have to have instant gratification of each and every desire or impulse that arises.
- More and more I am (*in a relaxed way*) thinking about planning what to do tomorrow—one day at a time.
- I am learning more and more to distinguish reality from fantasy, wishful thinking, and mania.
- I am taking one step at a time, and no step is too small.
- More and more I am willing and able to recognize and manage my problems.
- I don't have to immediately say anything or everything that comes into my mind.
- I can increasingly be here now without escaping into fantasies, obstructions, illusions, nightmares.
- More and more I am learning how to structure my own time.
- Doing something is better than doing nothing at all: I am learn-

ing to quit the habit of not acting from fear of failing. More and more I am looking for what *I* want to do and see.

On letting go, she listed:

- Gradually I am opening myself to more pleasure and good feelings.
- I am feeling more positive about myself, other people, and life every day.
- I am easy with good feelings.
- I am gradually increasing my tolerance of reasonable amounts of tension, uncertainty, ambiguity.
- I am gradually becoming more and more flexible.
- Life begins when I let go and give up. I must quit trying to control everything.
- I will not constantly defer here-and-now enjoyment for that "big payoff."
- I am more and more aware of, willing, and able to let go, enjoy myself, and have fun.

On relaxing, she listed:

- I will *practice* holding still, slowing down.
- I am more and more aware of, willing, and able to relax.
- I am willing and able and aware of breathing deeply and easily.

On practicing social skills (increasing the probability of effective performance of overt behavior), she listed:

- More and more I am seeing people as they are, without labels.
- I am appreciating and enjoying and understanding men as people more and more.
- I am gradually increasing my eye contacts—with practice.

Finding Our "Self"

As the above case illustrates, by learning to precisely pinpoint the nature and content of our thoughts, we can turn them from destructive, self-defeating patterns to useful, constructive aids. The images and self-statements will be different for each of us, depending upon the nature of the concern, and the nature of what is reinforcing.

What follows is a general framework integrating several Eastern and Western strategies, which may serve as a useful guideline in areas involving our "self." These areas include developing a more positive self-concept, overcoming self-consciousness, and striving to become egoless. A related framework, involving assertiveness and yielding, is also included.

One of the first steps in any self-change project we undertake is to observe our "area of concern." Below are several possible areas related to the self and phrased in such a way they can be observed (refer back to self-observation instructions). Pay special attention to:

- times when you use negative traits about yourself, or make negative self-statements
- number of positive things you say to yourself and do for yourself (self-reinforcement)
- times when you play petty, trivial, ego games: i.e., times when your "self-esteem" gets in the way
- times when you act egolessly, flow with a situation, and feel good about it
- times when you feel put down and don't stand up for yourself
- times when you stand up for yourself and feel good about it
- negative trait feedback that you have received in the past from others (Go over this list and check what you yourself believe to be true, then monitor the items on the checklist for a week to find out the specifics of when in fact you find yourself engaging in these behaviors.)

Increasing Positive Self-statements and Pleasurable Time for "Self"

As a result of your monitoring, you may decide to increase the amount of reinforcement you give yourself. For example, you may wish to reinforce yourself more liberally for the tasks you perform—complimenting yourself on your competence, productivity, uniqueness, ability to control events. You may also want to take time from task-oriented activities for pleasure, events you enjoy. For example, here's a list of enjoyable events I made for myself:

Behaviors by Myself	*Behaviors with Others*
Playing music	Dinner with spouse
Paint	Going to movie
Write poetry	Playing tennis
Nature hikes	Massages
Walking on beach	Playing in park with daughter

You may wish to increase the frequency and duration of activities that are reinforcing for you—both external activities and internal activities.

It may be helpful to put up pictures around the house or office to encourage you to take that extra time to be with yourself or others (this is environmental planning). These pictures may serve as cues, reminding you to step back from your tasks, to take a *kairos* break during your hectic daily schedule.

In addition to increasing the amount of reinforcement you give yourself for the tasks you perform, you may also wish to increase the frequency of global positive statements about yourself—that is, to accept, to love your "self" without regard to the task you perform, or the actions you accomplish: "the big cuddle." By increasing the amount of specific and global reinforcement you give to yourself, you will build a strong, more positive self-identity.

Overcoming Self-consciousness

List situations or memories in which you have felt self-conscious. For example, do you remember as an adolescent when one of your parents asked you to perform on a musical instrument for invited guests?

Think of other situations—e.g., trying to decide whether to contribute to a group discussion; public speaking; walking into a party. I remember that once while I was playing tennis, my wife—then girlfriend—came to watch me play, and although up until that time I had been playing well, I began to have difficulty. I soon realized that the problem was that I was focusing on me—not on tennis—making covert statements such as, "If I play well, will that look as though I am showing off?", "What if I miss a shot, will she think I'm less wonderful?", and so forth. When we get those feelings of self-consciousness, we should remember the following:

1. They are normal. They are part of ordinary awareness. Therefore, we should instruct ourselves as follows: Don't worry; this awkwardness is normal/natural. Stick with it, it will pass.
2. We should note where our attention is focused. If we are focusing on ourselves in an unproductive way (e.g., feeling awkward at a party), we should choose to redirect our focus:
   - to the task at hand: "Come on, let's go meet some people at the party."
   - to more productive evaluations: "This should be fun."
   - in a nonevaluative way, like a mirror: "Let's just be, enjoy, experience; let go of thoughts."

Below are listed some possible ways for overcoming self-conscious behavior (or negative statements) and giving ourselves the freedom to take risks:

1. Assess the reasons for hesitancy (e.g., consequences, such as fear of failure, etc.)
2. Decide to take the risk (decision making: existential choice)
3. Rehearse your behavior (imagine through covert modeling of yourself performing the risk-taking behavior), prepare through imagery and self-statements
4. Give appropriate self-instructions: e.g., "Don't think about it, you've made your decision; do it"; "Let go, trust yourself"
5. Use thought stopping to eliminate hesitancy statements
6. Make your mind empty like a mirror; let go of self-statements altogether, and trust yourself

Developing Egolessness

Finally, we have also suggested the need to let go of our concept of self, not to be self-preoccupied, not to feel we need to control all events, or constantly evaluate our own uniqueness.

If you have monitored this area, and would like to decrease the frequency of self-preoccupying thoughts, ego games, etc., it may be worthwhile to practice making self-statements such as "yield, let go, don't let it hassle you," and, in addition, to practice techniques, such as meditation, to reduce all thoughts.

We have discussed several different techniques for areas of concern dealing with self. These areas are summarized in the following table:

Positive Self-focus: Adding Pleasure to the "Self"	*Decreasing Self-consciousness*	*Becoming Egoless*
self-observation	self-observation	self-observation
commitment to increase	self-instruction to let go	meditation
set goal	change evaluations	self-instruction to let go, realize trivia
list reinforcing behaviors	be nonevaluative	
list global and specific self-reinforcing statements		
environmental planning		

Closely related to issues of positive self-image and egolessness is the area of assertiveness and yielding. The following list gives a six-step procedure which integrates both assertiveness and yielding.

1. Self-observe situations in which you feel you should be more assertive (e.g., waiter bringing burnt food; someone taking your parking place; standing in line waiting for a movie ticket and someone cuts in front of you; your co-equal at work was just given a promotion and you weren't).
2. Note what you're saying to yourself. Do you feel slighted? Put down? Do you feel the other person is being inconsiderate of your feelings?
3. Try to assess the importance of the issue in the larger scheme of things. Is it really that important? What difference does it

actually make if someone took your parking place? stepped in line in front of you? Are you merely playing a trivial ego game?

4. Take a few breaths; relax. Practice a few cosmic chuckle exercises (see detached observation techniques at the end of this chapter).
5. If you still bothered, buy an assertive training book and deal with the issue calmly and directly.
6. If you're not bothered, and have put things in perspective, deal with the issue calmly and directly.

Don't pretend you're not bothered when you are. We can't force our "egos" away. Keep practicing step four, and be patient. Soon the cosmic chuckle perspective will win out.

Developing Thought-stopping Techniques

In the first case example, we mentioned the importance of thought stopping. Both the East and West would agree that unreasonable negative thoughts are not productive. However, Western philosophy would advocate trying to *stop* the *thoughts*, *substituting* more positive ones. This was the method used in case number one. Eastern philosophy, however, would suggest that thoughts, by their very nature, are bad, and we should let go of them, thereby stopping all thoughts, even the positive ones.

Without the proper techniques, it is not easy to stop thoughts. For example, let me ask you to try the following exercise.

Stop thinking of elephants.

Well, what went through your mind? Elephants! There are many difficulties involved in *trying not to think*. Our first reaction is to block out the image, which only makes us think about it more.

Below are several different techniques that have been developed in Eastern and Western settings for stopping thoughts:

1. Meditation, in which we just let thoughts "flow away" down the river (see Chapter 1).
2. Behavioral thought stopping, in which every time you become aware that you are having an aversive, unwanted thought, you yell "stop!" (at first overtly, later covertly).

3. Relaxation of the vocal cords (see relaxation instructions for throat, Chapter 2).

4. Focus on an alternative response, such as a specific object (e.g., meditation; alternative focus); or you can imagine a big light switch which you click off to tell your mind you will no longer accept negative, unproductive thoughts. After you switch off the light switch, imagine a favorite natural scene and imagine yourself magically transported there.

These techniques may be used to stop several different types of thoughts. First, they may be used to stop useless rumination (e.g., taking our business home; perseverating about a past occurrence; putting ourselves down). Second, they may be used to interrupt thoughts that will lead to maladaptive actions (e.g., an overweight person after dinner having the thought that there is some delicious ice cream in the freezer). Third, they may be used when we are having two sets of ideas going on at the same time: e.g., trying to work on a task that we need to finish, yet wishing we were sailing.*

Case Two: Overcoming Anxiety

In Chapter 2, we discussed the case of a man who had "free-floating" anxiety. He described this anxiety as "overpowering feelings of being bounced around by some sort of all powerful forces, themselves neurotic." He was instructed to observe his own anxiety for two weeks, in order to pinpoint what might be causing it and when it was occurring. After reviewing the information gathered from *self-observation*, we devised an intervention strategy to help him deal with the anxiety.

*In the sailing/task dilemma, we may realize that images of sailing are pleasant and rewarding (high-probability behavior), whereas the task seems tedious (low-probability behavior). Rather than doing two things at once and neither one well (e.g., trying to perform a task and thinking about sailing), you may choose to do them separately. Following the Premack principle, you can let the more enjoyable behavior (high-probability behavior—sailing) be the reinforcer for the low-probability behavior (a certain quantity or amount of time of task completion). Covert strategies may also be facilitated by environmental planning. For example, every time an off-task thought occurs (e.g., sailing, etc.) you may get up, leave the desk (work environment). Thus, the desk becomes a cue for on-target attention.

First, he was instructed to practice *formal meditation* two times a day regardless of whether or not he was feeling anxious at that particular moment. Second, he was instructed to practice what we called "contingent informal meditation." This contingent informal meditation involved the following: (a) doing an "opening-up" *informal meditation* throughout the day; (b) paying particular attention to internal cues that told him that he was anxious; (c) bringing his attention to his breathing as soon as he recognized any internal anxiety; (d) closing his eyes and imagining himself feeling calm and relaxed (self-modeling); and (c) giving himself instructions to relax, stay calm (self-instructions).

The results of this intervention are noted on the following graph. Particularly informative is the description of progress in the anecdotal data.

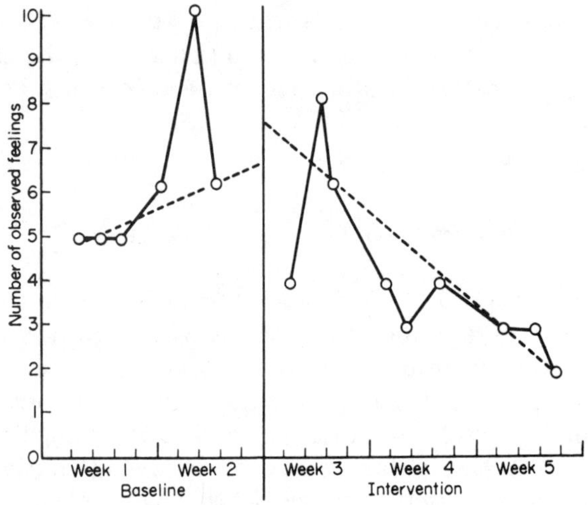

Daily self-observation of anxious feelings.

ANECDOTAL DATA:

1st Week:	...overpowering feelings of being bounced around by some sort of all powerful forces, themselves neurotic. (sic)
2nd Week:	I find the anxious periods can be timed-upon awakening and before English class in the evening. As if I'm conditioned to be anxious at those times. (sic)
3rd Week:	By focusing on breathing, I realize the trivia of my anxiety.
4th Week:	Self-control is growing as I feel I am starting to beat anxiety. I fall into breathing meditation much more automatically. At first informal meditation involved concentration on my breathing, but I don't even need to do this anymore. Just the recognition that I am anxious is a signal to dismiss my thoughts and worries. It's something like just recognizing that I am becoming anxious is a signal for calm.
5th Week:	I can direct myself out of anxiety very well now. Enormous improvement.

Managing Stress and Reducing Anxiety: Becoming "Centered" and "In Flow"

Case two illustrated the usefulness of integrating meditation and behavioral self-control techniques.We present here a general "how-to" plan for combining these two strategies. (The theoretical rationale for combining these techniques is described in Appendix 3.)

Step One: Self-observation

As in almost any self-change project, the first thing we must do is gain a greater awareness about the area of concern. The following concern times related to anxiety and centeredness which you may wish to observe in yourself:

- times when I feel centered, relaxed, "in flow with things"
- times when I feel "off-center": anxious, upset, tense in a non-productive way
- times when I feel helpless, out of control: when I feel my "willpower" slipping away
- times when I feel myself "overly controlled," too programmed
- times when I feel myself acting spontaneously and joyously: self-celebrating

If reducing anxiety (become more centered, more relaxed) is an area that you would like to work on, first you need to gain additional information about what *you* mean by your terms. In order to do this, follow the instructions on self-observation. There is a data collection chart specifically related to the area of centeredness and anxiety on which you may record information about your self-observation. At the end of each day, it is worthwhile to count up the frequency with which the behavior occurred (e.g., frequency of anxious feelings; frequency of relaxed feelings) and record that information on the chart. This will give you a graphic visual picture of what is occurring, similar to the anxiety graph. It is also worthwhile at the end of the day to spend some time thinking about what you learned from the self-observation: e.g., what are some of the situations that increase the likelihood of your becoming tense and off-center? What are some of the ways

NAME ______________________ DATE ______________

BEHAVIOR RECORDED* ______________________________

*Times when I feel centered, relaxed (X)
Times when I feel anxious, tense (O)

BEFORE	AFTER								
Where? Who was present? Doing what?	How did situation change as a result?	SUN	MON	TUES	WED	THURS	FRI	SAT	TOTAL PER TIME SLOT
		7-9							
		9-11							
		11-1							
		1-3							
		3-5							
		5-7							
		7-9							
		9-11							
		11-7							
	TOTAL PER DAY								

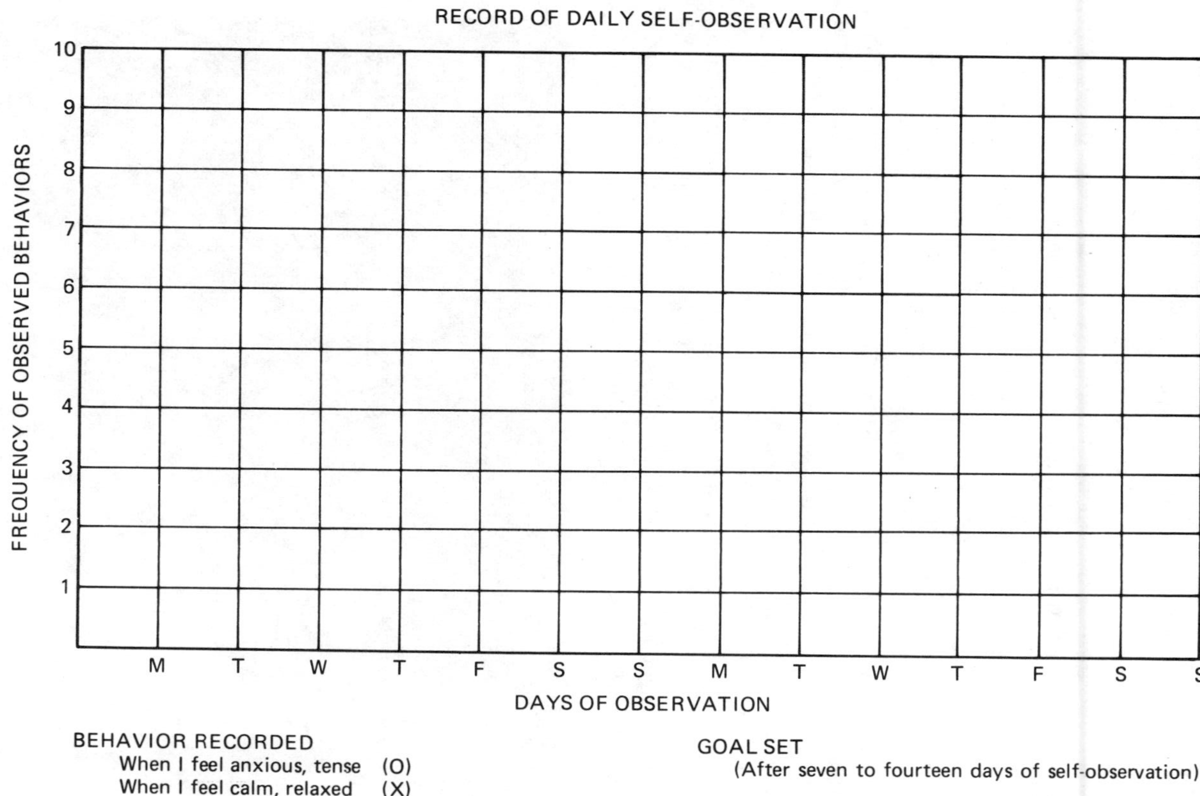
RECORD OF DAILY SELF-OBSERVATION
FREQUENCY OF OBSERVED BEHAVIORS
10
9
8
7
6
5
4
3
2
1
M T W T F S S M T W T F S S
DAYS OF OBSERVATION
BEHAVIOR RECORDED
When I feel anxious, tense (O)
When I feel calm, relaxed (X)
GOAL SET
(After seven to fourteen days of self-observation):

you react when you get tense? What are situations that increase the likelihood of your feeling calm, relaxed?

Step Two: Self-evaluation and Goal Setting

After you have sufficient information from your self-observation, look at this information, evaluate it, and set a goal.

Step Three: Techniques for Reaching the Goal

Environmental Planning. In order to individually tailor techniques to our own particular situation, we have to know what that particular situation is. Once we gain this information through self-observation, we can begin to look for how best to deal with the area of concern. For example, we may decide to use environmental planning to deal with the area of centeredness and tension. We may avoid situations that make us tense, and seek out situations in which we feel relaxed. We can put cues around our home and office to remind us to check ourselves for feelings of relaxation (e.g., are my shoulders hunched? Do I feel calm in my stomach? Am I engaging in a positive, accepting dialogue?). Below is a picture I often use as a cue to relax.

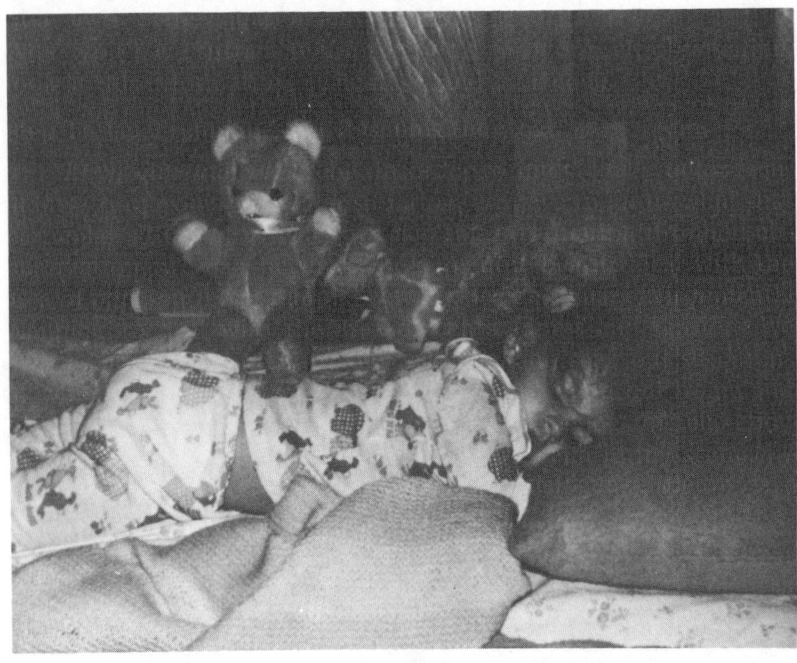

We can let these cues remind us to take a relaxation break: a moment to pause and appreciate, to just let go and "feel good."

Meditation, Progressive Relaxation, Systematic Desensitization. Other strategies that may be useful to help us relax are meditation, progressive deep muscle relaxation, and systematic desensitization. Each of these may be practiced twice a day for about fifteen to twenty minutes. These three strategies are similar in that they occur at certain fixed points throughout the day, regardless of the amount of tension or anxiety that you may be feeling at that particular time.

Time-out; Informal Relaxation. There are other strategies, however, that can be used informally throughout the day when we recognize that we are tense and anxious. One of the easiest ways for dealing with a tense situation is to leave the situation, a self-imposed "time out." Another strategy involves trying to interrupt the situation and practice a quick, informal relaxation exercise, which may be referred to as contingent informal meditation.

Contingent Informal Meditation. As a way of illustrating contingent informal meditation, let me ask you to think of a current personal situation which causes you to be somewhat tense. Take the situation and see if you can make it as specific as possible. Who is present? Where are you? What kinds of things are you doing, saying, thinking? Now close your eyes and imagine yourself in that situation, and allow yourself to experience the tension that you normally feel. Observe your tension. It's all right to let yourself feel anxious. You're in a safe place here, and the tense scene is not actually happening. Continue to observe your tension, noting where in your body you feel tense: Is your heart beating faster? Is your breathing more rapid? How does your stomach feel? What kinds of images do you have in your head? What sort of things are you saying to yourself? Are you saying things like: "I am helpless; I am not competent to handle this situation"? Let yourself go and just experience all that is happening to you.

Interruption of Sequence and Alternative Response. Once you have observed these thoughts and actions, say "stop" as you clench your fist and tighten your jaw. Then relax your fingers and your jaw and imagine yourself beginning to do an informal breath meditation: You are closing your eyes and beginning to focus on your breathing. Now, actually take two deep breaths through your nose, and, as you exhale, let your "center" of attention sink into your stomach. Say to yourself:

1. "I am (your name)."
2. "I am breath" (and take another deep breath).
3. "I am calm and relaxed and am in control" (and take two more deep breaths, letting your "center" sink to your stomach as you exhale).

Now imagine yourself becoming more and more relaxed; imagine yourself meditating, feeling calm, and in control. After a few more seconds, open your eyes, and just let yourself enjoy the calm, relaxed, and wide-awake feeling.

We're focusing on breath meditation because breathing is the simplest and most basic action we do. If we didn't breathe, we wouldn't be alive. If we weren't breathing, we wouldn't be able to get angry or upset or tense. As a rule, when you get anxious, all you have to do is remember that you are "just breath" and return to that simple behavior.

Some Final Thoughts on Relaxation and Centeredness

Centeredness may be seen as an attitude, a way of perceiving the world. We may learn, through several detached observation techniques, what things are important to us, and what things are not. In addition to this discrimination, we may learn to keep a perspective about all aspects of living.

When we catch ourselves becoming off-center, we must be accepting in our reaction, even if how we feel is a result of our own imperfection. Otherwise, we may commit a second fault, that of overreacting to our own imperfect humanness.

When you have a feeling you don't like, don't argue with the feeling. It exists. It is a true feeling: *you* are having it. Try to become aware of it. Accept your imperfections. Don't fight them, as in karate; flow with them, as in *aikido*.

As Gandhi noted, to cease being an angry man takes only two things: patience and hard work. Let's remember that Zen suggests we shouldn't become upset at our imperfections, but rather be able to accept them and, at the same time, work on changing them. The Zen way also advises that we should only do one thing at a time; and when we do it, *We Do It.*

If you catch yourself getting upset over trivia, and then getting angry at this lack of centeredness tell yourself to "let go, ease up, breathe deeply."

To stay centered and relaxed, you can:

1. Observe the times you get off-center—behavioral self-observation, informal meditation.
2. Make decisions about whether the issue is worth being upset about—detached observation, obtaining a perspective.
3. Use formal strategies for change—meditation twice a day, progressive relaxation twice a day (general relaxation), systematic desensitization (specific concern).
4. Use informal strategies for change—environmental planning (staying away from the situation, putting up cues as a signal to relax), interrupting sequence (leaving the environment, thought stopping, informal relaxation strategies [cognitive refocusing on breathing, covert self-modeling and self-instructions to be calm and let go and obtain a perspective]).

You can also:

1. Use mental aikido—practice flowing with an unpleasant situation, look for positive aspects.
2. Cut out relaxing pictures, images that make you feel good, and paste them up where you will see them frequently.
3. Make up a double-column self-instruction form so you can learn from your mistakes, one column listing the situation and how you acted, the other column listing your self-instructions and model for next time.

Case Three: Overcoming Depression

The third case we are going to discuss involves a male high-school adolescent who was described by his counselors and teachers as frequently listless, unmotivated, and uninvolved with any of the school's activities. When I talked to the student, he told me that he felt depressed all the time, and that there were only negative things around him—the smog, the traffic, the noise of the city. He also said that he had a lot of feelings inside himself, but whenever he tried to express these emotions in words, he became confused and frustrated.

I decided to develop two complementary strategies in working with this student. First, I wanted to help show him that he was selectively perceiving the negative things around him, and ignoring the positive; and second, I wanted to provide him with the means for communicating and expressing his internal feelings. He was a sensitive and warm person, and it seemed important for him to find ways of sharing this warmth with others.

Let me briefly describe the different types of structured experiences which I used with this student.

Realizing Selective Perception. To get him to practice self-observation of the "positive" in the external environment, I asked him to go to a park, and write down everything that made him feel good. He was instructed to also write down things that made him feel bad, but for every bad thing he noticed he was to list one good thing in a column next to it.

He returned with the list below:

benches

tables

fences

the willow trees not being allowed to grow naturally, trimmed so they can't hang to the ground

the cement creek that runs through the park

the hazy shades of gray within the sky

shrubs trimmed in columns

the shades of greens and yellows

people seeming as if they're enjoying themselves; child playing with her mother

yellow and pink flowers

the small creatures that, surprisingly enough, still roam between the blades of grass

birds

He didn't like the fact that men *clipped* the willows and didn't allow them to grow naturally. He also didn't like tables, fences: the human intervention. However, he was surprised to find how many things he did like: the green and yellow shades of grass; the living creatures hidden in the grass; a young child playing. Also he liked the columns of bushes even though they were artificially shaped by man.

The assignment (goal) for the next week was for him to write down, *each day*, at least three positive things that made him feel good. When he came in the next week, he brought the following list:

- camping, full moon, much wildlife
- the leaves seeming to be getting brighter, yellowish, and reddish
- very clear and colorful sunset
- day went very slowly
- a very illuminated rainbow, wind, stars exceptionally bright
- clouds, wind, rain
- camping, sunset, noises of the wind

He told me he had felt much better that week. "I know I'm feeling better—I went camping . . . just haven't wanted to go camping this year because I've been feeling so down. . . ."

During subsequent weeks, we talked and experienced many different modes of perceiving the positive things around us. We practiced meditating on our breathing and on the beauty of our internal body. As he noted, "I became more aware of the rhythmic processes and actions within me."

We practiced ear meditation on silence, on the sounds of a flute. We practiced eye meditation on inner visual imagery. We practiced opening-up eye meditation, in which he enjoyed "the intensity of color, like seeing for the first time." Toward the end of our sessions together, we practiced *mindfulness meditation* during a shared meal. This mindfulness meditation included being aware and observant of everything we were doing during the preparations of the meal: cutting carrots, celery, tofu, bean sprouts. Afterwards we tried a sensory awareness exercise with an orange, to practice living in the moment. We each took an orange, and focused on its texture, feel, form, spending several moments "getting to know" this orange. At the end of this experiment, he commented "Far out. I've only *eaten* oranges before." (He'd lived most of his life in Florida where they'd eaten oranges every day. But this was the first time he felt he'd ever really *seen* and experienced one.) This exercise helped make him aware and appreciative of the intricacy and beauty of everyday "objects."

Learning Different Modes of Self-expression. He had told me he had difficulty using words to express his feelings, so we also focused on this problem. First, I taught him brush-stroke painting (*sumi-e*) as one outlet for his emotions, one way for him to express his feelings without words.

His first painting was the face opposite.

We talked about this gloomy "Sun-Face." He said it felt good for him to get that out of his system.

He then proceeded to paint some other pictures, two of which follow. These pictures showed him the delicacy and sensitivity he also had inside him.

We also spent some time learning to label emotions. We cut pictures out of magazines and described how the people felt. This was done as a means of teaching him to correctly label his own internal cues. This successive approximation technique was used because it is often easier to label someone else's emotions than one's own.

Finally, we worked on having him describe and express his

own internal feelings in words, through the use of writing *haiku.* He wrote down his feelings and thoughts in quick sentences, not worrying about exact form.

Green leaves
Inhale sunlight
let me breathe

Red bottle brush blossoms
dancing to the whistling wind
always thought winter changes were heavy on me
but not so, as to a yellow tree

Leaves falling down
Only to be swept up by the wind
and scattered throughout

Caught a glimpse of sunset
as I turned to follow it disappeared
Listening to the silence and crickets
Darkness and stars

At the end of two months, this student had learned many things:

1. He had learned to precisely label and express his internal feelings.
2. He had learned many different modes of expressing himself—through words, through his breathing, through painting.
3. He had learned how he was selectively focusing on the negative, and was now able to use this habit as a cue for looking at what was positive and beautiful around him.

Through Eastern techniques (*sumi-e*, *haiku*, meditation), and Western techniques (self-observation, precise labeling), and combination techniques (sensate focus, selective perception), he had learned to once again enjoy himself and his environment. He was no longer depressed, apathetic. The school commented on how motivated he was. He noted how personally good he felt, especially with his renewed interest in camping, "where I can be in nature and have so many ways to play creatively."

Different Focus for Different Folks

In case three, several different types of awareness exercises were used.

Let me ask you to do a little experiment to illustrate the way in which different types of focus affect our experiencing. Next time you eat an ice cream cone, practice the following: (1) First, lick the ice cream as you normally would—e.g., while talking to a friend, walking, looking for a place to sit, looking at clothes in windows (ordinary awareness—many random stimuli). (2) Stop and *focus* on the ice cream; feel the texture, note the coldness (selective awareness). (3) Then focus on the ice cream and say to yourself, "This tastes good, I'm sure having fun eating this ice cream" (selective awareness with positive evaluation). (4) Focus on the ice cream, lick it, and say nothing, evaluate nothing, just experience (pinpoint meditation). (5) Finally, focus on everything around you—hand, ice cream, people, floor, ceiling, shops, cars, smells (opening-up meditation). Are some combinations more effective than others? Which do you prefer when you are eating ice cream? As can be seen, the effectiveness of a particular combination depends on your goals. It may be that certain combinations are more effective, depending upon the behavior being engaged in, and the goals of the behavior.

For example, sometimes we may find ourselves in a situation in which there is too much stimulation. We may be in a noisy city, with a lot of traffic and pushy crowds. We may be taking an exam and trying to concentrate while someone else is tapping a pencil on a desk. At these times, when we feel "too sensitive" it may be useful to try a type of selective awareness, in which we learn to tune out distracting stimuli. At other times, such as when we are out in a beautiful natural setting, we may wish to practice an opening-up awareness, in which we let ourselves tune in to all the stimuli around us.

Below are some additonal exercises that you may wish to practice, and which you may find enjoyable. These exercises involve different types of focusing procedures, and may help you learn more about which focusing procedures are most enjoyable and effective for you in different kinds of situations.

Eyes: Selective Awareness. Try pinpointing your focus amidst the plethora of stimuli around you: watch a bird flying, an ant crawling, the eyes of a child.

Eyes: Opening-up Awareness. Don't focus on any one thing. Rather, try to see everything simultaneously, like a mirror.

Eyes: Twinkle. Look at yourself in the mirror. Note your eyes. Note your mouth. Now twinkle your eyes. Really let them shine. Note what happens to your mouth; note what kinds of thoughts occur when you twinkle your eyes.

Ears: Selective Awareness. Try to selectively perceive: tune in to the notes of a flute or the song of a bird. Choose what you want to focus on, and concentrate your entire attention on it.

Ears: Opening-up Awareness. Listen. Make your ears like a

mirror. Try this in nature. Even try it in noisy traffic. Hear everything, but become attached to and bothered by nothing. In traffic, listen to the different car sounds, the tire squeaks, the honking; hear it all; don't dwell on any sound—let them all merge and pass. In nature, hear the birds, crickets, rustling leaves—merge and pass.

Smell. Note the smells when you next walk into a kitchen before dinner, or into a flower shop. Note also how long the smells last before you habituate to them.

Touch: External. Focus externally on various objects: use your hands, tongue, feet, and spend some time appreciating textures, sizes, shapes. What are you touching right now? With what? How does it feel?

Touch: Internal. Practice tensing and relaxing different muscles.

Touch: Combination. Have a good friend massage you. Try to make your body into a mirror so you can feel the hands massaging the inner surface of your skin.

You may play with any number of senses: smell, taste, touch; either with an opening-up or a selective awareness. The goal of these exercises is to develop the type of awareness you want, to teach your senses to focus selectively when you want them to, and to be open like a mirror, when you choose that.

Law of Reverse Effects[2]

As we tune into different types of focusing, we realize that awareness sometimes plays funny tricks on us. For example, here is an exercise to try. Stand on one leg. Imagine a canyon on your right side, and say to yourself "Don't fall into the canyon on the right side."

Well, what happened? Where is your "center" of gravity now? Watch how you fall.

Similarly, when a person focuses on something he/she doesn't want to do (e.g., eat), (s)he often seems to engage in that behavior more frequently (e.g., eats more).

This can be easily explained by the variety of the different types of modes of awareness that are possible. For example, try the above example of the canyon again, only this time focus your attention inwardly, right above the navel, "on your center," and practice breathing easily. Note your increased stability. *Where* we focus may have a pronounced effect on our behavior.

Similarly, *how* we focus may have a pronounced effect on our behavior. If, in the above food example, we say to ourselves, "I'm sure suffering a lot; I'm being deprived; that food sure looks good," then focusing on food will cause us to eat more. However, if we focus on food and tell ourselves how healthy we are for not eating, how the excess food is not good for us, then we will be more likely to resist. The effects of how we focus was illustrated in a study by Walter Mischel and his colleagues at Stanford University.[3] Students were asked to look at pretzels, and told that if they didn't eat the pretzel now, they could have a larger, better treat later. One group of students was told to imagine the pretzel's salty good taste. The other group was told to describe the pretzel to themselves as a piece of wood that was rotten and not edible. The second group was able to wait significantly longer for the pretzel. Even though both groups were focusing on the pretzel, the *manner in which they were focusing* determined the degree of self-control they evidenced.[4]

Focus Well!

Sometimes how we focus, or what we focus on, is not as important as the fact that we do it "wholeheartedly," and don't jump back and forth between strategies. This is illustrated by the different ways in which we can learn to increase our tolerance of pain.

One method was illustrated in a case study of a Latin American who was able to pass sharpened bicycle spokes through his body.[5] During the time the spokes entered his skin, he maintained a Zenlike attitude: *unfocused, without evaluation.* His EEG registered alpha both before and during the time the spikes were in his body. He had learned to disassociate himself from the pain; that is, he gave no evaluative commands, but simply observed everything in his internal and external environment, without comment.*

*Frontal lobotomy patients register the same amount of pain physiologically before as after the operation; however, after the operation, they *evaluate* the pain as less.

Another method of reducing pain is illustrated by a case study describing a karate expert who was able to hold a twenty-five-pound pole tied to a spike stuck into the fleshy part of the skin of his forearm below the elbow. He explained that he was able to do this by taking his *ki* (center) and focusing total energy on the point at which the spike went through his flesh. This involved a very active concentration, a selective focus on the single point of pain. The karate expert's EEG remained at beta (active brain wave); he was pinpointing his attention totally on the pain, with no evaluation.[6]

Still another method of pain reduction and pain tolerance involves having subjects focus on a competing response in either the external or internal environment. In Western settings this has been demonstrated by Kanfer and Goldfoot,[7] who showed that an individual who had his hand submerged in cold water was able to withstand pain longer if he was allowed to focus on external slides that he presented to himself. This method has also been demonstrated with the use of hypnosis as an analgesic.[8] In the LaMaze childbirth technique, the stimuli (contractions) are relabeled from "pain" (internal process) to "beauty of a child about to be born" (external goal). Simultaneously there is a focus on breathing as a means of shifting attention (from the pain stimulus to breath). In Eastern settings, the effects of focusing on a competing response were tested with Raj yogis who pinpointed attention on the tip of their nose, or a point on the back of their skull. These yogis did not react to cold water, bright lights shining in their eyes, or a tuning fork presented to their ears.[9]

Thus, there are three possible models (with accompanying techniques) to achieve pain reduction and tolerance: (1) cognitive focusing on objects other than those which are causing the pain (competing response); (2) a nonfocused awareness on no particular object, with no evaluations; and (3) pinpointed attention on the stimulus that is affecting one, but without any evaluations.

The important point we make here is that there may be no one right type of awareness. Several different models may work equally well. The element which each of these methods of focusing has in common, however, is that the effectiveness of the focus in the studies was related to the disciplined awareness and concentration of the practitioner. Therefore no matter where or how you focus, focus well!

Detached Observation: Obtaining a Perspective

I would now like to turn to several techniques which may be helpful in teaching us to achieve a perspective. These techniques are related to the section in Chapter 5 concerning detached observation (nonattachment) and caring love.

We talked in Chapter 1 about how meditation could help us attain a detached observation of ourselves. We may also use covert self-statements to effect a similar type of focus:

Lucy, though not perhaps with the status of a Zen Master, is moving along the continuum toward "immovable wisdom." By observing herself in the third person, as merely an object in the environment, she achieves a type of detached observation, a perspective on herself. Describing our behavior in the ongoing present may help us step back from the action, and gain a perspective. This is similar in certain respects to a "mindfulness" meditation, in which we maintain a perspective on all our actions and label all events that come into awareness. Mindfulness meditation focuses our attention on the act and the sensations. For example, Lucy, if she were doing a mindfulness meditation, might be saying: "Anger, anger, fluttering in stomach, tightness in throat, frustration, tension in neck, vocal cords beginning to vibrate, yelling. . ."

Mindfulness meditation, which involves a process of noticing (discriminating) and labeling all cues that come into awareness, may help detach us from the sensations themselves, and let us see them "out there." Lucy, in the cartoon, observes "herself": the composite of the sensations. She observes her entire self in a detached way, as if she were a third-party narrator.

To facilitate our developing and maintaining this detached observation, we may find it useful to instruct ourselves to keep a perspective; stand back; notice what's happening, etc.

An individual may also gain a measure of detached observation by forming a covert image of him/herself performing an action in the ongoing present.

In addition to meditation, self-instructions, and covert imagery, there are several additional techniques that may be useful in obtaining a perspective.

Writing About Ourselves in the Third Person: The Novel

Lucy, in the last cartoon uses verbal self-statements as if she were a narrator: "She knew not how to suffer in silence." Many authors have pointed out the potential therapeutic benefit of actually writing about personal experiences in the third person. Rilke, in the *Notebooks of Malte Laurids Brigge*,[10] only begins to recover his sanity and physical health when he can begin to detach himself enough from his experiences to gain a perspective. In so doing, he shifts his literary style from first-person "I" to third-person "he." Sartre's character, Rastignac, decides to fight the nausea he is feeling by writing a book about "nausea." Perhaps the most dramatic example occurs in Albert Camus' *Plague.* The narrator of the book describes in vivid detail how a plague attacks a small town, killing many inhabitants. The narrator is like a reporter, maintaining an objective distance from the story. Later, however, we discover that the narrator is Dr. Rieux, who lived in the town and fought valiantly against the plague. Rieux was both an actor within the drama *and* the narrator of the book. In order to be intensely involved in the life-and-death struggle against the plague, in order to be able to see his friends and loved ones die and still be able to continue to fight, Rieux needed to simultaneously stand back and maintain a distance from his actions, to observe "objectively" what was happening. Rieux wrote his book in order to fight the plague. In this book both the artist and his art were revealed. He both fought the plague and watched himself fighting the plague, living intensely in the here and now, *and* maintaining a detachedness, an "immovable wisdom."[11]

Similarly, reading about or hearing of others who face similar problems can help give a perspective. As Rastignac noted, his purpose in sharing his encounter with nothingness was to show others they were not alone.

Writing About Ourselves in the First Person: The Personal Journal

One of the reasons a journal or diary may be therapeutic is that when we write about events, we may gain a certain kind of objectivity, a certain removal of the emotional intensity of day-to-day events. Daily events, which may be confusing, are put on paper, outside our heads. We may begin to at least organize the confusion in black and white. Further, as Ira Progoff suggests,[12] the journal may give us a sense of continuity about our life. In the journal, we write freely, without censure or judgment.

The One-Year-After Technique. It is also important to reread one's journal. This can show that events which at one point were of great importance and intensely emotional become, with the passage of time, less emotionally laden. Things go on, things end, and new things take their place. Rereading our journal may also help us discover a progress, "flow" to our lives, which might not otherwise be apparent on a day-to-day basis.

Writing Your Obituary

Awareness of our own death may help us live our lives more fully, and obtain a perspective on what is truly important to us in this life. One way to do this is to write our own obituary. Put down how you would like to be remembered—personally, professionally, in human terms—and see how your goals relate to how you are currently living and acting.

____

____

____

____

Writing our obituary may help put many of our goals and life plans into perspective. There is a related technique, involving death, which has also been frequently used in the East: *Pretend that you are going to die the following moment.* Imagine that you have only a few more minutes to live. Note which things become important to you and which become insignificant. Look around you and see if you don't experience a freshness of vision. (Increase the time: a few minutes, a few hours, a few weeks, a few months, a few years. What changes do you notice in your priorities?)

Poetry

Similarly, many people use poetry as a means of expressing painful emotion in a constructive and creative way. As Rastignac noted about literature, so too may poetry be a vehicle for sharing common emotions and feelings with other individuals. This may help us as writers, by putting feelings on paper; it may help us as readers, by seeing we're not alone and that others have also felt our joys and sorrows. For example:

When he realized the past was nothing
more than this photograph of his daughter,
he sang softly with tears.

Once soon her new child's face,
unborn yet, would be the song of the past,
With fresh tears.

Let the images of your life flow past, and write a poem:

____

____

____

____

"Oh, How Lucky I Am" Experiences

Often, through some event, we realize what good and lucky lives we lead. This realization is the source of the old adage: "I cried because I had no shoes until I met a man who had no feet." Even though it may sound trite, looking at our advantages, which we usually take for granted, is quite helpful in gaining perspective.

Spend a few minutes listening and appreciating some of your "oh how lucky . . ." experiences.

____

____

____

____

Appreciation of Small Things

There are a myriad of examples of delicate, quiet, small events that help give perspective and joy. Try listing a few, like the following:

- The fine threads of a spiderweb
- Water dripping from a freshly watered plant
- My older daughter sharing a donut with her sister
- An ant crawling
- The warm touch of a friend

Here is an example of a small thing to appreciate.

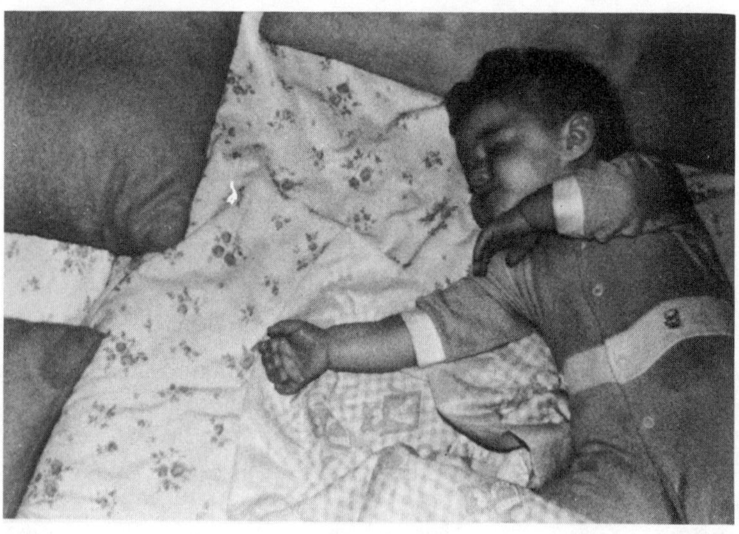

Where Did We Come From; Where Are We Going?

In the first chapter there is a picture of a man on a bridge. In our discussion of that picture, we noted that we don't know what is to the right of the bridge (where he's come from); nor do we know what is ahead, in the mist. Often certain events, or thoughts, may "jolt" us into this larger perspective, this realization that in many ways our world is like a bridge. We neither know where we have come from. . .

. . . nor are we sure where we are going.

And where does the bridge lead? Ronald Bracewell suggests that 300 years from now we may be able to put voyagers into interplanetary space. "After the planets are mined and space near the sun is crowded with orbiting societies, a few will shove off for nearby stars. It will take several generations."[13] What would life be like in a self-contained capsule? In terms of life's meaning? What goals will these travelers have? How are we on earth different from people in a space capsule cut off from everything? Where are *we* heading?

The Role of Humor: A Part of Detached Observation

Often humor helps give us a perspective on events. I'd like to share several ideas and stories that may be useful:

1. Keep a picture of the earth from the moon. When you get angry, find where you would be located on planet earth, U.S.A., state, county, city, building, room. Make a dot, and caption the entire picture in bold letters, stating your complaint.
2. Irreverence: Imagine yourself acting subtly inappropriate in a social situation to make sure you're not taking it too seriously.
3. During an afternoon lecture at Stanford, Rabbi Abraham Heschel reported there was to be an earth-shaking event of immense proportions within an hour. Everybody wondered whether he was a prophet. He was. The sun set.
4. Next time you have an important interview or conference, and feel nervous, try the following: when you meet those who are to interview you, imagine that they are wearing long red underwear under their "professional apparel" (to help you remember that we are all human beings under our clothes and roles).
5. *The day the sun didn't set:* Watch the sun set. However, instead of imagining the sun going down, imagine the earth rotating as you flip upside down.
6. Take a fear or concern you have, and give it a shape, a form, a color. Put it out on the table and play with it, pat it, scrunch it, bounce it. Get to know your concerns, play with them . . . make friends with them.

Additional Areas to Observe

Below are listed some additional areas and exercises related to focusing and detached observation (nonattachment) that you may wish to make use of.

1. Choosing awareness
   - Note when you catch yourself doing two things at once, (e.g., trying to work on a task and thinking of sailing).

- Note when you catch yourself dwelling in a future-oriented way on things that you can't really act upon or didn't intend to act upon, and so worry needlessly.

2. Detached observation and caring love—possessions

- List times when you have felt pain at the loss of a possession.
- List times when you have felt nonattachment (in a positive sense) to a possession.
- List times when you have felt nonattachment (in a negative sense) to a possession, a kind of indifference or numbness.
- List times when you have been attached to a possession, and as a result, have taken exceptionally good care of it.
- Do any of these past examples suggest areas worth monitoring in the present?

3. Detached observation and caring love—other people

- Note when you use negative trait descriptions about other people.
- Note times when you relate to only a part of a person (i.e., fitting them into preconceived categories).
- Note times when you feel you are relating fully to somebody.
- Note the positive statements you make to a spouse or close friend.

We live in the ways of the world, yet sometimes become so caught in them that we lose the broad perspective and the momentary beauty. We have described several techniques by which we can gain a broader perspective on our life. It may be worthwhile to set up cues to remind yourself to "get a perspective." Think of things that give you a perspective, specific examples to call up, when you see a cue. Perhaps you could monitor the amount of times you experience "detached humor," and try to increase the number. Enjoy the perspective. Learn to watch and to participate with humor, and with wisdom.

SUMMARY

In this chapter, case studies of three individuals were presented. These three cases respectively involved problems of low self-esteem, anxiety, and depression. Techniques that integrated Eastern and Western strategies were discussed as they applied to each case. In addition, information was presented for ways in which the reader could apply these integrated techniques to their own lives. Specific areas discussed included (1) those related to the "Self": increasing positive self-statements and pleasurable time for the self; overcoming self-consciousness; developing egolessness; balancing assertiveness and yielding; (2) those related to reducing anxiety and becoming "centered" and "in flow"; and (3) those showing the relationship between different types of focusing strategies—selective awareness, opening up awareness, detached observation—and our experience of reality.

7
Education: Having the Self-soar

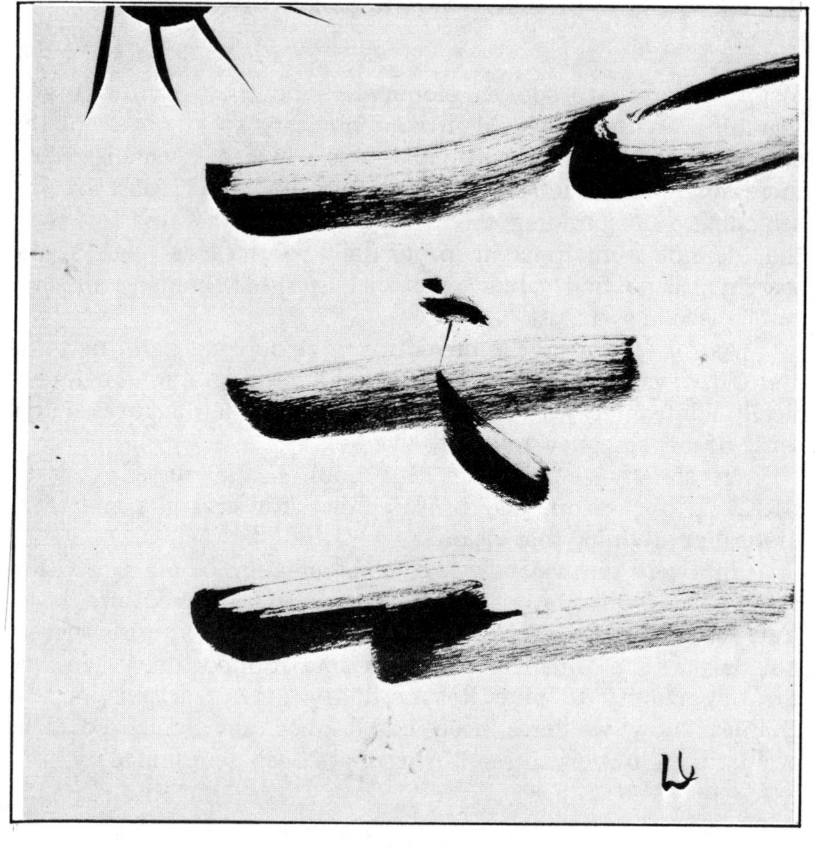

LETTING YOURSELF SOAR

Many writers have spoken eloquently about the confusion and searching of the individual in contemporary society. Part of the searching is for the warmth and love which a mechanized and increasingly bureaucratic society does not offer; part of the searching is for finding the poetry, the joy, the zest for living that do not seem apparent in our daily routines; and part of the searching is to find values—personal, spiritual, human—that we can believe in and trust.

As our social myths break down, as our past habit patterns and old ways of acting no longer seem appropriate, we are dramatically confronted with the need to search for new answers, a new sense of meaning, new myths to live by.

In step-by-step fashion this book has discussed how to CREATE our vision, and provided us with strategies and techniques for attaining that vision.

In a very real sense, we begin the creation of our new vision at a time of Crisis, a crisis on both a personal and cultural level. Yet, as we saw in Chapter 3, the two characters for crisis suggest not only a time of danger but also a time of opportunity. We have the opportunity to take Responsibility for our actions, and to Evaluate how we have been conditioned and socialized. This evaluation allows us to see how we have been determined by both our heredity and our social environment, the two characters which make up the Chinese word for fate.

By taking responsibility, and by evaluating our reflex responses and habit patterns, we have an opportunity for a new awareness. As suggested in Chapter 4, this awareness, this mode of knowing, can and should "bridge the hemispheres" and encompass both an Eastern intuitive holistic approach and a Western scientific analytical approach. For example, at the start of Chapter 3, I asked you to do an informal self-observation of times you felt free, and times when you did not feel free. Behavioral self-observation provides a precise, causal, sequential relationship between our behavior and the environment. We can see that certain situations (antecedents) are facilitative of freedom, and certain others are not. Look at that self-observation again and reread what you wrote on page 123 in your lists of antecedents, behavior, and consequences. As part of a self-change project you may wish to think of ways you could alter one or all of the feelings in those columns to increase your personal freedom.

A second skill that allows us to gain a new awareness about our conditioning is meditation. As we pointed out in both Chapter 1 and Chapter 4, meditation helps us to uncondition ourselves to our normal modes of awareness, to the normal socializiation process, and to reprogram ourselves to our own inner-directed drummer.* By helping us remove the preconceptions of ordinary awareness—our concensus reality—meditation may allow us to experience and realize the much wider and greater depth of our potential capabilities. For, we need to remember that in the creation of our cultural myths and belief systems, we are limited, to a large extent, only by the reality we create in our minds. As John Lilly noted, "In the province of the mind, what is believed to be true is true, or becomes true, within limits to be found experientially and experimentally. These limits are further beliefs to be transcended. In the province of the mind, there are no limits."[1]

*Meditation teaches a method of unconditioning ourselves to societal mores in two ways. First, during meditation, the individual practices spending time alone, apart from society. Second, the process of detached observation may help teach an individual about the process by which he is conditioned: i.e., learning about the ways our culturally acquired language may cause us to act, feel, and believe. (For a further discussion of "unconditioning" see Chapter 5, footnote on internal and external reinforcement.)

With our new awareness, we are able to look for new Alternatives. We have the opportunity to choose and affirm our newly created vision, our path of heart. Part of this new vision comes from the knowledge and wisdom of the Eastern esoteric and mystical traditions; part of the vision comes from the knowledge and wisdom of Western psychology. As we suggested in Chapter 5, each of these traditions makes certain assumptions about human nature, our capabilities, and the best way to obtain knowledge about ourselves. A new vision of human potential, of holistic health and healing, combines the best of both of these traditions.

Once we have created the vision, we have to deal with the questions of how to achieve it. Can we actually develop the skills to enhance our willpower, our sensitivity, and openness to ourselves, to nature, to other people? The answer is yes. By using a combination of self-regulation techniques from the Eastern spiritual disciplines and Western psychology we can learn to achieve our self-chosen goals. In Chapter 6, we discussed the Techniques that may be used to help us reach our path of heart. We illustrated the way these techniques could be integrated by means of three case studies: on low self-esteem, on anxiety, and on depression.

However, the possibility of reaching our vision brings us to a seeming paradox involving the question of free will, fate, and determinism. As noted above, the Chinese word for fate consists of two characters, one meaning heredity, one meaning social environment. The Chinese believed that we were bound by the limits of fate, determined by our heredity and social environment. This is similar to the view suggested by B. F. Skinner in *Beyond Freedom and Dignity*, in which our determinism by environmental conditions is strongly underscored.

Yet if we are determined by fate, what hope is there for developing the freedom, the responsibility, and the skills to take control of our own lives?*

*One of the primary disadvantages of belief in a deterministic world is that if we give up our sense of control we may feel like helpless, passive creatures. We may ask ourselves, "Why act, why try to change, if everything is determined?" However, this is not a necessary result of a belief in a deterministic world. I would like to suggest that once we can give up the illusion of freedom, once we can accept that we live in a deterministic world, there may be several positive consequences that will, paradoxically, give us *increased* freedom. First, by letting go of our illusory sense of freedom, we can learn to *honestly* evaluate how the environment influences us. This will allow us to

This paradox can be resolved by reference to the Chinese concept of Education (learning). The Chinese word for "to learn" consists of two characters. One character is the picture of a nose, meaning self. The other character is a pair of wings, which rests above the self. To the Chinese, education was to have the self soar. By learning about our habit patterns and conditioning, by learning how the environment affects our behavior, by learning how to choose a vision for ourselves, and by learning the skills to reach our vision, we educate and CREATE ourselves—literally and figuratively, to soar beyond our fate, to become an "artist of life."

HOW TO CREATE YOURSELF

Both the Eastern and Western schools tell you that you are a creature of habit, bound by fate. You have no control over your life, even though you may think you do. You are merely living in an illusion of freedom.

1. Have a Crisis. (It may be a small concern, a large problem or an area in which you would like to grow and develop your human potential more fully.) If you have already had one, go on to step 2. If you haven't had one yet, look at chapter 3 to get an idea of what you have to look forward to.
2. Responsibility and Evaluation—you may have a choice at this point. You may choose to decide not to learn from your crisis, thereby deciding for the time being that it is simpler to return to your ordinary habit patterns. If this is your choice, return to the beginning and wait for your next crisis. (You may also

---

deal creatively with what *is*, rather than what we would like to believe is. Second, I believe that without control (determinism), there is no freedom. (For example, let us look at the sport of skiing. To let go, to be free going down the slope, you need knowledge of the *skills* of skiing (e.g., gravity, balance, how to distribute your weight, etc.) It is only by acknowledging and working within the limits of these determinants that we can truly let go and be free. A third advantage of acknowledging a deterministic world is, when we choose to act, we realize the *illusory nature* of our choice. Therefore, we may be willing to hold "our" ideas more loosely, cling to them less tenaciously as ours. This may help bring us closer to attain the Eastern goals of yielding, nonattachment, nonpossessiveness, and egolessness.

wish to peek at Chapter 5, and the Epilogue to see what fun you're missing).

You also have the opportunity for rebirth, for a new awareness, a new alternative. If this is your choice, and you are willing to take responsibility for your actions, go on to number 3.

3. A new awareness and a new Alternative—good choice! But not an easy one. To help see how you are conditioned, practice both modes of awareness: meditation and behavioral self-observation.

   But what to self-observe? What is the new alternative. Good question! On the next three pages, we list every area of the vision discussed in the book. You may also want to look back at your own goals, your own ideal self, times when you haven't felt free. Don't let yourself be limited in your vision—let yourself believe in the possibilities of your mind.

   Having trouble making a decision? That's part of it.

   Affirmation? You can do it if you want to. Do you want to? After choosing, you've got to be honest with yourself about whether it's really worth it to you to commit to attaining your "path of heart." As part of your affirmation, you may wish to make a contract with yourself. In this contract, put down what you're going to get out of this effort. For the techniques to put down in the contract, go to number 4.

4. But before going on to techniques, here's a word about acceptance: as Zen suggests (Chapter 5), we are a gift and a blessing just by being. We need to accept and love ourselves just as we are, with all our imperfections, all our not yet developed possibilities. As Tillich wrote "Accept that you are accepted." We don't need to prove anything; we don't have to chastise ourselves for failure, or compare and evaluate ourselves with others who are "succeeding more"; we don't need to type or categorize ourselves, or give ourselves trait labels. There is nothing to prove. We are unique and of worth just as we are.

   Stop and appreciate the beauty of you, just as you are. Just the way you are now. Not your role in life, or your job or your achievements. Just you. Stop. Just appreciate you as you. Let yourself feel loved for the unique gift and blessing you are just as you are. Use what you have learned about stopping negative thoughts and increasing the amount of self-accepting statements you make to yourself.

Okay, now you may go on to techniques. Within the framework of acceptance and being, learn the joy of striving for excellence, reaching beyond your grasp, daring to be great—the joy of becoming.

4. Techniques—we've presented some of the most powerful self-change strategies from East and West. They're yours for the asking. Take whatever is appropriate for your needs and your own personal goals. They work. (P.S. remember, if your new way of acting feels awkward at first, that's okay, and even expected. Keep at it; soon it will feel natural.)
5. And now we're at the E of create. We have learned to Educate ourselves to reach our vision. We have begun the process of becoming our own Zen masters, our own Grand Conditioners. We have chosen how we want to live. We have begun the process of learning to have the self-soar, of becoming an "artist of life." Much deserved congratulations. Let's don't ever stop "creating ourselves."

You may wish to pull out certain sections of the book referred to in the above 5 steps that are particularly appropriate for you, thereby making your own individualized "Owner's Manual." This smaller owner's manual can become a foundation for your own personal journal. The larger book, *Precision Nirvana*, can then serve as a reference guide, offering elaboration on certain instructions, concepts, areas of the vision.

SUMMARY

Areas of the Vision

East

(Chapter 1)

overcoming awkward self-consciousness

self-regulation: stress and tension management; overcoming fears and phobias; reduced blood pressure;

West

(Chapter 2)

becoming aware of our conditioning: social environment, physical environment, internal environment

setting goals for ourselves

Areas of the Vision (continued)

East

(Chapter 1)

reduced dependence on drugs, cigarettes, alcohol

obtaining a perspective

sense of timelessness; kairos moments

lack of goals; living in the moment

lack of language/analysis; openness to nature, to others, to ourselves—hearing the bird in our breast sing

(Chapter 5)

nonjudgmentalness; acceptance

nonattachment; yielding

West

(Chapter 2)

learning self-regulation skills for anxiety, for fears and phobias, for strong sense of self, for positive attribution of control

(Chapter 5)

learning to obtain a perspective

learning to see peoples' behavior without the need for traits

(Chapter 6)

pain reduction

thought stopping

Integration

(Chapter 5)

egolessness and strong sense of self

naturalness, spontaneity, and self-control

centeredness and productivity

yielding and assertiveness

nonattachment (acceptance) and caring love

living in the moment: ordinary awareness and altered state

Techniques

East

(Chapter 1)

formal meditation instructions: Zen breath meditation; counting 1-10; shikan-taza; koan; chant

concentrative meditation: internal focus; external focus

West

(Chapter 2)

behavioral self-observation: data collection sheets

self-evaluation

goal setting

environmental planning: rearranging stimuli

Techniques (continued)

East

(Chapter 1)

informal meditation:
just listening/watching;
tea ceremony; mondo

additional techniques:
sumi-e; haiku; mindfulness meditation; hatha yoga; kwat

(Epilogue)

Zen laughing meditation

West

(Chapter 2)

preprogramming: time out; contracting

learning skills: progressive relaxation; systematic desensitization — fear survey schedule

behavioral programming: reinforcement — successive approximation, Premack Principle, big cuddle; punishment (negative feedback) — the sandwich

self-instructions; self-modeling

(Chapter 5)

communication skills

Combinations and Additional Techniques

(Chapter 6)

Case One: overcoming low self-esteem and self-consciousness; developing a strong self of self, self-acceptance and egolessness; assertiveness and yielding; thought stopping

Case Two: reducing anxiety; becoming centered, relaxed, "in flow;" contingent informal meditation

Case Three: overcoming depression; learning different modes of self-expression

Selective Perception

eyes: opening-up awareness; selective awareness; twinkling

ears: opening-up awareness; selective awareness on silence, on flute

tactile: external; internal; combination — massage as mirror

Detached Observation

the personal journal

writing obituary

poetry

"Oh, how I lucky I am" experiences

humor

SUMMARY OF A SUMMARY

All books should be able to be summarized in one sentence. In the *Bhagavad Gita*, the wise person is said to be one who has not a hair's breadth between will (what (s)he decides to do) and action (what (s)he does). The essence of this book may be summarized similarly:

Decide what you want to do,
*and do it.**

*There are many skills necessary to make this decision a reality. To *decide what you want to do* (a) it is necessary to be aware of when you are acting by habit and reflex (see Chapter 5), so that you can become aware of the many choice points that exist at every moment; (b) you also have to be willing to take responsibility for your actions and choices; (c) you have to develop the skills to perceive increased alternatives; and (4) you have to acquire the skills of decision making (including the skill of affirming and getting behind your decision 100 percent). To *do it*, you need the self-regulation and self-management skills to carry through with your decision.

It should be added that this is not meant to be an amoral sentence. Quite the opposite. The assumption is made that the person of wisdom has a highly developed sensitivity toward all forms of life. Therefore, decisions would be made within the framework of values that place a high respect on the rights and freedom of others.

III
Epilogue

8
Self-celebrating: The Art of the Cosmic Chuckle

SOME COMMENTS ON NIRVANA

> I stand once more beneath the sun, as I once stood as a small child. Nothing is mine. I know nothing, I possess nothing. I have learned nothing. . . ." Now Siddhartha stood empty and naked. . . he felt a great desire to laugh.[1]

Nirvana, which may be seen as the Eastern analogue of our "heaven," literally means "blow-up," or "extinction." In terms of our meditation model, this extinction refers to an absence of thoughts and images. When we have no thoughts, we also have no concepts such as "I" or "self." We are like a mirror, empty. This emptiness allows us to more freely see and participate in our everyday life. Since in Zen belief the only "heaven" that exists occurs in this everyday life, the emptiness of nirvana allows the enlightened person to see the fullness of everyday life (*samsara*). As a Zen Master noted: to find the infinite, search the finite in all directions.

This relationship between enlightenment and ordinary activities is illustrated in the following poem, the first two stanzas of which were presented at the start of Chapter 4. The poem consists of *three* stanzas.

> When one is unenlightened, the snows of Mt. Fuji are the snows of Mt. Fuji and the water of Tassajara is the water of Tassajara

> When one seeks enlightenment, the snows of Mt. Fuji are not the snows of Mt. Fuji, and the water of Tassajara is not the water of Tassajara
>
> When one has attained enlightenment, the snows of Mt. Fuji are the snows of Mt. Fuji, and the water of Tassajara is the water of Tassajara.

This poem is full of hope; it is an affirmation. When we seek enlightenment, when we suffer a crisis or jolt, all seems confused. Our traditional "ground of being," our normal support systems no longer suffice. However, the poem suggests that there is another side to the confusion and existential abyss. The search is worth it. We may appear the same, but things have changed:

When the ordinary man attains
Knowledge he's a sage,
When the sage attains
understanding he's
an ordinary man.

This belief does not mean that one is hiding from existential questions. Rather, it represents what Kierkegaard called the "double movement," what Sartre referred to as being on the other side of nothingness.

On the one side, a jolt is a crisis. On the other side, it is part of what might be called the *cosmic chuckle*—the ability to stand back and observe the events of one's life with humor: both the wry humor which acknowledges the absurdity of life and the joyous, happy humor which recognizes its grandeur and beauty. On the one side, the self is nothing, empty, confused; on the other side, the self is egoless, empty, joyful. Mind full; mind empty; mindful. On the one side, naturalness is reflex conditioned habit patterns; on the other side, our self-chosen habits are "paths of heart." We have learned new "mental" ways of acting, new ways of labeling and attributing causality. We work to develop control of our own lives, yet we will eventually die. We are helpless in the long-term sense to really be effective. Nature and the natural order of things win. If we see ourselves pitted against this order we will quit because in the present there is little we can do that will change the course of the future. However, if our goal is to achieve fullness of life within the present, then we have the opportunity to make constructive changes. This is a very important distinction. It is not an avoidance of the future. Rather, it is a confrontation of that future, realizing and accepting our limitations, then coming back to the present to bring as much fullness of life as we can to ourselves and to others.

SOME COMMENTS ON PRECISION NIRVANA

Unless we decide to retreat to a cave in the Himalayas, we live in the ways of the world. To survive, we need certain skills. We must learn skills that enable us to earn a living; we need to learn the mores and customs of the society so that we can interact with our fellow human beings. We need to see clearly how our behavior is affected by other people, as well as how we affect others. We need to learn to set goals for ourselves, to meet deadlines, to receive feedback about our performance, and to make improvements based on that feedback. We need to teach our children these skills; to reinforce them systematically for specific skills they have learned; to socialize them to the importance of accommodating and compromising so that their freedom doesn't overly impinge on that of others. Similarly, we need to learn which foods are healthy for us to eat, and which not; which people are healthy for us to be with, and which not. All these skills are examples of the *precise* awareness involved in behavioral self-management strategies.

However, we also need to learn more. We need to learn how to avoid becoming trapped by the goals we set for ourselves, or by the goals that society sets for us. Although future planning may be important and functional, it is also important not to live only in the future. If we live only in the future, we sacrifice the spontaneity and joyfulness of the present moment—the smile of our child; an ant crawling; the wind blowing a leaf to the ground; morning dew.

Further, we need to learn to let go of our self-evaluations; to get off our own backs. Feedback is important for learning, but analyzing and evaluating, categorizing and labeling inhibit experiencing. We need to learn to let go of the security of our labels, the security of our ordinary ways of perceiving reality, and just experience. Sometimes we need to trust our learning, let go, and float on the river, even though we aren't sure where it leads. In addition, we need to reinforce our children and ourselves in a total holistic way, for no reason—for no accomplishment—except that they are, that we are: the big cuddle, a warm bear hug of closeness. All these skills are examples of the global, nonprecise *nirvana*-type awareness that may be achieved with meditation.

What I am suggesting is that neither of the above modes of awareness *is* reality, neither mode is higher or better. Neither meditation nor behavioral self-management skills provides a final answer. Rather, both are necessary. Therefore, we need to learn a *precision nirvana.* By this I mean three things: we need (1) the skills of applying ordinary awareness and self-management strategies,* (2) the skills of applying altered states and meditative strategies, and (3) the ability to know, intuitively and accurately, when which modes of awareness are called for.

By being able to use both modes, we learn to be master of both. We learn that reality is a fiction created by our mode of perceiving. As Chuang-tzu noted:

> One night I dreamed I was a butterfly, fluttering hither and thither, content with my lot. Suddenly I awoke and I was Chuang-tzu again. Who am I in reality? A butterfly dreaming that I am Chuang-tzu or Chuang-tzu imagining he was a butterfly?[2]

Through both Eastern and Western modes, we learn to maintain a perspective on ourselves when we act in the ways of the world: we set goals, but do not feel enslaved to them; we use feedback and evaluation as a means of learning, but do not forget to experience; we give precise reinforcement to optimize performance and skill learning, yet we also give the big, noncontingent cuddle. We learn

*Notice that philosophically we are still talking about a world of cues and consequences, cause and effect. However, we are saying that certain states of consciousness—i.e., those which don't involve evaluations and a search for causality—may have positive consequences. Therefore, we need to teach (condition) ourselves to use both states of awareness. This does not imply that we live in a world in which causes can't be determined. Rather, it suggests the importance of acting, at certain times, "as if" we believed in such a world.

to notice which situations cause us the stumbling self-consciousness, which situations make us tense; and, at the same time, as in meditation, we learn to let go, relax, and move beyond the early steps of self-consciousness and tension. We strive for the goal of excellence, yet we see perfection as a playful game of becoming. Free, yet specific; within the world, of the world, and enjoying the world, we have learned the skills for obtaining *precision* and the skills for attaining *nirvana*.

SOME COMMENTS ON CARE AND MAINTENANCE OF THE MIND

This book has been concerned with what goes on inside our "mind."* We have seen that according to Eastern belief we should decrease the images and thoughts that we have in our mind. Therefore, we can use Zen techniques, such as breath meditation, in which we try to remove all thoughts; and techniques, such as the *koan* and *mondo*, which use words to show the limits of words.

According to Western belief we should decrease the negative, unproductive types of thoughts, and increase positive, reinforcing thoughts. In the West we are told that through self-observation we can learn to use words to best advantage, to find causes for events, to analyze and better define and understand reality.

We have mentioned the research that suggests that each of our two brain hemispheres may have "its own private sensations, perceptions, thoughts, feelings, and memories." Most of our language function is considered to be "in" the left brain hemisphere, which is apparently better able to deal with verbal, sequential analytic thinking.[3] This mode of awareness is that which is involved in behavioral self-observation and self-management skills.

The right brain hemisphere, on the other hand, seems specialized to deal with spatial relationships: relating parts to wholes; nonverbal, holistic thinking, based on direct, perceptual, intuitive experience.[4] It may be that meditation is a mode that is primarily governed by the right hemisphere.[5]

*I am using the word "mind" here as a descriptive phrase.

If this relationship is borne out by further research (and I must acknowledge the speculative nature of what I am now going to say), then the Zen Master and the Grand Conditioner may be nothing more than cultural representations of our two brain hemispheres. The East emphasizes the holistic right brain perception; the West, the logical, analytical, left brain perception. When these two figures—the Zen Master and the Grand Conditioner—bow to each other and shake hands, we have poetry. For, as we noted when discussing haiku poetry, there is an intimate connection between an intuitive, holistic experience (right brain—Zen Master) and a logical, intentional description of that experience in words (left brain—Grand Conditioner).

Through a combination of the Eastern and Western techniques, we may learn to control our mind—to analyze, think, and set goals when it is necessary; and to stop thoughts and stop analysis when that is useful. We learn to work our mind hard for progress and productivity, to play and have fun with it through fantasy and images, and to integrate its two sides for creative synthesis. In so doing, we truly learn the "care and maintenance of the mind."

AND NOW IT'S YOUR RESPONSIBILITY: AN OWNER'S MANUAL

In our left hand, we carry nothing; in our right hand we carry a self-observation data chart. And this is as far as this book can take you. The rest is up to you. Only you know what vision is of most interest to you. Go through the areas of the vision and see which seem most relevant. Practice the various techniques we have described that relate to your vision.

The techniques presented are like a delicious smorgasbord: meditation, guided fantasy, role-playing, different sensory awareness exercises, relaxation and self-control strategies, communication skills, poetry writing. You have to decide which techniques work best for you; which ones feel comfortable for you; which techniques seem relevant in reaching your own self-chosen vision.

Begin your own journey, your own search*; experiment with different combinations of visions: being both a spontaneous, joyous child *and* a disciplined, creative, empirical scientist. Follow your journey, structured and free, poetic and ordered, as an unfolding within and without. You are choosing to play your own game, your own dance with life. Listen, and enjoy the melody.

Zen Laughing Meditation

I would now like to conclude with a brief meditation—a Zen laughing meditation, which I made up while giving a talk on the question of "Is there humor in Zen?" I suggested that there were three answers to the question; and that these three answers corresponded to different steps of meditation.

*As we have noted previously, if you find yourself dealing with an issue or area that seems too difficult or overwhelming, it may be useful to seek professional psychological support and assistance.

Humor	*Meditation*
answer one: no	step one: stumbling self-consciousness
answer two: yes—quiet joy	step three: effortless breathing
answer three: ______	step five: mind as mirror

As can be seen from this, the first answer to our question is "no"; the second answer is "yes"; and the third answer is—well, we'll get to that.

Answer One: No. When we are at a stage of little consciousness of ourselves, there is little humor. For example, let's try an experiment. For the next ten seconds, I'd like you to be humorous.

Pause and be humorous.

Well? Probably you noticed that the old reactive self-consciousness effect took over, similar to step one of meditation. Thus, the first answer is "no," there is not humor in Zen, since there is little humor when there is self-consciousness.

Answer Two: Yes. The second answer is "yes." As we move toward a new awareness, a greater consciousness of ourselves and the world around us occurs. We come to realize the limited nature of the reality in which we have previously believed; our constructs begin to topple. For example, when asked by the monk, "How do you see so clearly?" the Master replied, "I close my eyes."

Ordinary reality is a construct formed by our perceptions. When we realize that we can create a meaningless reality, and then believe in it, that's funny. For example, when the monk asked the Master to play a tune on the stringless harp, the Master agreed. After a few moments, the Master said, "Do you hear it?" "No" the monk replied. "Why then, didn't you ask me to play louder?"

This "humor" of Zen needs to be seen in the broadest sense of the word—as a kind of joy, a celebration of the moment. This is illustrated in the following poem by Pao-tzu:

Eating rice
Drinking tea

Passing time as it comes
Looking down at the stream
Looking up at the mountain.[6]

This humor is similar to step three in meditation, the effortless breathing, the calm joy of just being.

In this regard let me ask you to do a short meditation, called a Zen laughing meditation. This meditation was passed on to me by a friend, and I share it with you.

> Get comfortable. Close your eyes. Take a minute to notice your breathing—feel your breath come through your nose—let it go out. Just let go—let the chair or the floor hold you up—there's nothing to be concerned about now—just relax—Now imagine you're in a spot that's a favorite spot for you. Make it somewhere outdoors, in nature—notice where you are, what's around you; make this a peaceful spot for you. Imagine that it's just before sunrise so that it's dark, but almost not dark. Watch the dark before the sunrise, and imagine, rather than the sun coming up, that you and the earth are rotating down. You are turning upside down and looking at the after glow of an imaginary candlelit dinner and watching as the candle-tip flames of the stars are snuffed. Imagine yourself in this pleasant spot of yours, and, as it begins to get light, do the following laughing meditation: Begin to smile, and notice the peaceful feeling within you. No loud laugh, but just a quiet joy as you see the light begin to flicker through whatever is around you—the beginnings of the morning. You're feeling very quiet and very nice. Take a few seconds as it begins to get a little more light, and enjoy the smile, as you appreciate that light. Feel a twinkle in your eyes. Now, let yourself go for a moment or two, and just enjoy. Later, as you feel comfortable, stir a little bit, open your eyes, come on back.

We realize that the second answer to our question of whether or not there is humor in Zen is "yes." As humor increases, so does our awareness, and our health.

Finally, we get to the third answer. This answer is represented by the fifth step of meditation—the step that goes beyond duality, beyond constructs. In the fifth step of meditation, we learn to go beyond the duality of yes and no. In the fifth step we go beyond distinctions of humor and not humor.

SUMMARY

We have learned to watch, *and* we have learned to participate, to be centered *and* productive, self-controlled *and* yielding. With practice, we shall learn to play our new game, and new role — the master game, the only dance there is. We have learned to let everything reinforce us. Therefore, may you work hard, may you enjoy the cosmic chuckle, and may you not know the difference.

> Now we have finished. Everyone stand and we will bow to the Buddha three times to thank him. We thank him, because even if we did not have a great enlightenment, we had a small enlightenment. If we did not have a small enlightenment, at least we didn't get sick. If we got sick, at least we didn't die. So let's thank the Buddha.[7]

IV
Appendixes

APPENDIX 1: A REQUEST TO READERS

My hope in writing a book like this is that you, the reader, will become actively involved and apply many of the exercises to your own life. I would appreciate it greatly if you would share your experiences with me. Please feel free to write and let me know which parts of the book were particularly meaningful to you, and which weren't. This feedback will help me in making future revisions of the book and will also allow a mutual sharing.

Thank you.

Your name: ______________________________

Address: ______________________________

____

Exercises that were particularly helpful to me:

____

____

Exercises that were not particularly helpful to me:

____

____

Areas of the vision that were particularly meaningful to my life:

____

____

Areas of the vision that were not too meaningful to my life:

____

____

What I like most about the book:

____

____

What I like least about the book:

____

____

Please send to:

Deane H. Shapiro, Jr., Ph.D.
P.O. Box 2084
Stanford, California 94305

APPENDIX 2: HARD-CORE ZEN

In preparation for writing this book, I reviewed the journals that I had kept while in the Orient. The following three anecdotes from these seem to capture an essence of Zen.

Finding a Bordello: The Beginning

We were being led by a Zen Master named Nishimura through the red-light district of Kyoto to find a bordello. He knocked on several doors; sometimes no one answered, sometimes he received a flat "No—nothing is available." Finally, he knocked on a door and an attractive older woman answered. They talked briefly, and an arrangement was made.

Yet things were not as they might at first seem.

Johanna and I had recently arrived in Kyoto, and were unable to find lodging. The Zen priest suggested we might find a temporary place to stay in the red-light district. The arrangement he made allowed us to spend the weeknights, but we had to leave on weekends because of the establishment's prior "business commitments."

So began our search for the spirit of Zen.

I'm A History Major: The Arrival

When we first arrived at Daitoku-ji monastery, we had an interview with the Master, Kabori Roshi. He inquired of my background, my college major, and what I intended to do once I returned to the States. I told him that I was officially a political science major, and that I had been accepted at Harvard Law School. However, I quickly explained that I had obtained nearly the equivalent of a religious studies major while in college, that I had chosen not to go to law school this year, and that I was on an intense "spiritual quest." I was eager to show him that I would be a good pupil, was committed to the path of the seeker, and should be allowed to study at the temple.

He nodded, rather noncommitally.

He then turned to my wife, Johanna, and said, "I suppose you too are on a spiritual quest, and were also a religious studies major."

"No," she said, "I was and still am a history major."

He laughed, bowed to her, and led us into the meditation room.

Rice Curry: The Answer

Near the end of our stay in Japan, we were talking to a young Zen monk-in-training about our plans to travel to India.

"I, too, plan to go to India soon," he added.

I was quite excited to hear this. It seemed to me that here was a fellow searcher; I felt an instant sense of brotherhood with him. Many of the young monks I had met seemed to be merely putting in time, going to vocational school, by being in the monastery. Much of the spiritual searching and questing that I felt seemed absent in them.

I told him that I had the names of several great Indian teachers with whom I intended to study. I asked him if he would like their names.

"No, thank you," he said.

"I don't understand," I replied, "Do you already have a teacher?"

"No."

"Then why are you going to India?"

"To eat the excellent rice curry."

APPENDIX 3: EAST-WEST TECHNIQUES— DIFFERENCES, SIMILARITIES, ADVANTAGES IN COMBINING

Differences in Eastern and Western Techniques

Types of Awareness

The awareness in self-observation strategies involves a precise labeling of certain events, a search for causality, antecedents and consequences, goal setting, and analysis and evaluation. In formal meditation, the type of awareness is present-centered, goalless, involves no search for causes, and is without evaluation and analysis. Although the beginning meditator may subvocalize such self-instructions as "Relax; keep focused on your breathing; your attention has wandered, better return to breathing again," the goal of meditation is to remove these verbal cues eventually and have an "empty mind"—that is, an absence of covert statements and images. In informal meditation, the individual observes *all* actions and behaviors throughout the day. In a behaviorally oriented stress-reduction training package, the individual is instructed to discriminate (notice) certain specified "anxiety-arousing" situations, and then to use those situations as cues for engaging in relaxation, covert self-modeling, and self-instruction activities. In informal meditation, although all cues are observed, the individual is instructed to "merely observe, as a witness" and to take no specific action after recognizing any particular cue.

Use of Covert Statements and Images

Western self-management techniques employ covert events and images in many of their strategies. An attempt is made to change maladaptive ways of thinking to more productive ones. This is done by stopping the nonproductive thoughts and substituting positive images and statements. In meditation, an individual "lets go" of the nonproductive chatter, but makes no attempt to substitute positive statements and images. In the East, when an image (e.g., third eye, image of Guru) or covert statement (e.g., *mantra, koan*) is used for concentrative meditation, it is focused on exclusively for a long period of time as a means of reducing surrounding inputs and covert chatter. In the West when an image (e.g., covert self-modeling, positive reinforcing image) or covert statement (e.g., self-instructions; self-reinforcement) is used, it may have several different purposes. Its purpose depends on its position in the behavioral sequence (e.g., image as antecedent, as behavior, or as consequence). Internal images and statements may be used as reinforcement or punishment for a behavior, as a cue to initiate a behavior, or as practice or rehearsal (self-modeling) of a behavior.

Similarities in Eastern and Western Techniques

We have noted that certain types of mindfulness meditation involve discriminating and labeling all stimuli that come into awareness. This is nearly identical to the detached observation effected in the West by covert statements. The fourth step of meditation, which may involve a global desensitization to whatever is on our mind, may be similar to systematic desensitization in behavior therapy (i.e., relaxation precedes the presentation of the feared image). The only difference between the two is that the prearranged, structured hierarchy in the behavioral model is absent in the meditation model.

There is also a similarity between certain types of thought stopping in the West, and the effect of the kwat in the East. Both may be used to stop thoughts, and/or to interrupt a maladaptive behavioral sequence.

Finally, it should be clear that the location of the meditation room and the location of the tea ceremony may represent a type of environmental planning to reduce unwanted external stimuli.

The table at the end of this appendix illustrates, in detailed form, a comparison and contrast of meditation and behavioral self-management techniques.

Advantages in Combining the Techniques

The intervention in case two involved formal meditation and a combination of informal meditation, self-instructions, and focused breathing. Below is a theoretical discussion of the advantages that may be gained by this combination.[1]

Informal Meditation Plus Behavioral Self-management Techniques: "Contingent Informal Meditation"

It appears that the technique of informal meditation may be made into a more powerful clinical intervention strategy by being combined with self-imagery, self-statements, and focused breathing. In this model, in addition to observing all events and behaviors occurring throughout the day (informal meditation), we also notice certain specified cues in the internal and external environment (e.g., tension, anger, anxiety, social events). Once we have noticed those cues, we then self-observe in a "detached" nonevaluative manner, as in informal meditation. However, we also focus on breathing and covertly initiate cues to relax, to feel in control, and imagine acting in a relaxed, competent fashion.

Formal Meditation Plus Behavioral Self-control Techniques

Learning to meditate properly may be facilitated if we borrow from certain behavioral self-management techniques. For example, individuals have been given a counting device (e.g., a golf counter) and instructed to punch the counter every time their attention wandered from the task of breathing. The punching of the wrist counter was then made a cue for returning attention to the task of breathing. In essence, what was occurring was that a tool used in behavioral self-observation (the counter) was taking the place of the *kwat* of the Zen monk.[2] It is possible that biofeedback techniques might also serve to facilitate the acquisition and proper performance of meditation.

Certain aspects of formal meditation may complement and facilitate behavioral self-control skills. For example, as discussed in Chapter 1, during formal meditation, the individual learns to unstress (desensitize) himself (step four) and to reduce the frequency and duration of internal chatter and images (step five). It is suggested that this ability to relax and have an "empty mind" gained during formal meditation will help an individual be more alert and responsive to stress situations occurring at other times, thus facilitating a person's performance of behavioral self-observation of internal and external cues throughout the day.

Second, formal meditation seems to give the individual practice in noticing when his or her attention wanders from a task. At first, in step two of meditation, there is usually a long time period that elapses between the time the attention first wanders and the *realization* that it has wandered. With practice, however, the person may learn to catch himself almost as soon as he stops focusing on breathing. Similarly, in behavioral self-control strategies, often several minutes or longer pass before the individual realizes that he is supposed to have noticed a cue and subsequently interrupted a maladaptive behavioral pattern. The chronic smoker illustrates this lack of awareness, as does the heroin addict. The practice of noticing a certain cue (e.g., wandering attention) developed in meditation may also be applicable to situations involved in behavioral self-control strategies (e.g., reaching for a cigarette, the "need" for a fix). Thus, the individual practicing meditation may be aided in eventually recognizing a certain cue as soon as it occurs, and is thereby placed in a much better position to interrupt a maladaptive behavior pattern.

The third way in which formal meditation might help behavioral self-control strategies involves the cognitive set that meditation can help give to the practitioner. Formal meditation allows the individual an opportunity for fixed reference points in the day during which he/she feels relaxed, calm, and in control. Therefore, when recognizing tension at subsequent points during the day, the individual should be able to say to him/herself, "I was relaxed, calm, and in control this morning," thereby attributing current stress to a specific situation rather than to an "anxious personality trait."[3] In this way the person may learn to increase feelings of self-control and learn to perceive him/herself as a responsible individual who has the ability to control his/her own behavior and actions.[4]

Fourth, although the physiological data are still equivocal,[5] aspects of the technique of formal meditation may make it more powerful than other self-management techniques in certain respects. For example, other self-control techniques, such as autogenic training,[6] self-hypnosis,[7] or relaxation with covert self-statements[8] employ certain covert images and self-statements (e.g., "I'm feeling warm; my right arm feels heavy; I am feeling relaxed"). In formal Zen meditation, the individual does not say anything to himself, nor does he/she attempt to engage in positive covert images or thoughts. It is this absence of preprogrammed covert thoughts and images that seems to allow the meditator to observe and become unstressed to "what's on his/her own mind" (step four). Repetition of preprogrammed statements and images would seemingly interfere with this process and would also seem to prevent the "mind from becoming empty" (step five). This "empty mind" (i.e., an absence of verbal behaviors and images) may be important in certain externally oriented situations, such as the counseling setting[9] and interpersonal relationships.[10] The empty mind may also be important for hearing certain internal cues, especially in clinical areas dealing with stress and tension, obesity, tachycardia, migraine, and hypertension.

Finally, because during meditation the individual seems to be able to step back from personal fears, concerns, and worries, and observe them in a detached relaxed way, it is possible to hypothesize that *after* meditation the individual should be able to think about the fears and evaluate how he or she wants to act without being overwhelmed or oppressed by them. Thus, even though during the process of formal meditation there is ideally no thinking or evaluation, subsequent to meditation the individual may be well prepared to think and make decisions. In this way, meditation might help produce "self-observation conditions such that inner feedback for behavior change is optimal".[11]

It appears that when informal meditation is made contingent on certain cues and coupled with covert self-modeling and self-instructions, it becomes a more powerful clinical strategy for an immediate problem. However, this is in no way meant to suggest that the combination of informal meditation with behavioral self-control strategies makes informal meditation more effective for the goal for which it was originally intended: "ongoing awareness of all cues."

Similarly, from a Western perspective, formal Zen meditation is often seen merely as a technique that may be useful when applied to certain clinical problems. However, from an Eastern perspective, Zen meditation is a way of "being" in the world: a total awareness of oneself, of nature, of others. Thus, it is important to note that the technique of formal Zen meditation may be being used clinically for goals other than those for which it was originally intended.

Topics	*Formal Meditation*	*Behavioral Self-management*	*Informal Meditation*	*Contingent Informal Meditation*
Environmental Planning where intervention strategy occurs	specified setting (e.g., room or in nature); reduced external stimuli to initially help individual focus on object of meditation	*in natural environment where problem behavior occurs; or symbolically in neutral environment*	occurs in natural environment	*same as behavioral self-management*
if stimulus cues are used	stimulus cues (control): e.g. incense; or, in case of concentrative meditation, the object of meditation as stimulus cue	*specified cues in natural environment (programming antecedent or initiating stimuli)* *self-regulated stimulus exposure*	everything is a stimulus cue for "awareness"	*same as behavioral self-management*
nature of physical posture	specified body posture: lotus or half-lotus, to reduce bodily distractions	*symbolic desensitization occurs in relaxed posture: e.g., reclining in thick armchair*	no specified posture	no specified posture
if preprogrammed punishments or reinforcers	"KWAT" as preprogrammed punishment for nonalert behavior	*preprogramming of certain punishments or reinforcements*	no preprogrammed punishments or reinforcers	sometimes preprogrammed punishment or reinforcement
Cognitive Variables effects of observation	in formal Zen meditation, focusing on behavior of breathing alters the behavior: a stumbling reactive effect (step 1); soon mind wanders, i.e.,	*behavioral self-observation alters behavior observed (generalization one); then there is habituation to task; subject forgets to monitor; when subject stops monitor-*	goal is that observation have no interference or interruption of daily activities	observation used as a discriminative stimulus to interrupt a maladaptive behavioral sequence *(see also behavioral*

	habituation to task of observing (step 2)	*ing, behavior returns to pre-self-observation phase (generalization two)*		*self-observation)*
what is observed	initially just breathing is focused on (steps 1, 2, 3); eventually openness and receptivity to all stimuli, internal and external (steps 4, 5) occurs	*functional analysis: observation of problem behavior, antecedents, and consequences*	all behaviors, actions, and thoughts are observed: global awareness	only specified cues (e.g., anxiety, stress) in internal and external environment are observed
how behavior is observed: self-evaluation and goal setting	thoughts, behavior, breathing, are observed without analysis; no charting, no evaluation, no goal-setting: i.e., "detached" self-observation	*parameters of behavior observed: frequency, latency, duration, intensity; behavior is counted, charted; systematic evaluation is made; and goals are set*	observation without comment and without evaluation	*same as behavioral self-management;* however, also try to maintain detached self-observation at same time
desensitization paradigm; when occurs	relaxation (step 3) precedes feared images (step 4); in formal meditation, a "global" desensitization with no specific cues formal meditation occurs at specified times throughout the day, regardless of antecedent stimuli	*relaxation precedes phobic scene (cf. Wolpe, 1958, 1969)*[12]*: involves subjective hierarchy of disturbing scenes; or, relaxation follows phobic scene (real or symbolically) and is contingent on discriminating certain cues (cf. Goldfried, 1973)*[13]	continuous discrimination of cues in daily environment	relaxation follows phobic scene or certain stress cues

Topics	*Formal Meditation*	*Behavioral Self-management*	*Informal Meditation*	*Contingent Informal Meditation*
cognitive statements and images; thought stopping	observation without comment (no self-statements); and without evaluation (no thinking); covert images are allowed to "flow down the river of consciousness" and are not dwelled on; focus on competing response of breathing helps remove thoughts (step 4)	*covert images and self-instruction used extensively: e.g. covert sensitization (images as punishment); covert rehearsal (images and self-instructions as successive approximation): self-modeling; covert self-reinforcement; covert behavior modification: either alter self-statements, or emit relaxing instructional self-statements; to stop thoughts, covert yelling of word "stop"*	no cognitive statements or images involved in the performance of actions.	use of covert images, self-modeling; and self-instruction: e.g., "I am breath," "I am relaxed, in control, I can handle this"
focused attention	in formal Zen meditation, attention focused on breathing (steps 1–4); the KWAT (step 2) helps return the wandering mind to the object of focus; in Raj Yoga (cf. Anandi,[15] Chhina, & Singh, 1961) note the use of internal focusing	*Kanfer and Goldfoot (1966)*[14] *discuss the use of external focusing as a technique for self-management of pain*	attention focused on the here-and-now action only	in contingent informal breath meditation, attention focused on breathing; in Transcendental Meditation, attention focused on covert sacred syllable
Breathing effects of; type	breathing from the abdomen; goal is effortless, autonomic	*"controlled" breathing; voluntary breathing from*	relaxed, aware autonomic breath-	controlled breathing in contingent

used	breathing plus awareness of that breathing; used as a type of relaxation (step 3); an aid in unstressing (step 4) and in thought stopping (step 4)	*chest/thoracic area; used in deep muscle relaxation*	ing from abdomen	informal breath meditation (cf. Shapiro, 1974a); nonfocus on breathing (but rather on sacred sound) in "contingent" Transcendental Meditation (cf. Boudreau, 1972)[16]
Contributions of the Strategies to Each Other	acquisition and proper performance of formal meditation is facilitated by a wrist counter, a device used in behavioral self-observation; naturalistic observation methodology of social learning theory is useful in understanding meditation as a series of behaviors under explicit contingency arrangements	*clear mind gained during step 5 of formal meditation helps facilitate a behavioral functional analysis of internal and external events throughout the rest of the day; practice of discriminating a stimulus (e.g., wandering mind) gained during formal meditation should help an individual interrupt a maladaptive behavioral chain earlier and more quickly; meditation involves a "detached observation" of concerns, thereby reducing the threat of the concerns and producing optimal conditions for behavior change*	in terms of a clinical intervention strategy, informal meditation is made more powerful by making its performance contingent upon certain internal and external cues, and by coupling it with covert imagery, self-instructions, and focused breathing	This technique is a combination of informal meditation and behavioral self-management strategies; covert imagery, self-instructions, focused breathing, functional analysis all come from the behavioral self-management strategy; however, at the same time the technique involves the use of "detached self-observation" derived from informal meditation

APPENDIX 4: BEHAVIORISM, HUMANISM, AND BEYOND

To My Humanistic/Existential Colleagues

On Preconceptions about Behavior Therapy

Below are listed some common preconceptions about behavior therapy. I enclosed this list as a way of helping us check to make sure our "cups are empty"; as the story of Nan-in in Chapter 4 suggests, it is difficult to discuss behavior therapy unless we first empty our minds and remove our preconceptions.

I have purposely put this list at the end of the book in hopes that by presenting what behavior therapy *is* first, the preconceptions will have been addressed and cleared up. In case there are some lingering misunderstandings, however, I have referred to the appropriate section in the text you may want to reread in order to "empty your cup."

Preconception One. Behavior therapists try to control another person's behavior, thereby taking away his free will. Whereas good therapies deal with the client in an I-Thou relationship, not manipulating or shaping the client, behavior therapists mechanically manipulate clients. Further, behavior therapists deal segmentally with only part of a person, not the whole person.

See the sections on teaching the client to take responsibility for his own actions; on getting the client to choose his own goals (Chapter 2).

As can be seen, social learning theorists work to increase a client's freedom. A good behavior therapist, as any good therapist, should use techniques within the framework of a supportive relationship. Otherwise, as behavior therapists have recognized, the client may not be willing to use the techniques.[1] All forms of therapy and education, in both the East and West, try to influence the client about certain goals. By working with the client to develop cooperative goals, by being open and honest about how certain techniques can help him/her reach certain goals, the behavior therapist, as any therapist, is merely being a good teacher.

Preconception Two. Behavior therapists don't deal with the emotions and feelings of a person, but only with observable, quantifiable behavior. They see feelings and emotions as part of a black box which isn't important.

This preconception has been fully covered in the text (see section on the importance of observing internal thoughts and images) and does not need further elaboration here.

Preconception Three. Behaviorists don't believe in concepts such as consciousness, awareness, free will, compassion; and behavioral goals are different from humanistic, self-actualizing goals of therapy.

The concepts of free will, awareness, etc. are talked about in Chapters 2 and 3. It shall be apparent that these concepts are of crucial importance to behavior therapists.

It is true that traditionally behavioral goals have been applied to specific patient problems: weight, alcoholism, smoking, fears and phobias, insomnia, anxiety. Normally, the goals of positive mental health have been ignored. Partly this makes good sense, for patients seen in clinics are usually hurting, and want relief from their hurt. However, there is no reason why target behaviors can't include health-giving "self actualizing" types of goals.[2] Goals of health may be conceptualized from a behavioral perspective; behavioral techniques can be used to obtain these goals.

Preconception Four. Behavior therapists deal only with symptoms of behavior, not underlying causes. However, once they "cure the symptom" it returns. only in a different form.

As we have noted in our discussion of self-observation, social learning theorists do look for the cause of behavior. However, they look for the cause in the here-and-now environment rather than in historical causes (e.g., Freud). In addition, there is an attempt to not only teach a person awareness of the problèm, but to give him or her the skills needed to deal with the problem. These skills include means of dealing with the current problems, as well as self-management skills which can be applied to other life problems as they come up. Finally, regarding symptom substitutions, Walter Mischel notes: "Behavior change programs . . . tend to be effective and the changed behaviors are not automatically replaced by other problems."[3] On the contrary, and not surprisingly, when clients are freed from debilitating emotional reactions and constricting crippling avoidance patterns, they may become more free to behave in new adaptive ways that in turn lead to more positive consequences for them. After reviewing the relevant literature on behavior therapy, Grossberg says about symptom substitution:

> The overwhelming evidence of the present review is that therapy directed at elimination of maladaptive behavior ("symptoms") is successful and long-lasting. . . . Unfortunately, psychotherapists seem to have stressed the hypothetical dangers of only curing the symptoms, while ignoring the very real dangers of the harm that is done by not curing them.[4]

Preconception Five. Behavior therapists don't dream.

Some of my best friends are behavior therapists. They tell me, unofficially, that they do dream. They just don't know what to make of the dreams.

Internal Self-examination

I'd now like to turn to some potential caveats within our own humanistic tradition. *First*, we should remember the advice of Confucius that the wisdom to perceive a truth is not enough. There are many awareness exercises in the humanistic/encounter group tradition. However, we need insight *plus* the skills to follow through with the insight. *Second*, we should be aware of the limitations of advocating "global" growth, without tying growth down to more specific goals. Growth is such an amorphous word that unless we are more specific, it becomes nearly impossible to evaluate our progress. *Third*, we should be aware of our own preconceptions of what "growth" is. For example, although it may be important to posit alternative models for our clients, it is also important to hear and listen to the client's concern as (s)he sees it. Not everyone who comes to us with a specific hurt (e.g., loneliness) needs to first experience facing existential angst.[5] It should not be beneath us to teach our clients the practical skills (social skills) to help them deal with their everyday hurts. *Fourth*, although I believe that (a) Eastern spiritual values are a necessary adjunct to our Western technology and science and that (b) the Eastern emphasis on intuition, spirituality, a holistic perception of the world, altered states of consciousness can provide us with a valuable knowledge and wisdom, I also believe we make a mistake if we unquestioningly embrace all aspects of the Eastern tradition, eschewing logic and analysis. As Alan Watts noted, Zen itself may become rigidified in the dogma of non-dogma, thereby developing a static quality and blinders of its own.[6] By using tools of Western intellect and analysis, we can come to see some of the blinders and the static quality that may have developed in the formal Zen tradition. Further, Western emphasis on intellect, reason, and analysis may provide us with certain tools that are useful in translating the descriptive terminology of Zen into terms more understandable to Western readers. These tools "demythologize" Eastern mysticism and help us get at the heart of why Zen techniques work. It further shows which techniques may be useful, and which not. This knowledge, provided by empirical evaluation, is crucial to practicing psychotherapists, educators, and people in the helping and healing professions.[7]

Finally, although we need to acknowledge that Zen, like the humanistic and transpersonal schools, provides us with a pleasing vision of our human potential, it may be just a *descriptive* vision, and not *a priori* scientifically true. We may not be innately self-actualizing creatures; we may not be innately born with free will. We may need the skills to attain these qualities of existential freedom; of developing warm and compassionate human relationships. We need to believe in the vision; but we must not let it blind us to the skills necessary to make the vision a reality.[8]

To My Behavioral Colleagues

On Preconceptions about Zen and Humanistic/Existential Psychology

Just as there may be preconceptions about what behavior therapy is, there are preconceptions about the humanistic/existential schools of thought and Eastern mysticism. These preconceptions often include the following three:

Preconception One. The concepts discussed are esoteric and have no practical significance in treating human problems.

Chapters 1 and 6 show the practical applications of Zen techniques to our daily lives and problems. As such, Zen techniques may be a useful way to expand the behavioral base of techniques. And, Zen values and teachings can provide for us alternative models and values of excellence which have a real practical significance in terms of the goals our clients set. We have discussed these issues at length in Chapters 1 and 5.

Preconception Two. Adherents of these disciplines are really "soft" scientists who don't take the time and effort to evaluate whether or not their techniques are really effective.

There is no reason why these techniques can't be evaluated with an empirical, data-based methodology for their effectiveness in areas such as stress and tension management, drug abuse, insomnia, and hypertension[9]

Preconception Three. The humanistic techniques increase our awareness, but don't give us the skills to deal with increased awareness.

We have shown in the case studies in Chapter 6 how Zen techniques can be combined with behavioral techniques to provide individuals with increased awareness and the skills to effect personal change.

Internal Self-examination

In addition, looking at behaviorism from a different philosophical vantage point may help point out whatever blinders and preconceptions there might be within a behavioral approach. Let me suggest some of the caveats that we as behavior therapists need to be aware of:

1. We need to be aware of an overemphasis on analysis, definitions, charts, data. Although a large section of this book was devoted to showing the importance of words and analysis (Chapters 2 through 5), we need to remember that words can't take the place of reality and of experiencing. Further, many people either can't or aren't willing to collect the data in the precise way we would like them to do so. Some of these people are quite willing to make changes, but find data gathering to be so difficult that it becomes more of a barrier than an aid.
2. Data collection, with its stress on analysis, causality, consequences, may be overemphasized, leaving the client with no concomitant ability to "let go" and just be.
3. Thus far there has been a lack of emphasis on the existential difficulty of choice and commitment.

"We examined the facts coldly, critically, objectively, and reached the wrong conclusion."

4. There is a danger of an overreliance on techniques. As Nolan wrote, "Without an independent basis for specific cultural goals, the technique itself is likely to dictate those goals."[10] It is important that we keep a perspective of the larger culture in which our techniques are used.
5. A behavioral view of our "self" as a blank slate that can learn is not as comforting as a view of our innate nature as "organismic" and "self-actualizing." Behaviorists can and should see this "self-actualizing" view as a model, a vision of who we can become. As we have suggested, believing in its worth as a vision may be at least as important as documenting it as a prior untruth (Chapter 5).
6. In working out contracts, it is important that we spend a large percentage of our time ensuring that there is a "spirit" behind the contract. Otherwise a contract, or a given set of techniques, may feel forced and confining.
7. We need to realize that for all our emphasis on scientific approach and empirical verification, we also use intuition and speculation in our hypothesis testing.
8. Contingent reinforcement for skill building is useful and necessary. However, we must also be able to use non-contingent reinforcement as a means of teaching self-acceptance (Chapter 2).

9. Finally, although it may be important to emphasize initially that we are determined by the environment and thus don't have free will, it is also crucial to teach people to believe "as if" they do have free will (Chapter 2).

To Researchers, Clinicians, Educators (Scientists and Practitioners)

Abraham Maslow, in *The Psychology of Science*,[11] noted that there were two particularly dangerous attitudes being developed with regard to science. One rejected the scientific approach altogether, and confused "impulsivity" with "spontaneity." The other was the belief in an amoral, value-free technological science. Behaviorists have accused transpersonal and humanistic psychologists of the former; the transpersonal and humanistic psychologists have accused behaviorists of the latter. In this book I have tried to show that it is possible to wed both values and a scientific approach to the study of behavior: to not only suggest a "new" (2000-year-old) technology that can help us cope with this society's cultural norms but also to suggest other cultural norms and values.

Thus, I have worn two hats in writing this book. One is that of the academician/scientist. This part of me would like everything tied to data—no statement would be made unless there were sufficient empirical research justifying its inclusion. This is an important position, for once we leave the data, we are in the realm of speculation and educated guessing. There may be a tendency, amidst the excitement of "new thoughts" and "new integration," to speak in slight hyperbole. The efficacy of many of the self-regulation techniques, though promising, needs to be further documented. There are problems of generalizability of techniques, long-term maintenance, placebo effects, and so forth.[12] Further, as we try to incorporate Zen into our daily lives, there is the problem that we may misperceive its meaning. For example, I recently saw an ad for "Zen bath powder—a total fragrance and way of being in the world." Without a proper philosophical perspective, we may rush to Eastern spirituality and skim off the top, without the essence.

I also wore the hat of clinicians and educators, who are on the front line, and who see people every day. We need to present these people with the best, most up-to-date skills and knowledge possible. Their concerns won't wait. So we go with our best, albeit incompletely documented efforts. We try to be honest with ourselves, and acknowledge the intuitive, "seat-of-the-pants" speculation that is often used in our efforts. At the same time we need to be honest in evaluating the effectiveness of our efforts.

On one level, this book has been speculative and heuristic. It has begun with the research data, but then it has gone beyond the data to (1) integrate an Eastern and Western vision of health; (2) develop a precise vision of Eastern goals that is understandable to the Western reader; and (3) combine this vision with Western goals. In formulating this combined vision of *nirvana*, there has also been an attempt to point out the limitations of words to describe certain experiences that are beyond the scope of words.

Precision here refers to determining the precise techniques from the East and the precise techniques from the West which, either alone or in combination, are most useful in attaining precise integrative goals of the vision we have called nirvana. The efficacy of this approach, though promising, necessitates further empirical documentation.

Psychology is currently undergoing a revolution in thinking and conceptualizing. There is an openness in the field, a breaking down of the traditional scientific paradigms. Although this makes for a confusing time within a scientific discipline, it also makes for an exciting time, for new approaches and new paths are being explored. We are giving ourselves permission to explore; we need to also take the time to verify the results of our exploration. It is in this spirit of open inquiry and searching, on both a personal and professional level, that this book was written.

On another level, this book has also tried to set to rest certain preconceptions that two major current schools of psychology (humanistic and behavioral) have about one another. Some of the preconceptions are accurate; there are real differences between the two schools of thought. Some of the preconceptions are not accurate, and seem to serve no useful purpose. Let me first suggest the similarities between the schools, with Zen representing the humanistic, transpersonal school and behavioral self-management representing the social learning theory viewpoint.

Both Zen Buddhism and behavior therapy involve teaching skills; both schools of thought hold that we can learn the skills; both schools involve, initially, a teacher who tries to influence us (educate us) to learn the skills so that eventually no teacher is necessary.

In both schools the teacher (therapist) needs an affirmation that the client (pupil) is willing to change; the therapist must use certain cues, statements, consequences to shape the client to feel he is in control of his own life; and he must also ensure that the client agrees with the goals of the strategies involved.

There are differences, too. Both the behaviorists and the humanists are carrying on a longstanding tradition over those differences. This tradition dates back to Confucius and Lao-tse in ancient China. As we have already noted, both men lived during a time of social chaos and revolution. Confucius believed the problem was that the society needed more and better labels, more precision, more "scientific verification" of principles. Lao-tse felt that Confucius' solution was acutely part of the problem, and advocated letting go of words and labels, opening ourselves to the "naturally" good way of things, the Tao, and following the way of water—flowing down the river. As we have suggested, Confucius' position is evidenced in the behavioral self-management literature, with its precise labeling, logical, causal, sequential processing of information (mode of our left brain?); and Lao-tse's position is evidenced in meditation, with its holistic mode of perceiving, a lack of goal directedness, an absence of search for causality (mode of our right brain?).

The behaviorists' approach is right. The humanistic/transpersonal/ meditative approach is right. Both are right. Both provide us with a unique and valuable way of knowing the world and perceiving reality. By literally and figuratively bridging the hemispheres, by combining both strategies in an integrative fashion, we may be able to develop a truly complete and comprehensive way of dealing with the whole person in educational settings, in therapeutic interaction, and in our own lives.

APPENDIX 5: SELECTED READINGS

On Zen Buddhism and its Relationship to Meditation, Altered States, and Western Psychotherapy

General Introduction to Zen Buddhism

SHINRU SUZUKI, *Zen Mind, Beginner's Mind: Informal Talks on Zen Meditation and Practice* (New York: Weatherill, 1976). A good beginning book, clearly and simply written by a noted Zen Master.

D. T. SUZUKI, *Introduction to Zen Buddhism*, Ed. William Barrett (New York: Anchor Books, 1956). A useful collection of Suzuki's writings. Gives background and information about Zen concepts, a brief history of Zen, and a comparison of Zen with existential philosophy.

ALAN WATTS, "Beat Zen, Square Zen, and Zen," in *This is It* (San Francisco: City Lights Bookstore, 1959). Watts' article suggests some of the misconceptions Westerners may have about Zen, some of the misconceptions Easterners seem to have about Zen, and what "true Zen" is.

Meditation and Altered States: General Introduction

CLAUDIO NARANJO and ROBERT ORNSTEIN, *The Psychology of Meditation* (New York: Viking, 1971). The first Western book to describe meditation in psychological terms. Useful survey of different types of meditation, including Taoist, Sufi, Yoga, Zen.

CHARLES TART, Ed., *Altered States of Consciousness* (New York: Wiley, 1969). The book that first coined the term "altered state." Outstanding collection of readings. Many of the articles cited in this text, such as Kasamatsu and Hirai's study of Zen meditation; Anand, China, and Singh's study of Raj yogis; and Deikman's study of meditation on a vase are included in this collection.

ROBERT ORNSTEIN, *The Psychology of Consciousness* (San Francisco: W. H. Freeman, 1972). A clear and well-written discussion of research on the right and left brain hemispheres.

CHARLES TART, *States of Consciousness* (New York: Dutton, 1976). The most definitive book yet on the different states of consciousness—ordinary awareness, altered states.

DAN GOLEMAN, *Varieties of the Meditative Experience* (New York: Dutton, 1977). A nontechnical, unbiased, clearly written account of the different schools of meditation, their goals, and their interrelationships.

DEANE SHAPIRO et al., Eds., *Meditation: Self-Regulation Strategy and Altered State of Consciousness* (Chicago: Aldine, in press). The most complete reference book on meditation research studies.

Zen and Western Psychology

Zen has been compared with almost every major Western psychotherapeutic school of thought. Below are listed some reviews of Zen and psychology in general, followed by a list of readings concerning the relationship between Zen and specific schools. Many of these articles are reprinted in Deane Shapiro, Ed., *Zen and the Art of Psychotherapy.* Zen may be viewed as a psychotherapeutic system in that it has the following: (a) a view of the individual (personality theory); (b) a view of the human potential; and (c) techniques to help individuals reach that vision of the human potential.

General Relationship between Zen and Western Psychology

EDWARD MAUPIN, "Zen Buddhism: A Psychological Review," *Journal of Consulting Psychology*, 26 (1962), 367-75.

EMANUEL BERGER, "Zen Buddhism, General Psychology, and Counseling Psychology," *Journal of Counseling Psychology*, 9 (1962), 122-27.

KOJI SATO, "Psychotherapeutic Implications of Zen," *Psychologia*, 5 (1958), 213-18.

ALAN WATTS, *Psychotherapy East and West* (New York: Pantheon, 1961).

ALAN WATTS, "Psychotherapy and Eastern Religions: Metaphysical Basis of Psychiatry," *Journal of Transpersonal Psychology*, 6 (1974) 18-31.

C. OWENS, "Zen Buddhism," in C. Tart, Ed., *Transpersonal Psychologies* (New York: Harper & Row, 1976). A good basic introduction to Zen and Western psychology. Tart's first three articles at the start of the book are superb.

J. FADIMAN and R. FRAEGER, "Zen Buddhism," in *Personality and Personal Growth* (New York: Harper & Row, 1976). This is the first time that Zen has been included in a Western psychology personality text.

Zen and Jung

CARL JUNG, Introduction to D. T. Suzuki's *Zen Buddhism* (London: Rider, 1949).

CARL JUNG and SHIN-ICHI HISAMATSU, "On the Unconscious, the Self and the Therapy," *Psychologia* (1969), 25-32.

Zen and Interpersonal Theory (Sullivan)

ALBERT STUNKARD, "Interpersonal Aspects of an Oriental Religion," *Psychiatry*, 14 (1951), 419-31.

ERNEST BECKER, "Psychotherapeutic Observations on the Zen Discipline," *Psychologia*, 3 (1960), 100-12.

Zen and Psychoanalysis

ERIC FROMM, "Zen and Psychoanalysis," *Psychologia*, 2 (1959), 79-99.

ERIK ERIKSON, "Zenanalysis," *MD Psychology*, 16 (1972), 184-88.

NORMA HAIMES, "Zen Buddhism and Psychoanalysis," *Psychologia*, 15 (1972), 22-30.

Zen and Existentialism

D. T. SUZUKI, "Zen and Existentialism," in W. Barrett, Ed., *Introduction to Zen* (New York: Doubleday, 1959).

T. HORA, "Tao, Zen, and Existential Psychotherapy," *Psychologia*, 2 (1959), 236-42.

Zen Meditation: How To Do It

PAUL WIENPAHL, *The Matter of Zazen* (New York: New York University Press, 1964).

PHILIP KAPLEAU, *Three Pillars of Zen* (Boston: Beacon Press, 1967).

Both these books are clearly written and give background to the practice of meditation, illustrations from people who have tried it, and practical instructions which the reader can use.

Zen Meditation: Additional Readings on Physiology and Psychology

T. HIRAI, *Psychophysiology of Zen* (Tokyo: Igaku Shoin Ltd., 1974).

T. HIRAI, *Zen Meditation Therapy* (Tokyo: Japan Publishing Co., 1975).

Y. AKISHIGE, Ed., *Bulletin of the Faculty of Literature of Kyushu University*, 1974.

AKIRA KASAMATSU and TOMIO HIRAI, "An Electroencephalographic Study of Zen Meditation (Zazen)," *Folia Psychiatria et Neurologica Japonica*, 20 (1966), 315-36.

Applications of Zen Meditation to Therapy with Adults, Children, and Therapists

A. KONDO, "Zen in Psychotherapy: The Virtue of Just Sitting," *Chicago Review*, 1958.

E. MAUPIN, "Individual Differences in Response to a Zen Meditation Exercise," *Journal of Consulting Psychology*, 29 (1965), 139-45.

D. SHAPIRO, "Behavioral and Attitudinal Changes Resulting from a Zen Experience Weekend and Zen Meditation," *Journal of Humanistic Psychology*, in press.

W. LINDEN, "Practicing of Meditation by School Children and Their Levels of Field Dependence-Independence, Test Anxiety, and Reading Achievement," *Journal of Consulting and Clinical Psychology*, 41 (1973), 139-43.

T. LESH, "Zen Meditation and the Development of Empathy in Counselors," *Journal of Humanistic Psychology*, 10 (1970), 39-74.

Comparison of Zen Techniques and Western Techniques:
Zen Meditation and Behavioral Self-control

D. SHAPIRO and S. ZIFFERBLATT, "An Applied Clinical Combination of Zen Meditation and Behavioral Self-Control Strategies: Reducing Methadone Dosages in Drug Addiction," *Behavior Therapy*, 6 (1976), 694-95.

D. SHAPIRO and S. ZIFFERBLATT, "Zen Meditation and Behavioral Self-Control: Similarities, Differences, Clinical Applications," *American Psychologist*, 31 (1976), 519-32.

D. SHAPIRO, "Zen Meditation and Behavioral Self-Control Applied to a Case of Generalized Anxiety," *Psychologia*, 19, No. 3 (1976), 134-38.

Zen, Autogenic Training, and Hypnosis

AKIRA ONDA, "Zen, Autogenic Training, and Hypnotism," *Psychologia*, 10 (1967), 133-36.

Zen in Play Therapy

MISAKO MIYAMOTO, "Zen in Play Therapy," *Psychologia*, 3 (1960), 197-207.

Morita Therapy

TAKAO MURASE and F. JOHNSON, "Naikan, Morita, and Western Psychotherapy," *Archives of General Psychiatry*, 31 (1974), 121-29.

Meditation and Psychotherapy

J. SMITH, "Meditation as Psychotherapy," *Psychological Bulletin*, 82 (1975), 558-64.

D. SHAPIRO and D. GIBER, "Meditation and Psychotherapeutic Effects: Self-Regulation Strategy and Altered State of Consciousness," *Archives of General Psychiatry*, in press.

D. SHAPIRO et al., Eds., *Meditation: Self-Regulation Strategy and Altered State of Consciousness: Applications to Medicine, Psychotherapy, Education* (Chicago: Aldine, in press).

Other Zen Techniques:
Haiku

MATSUO BASHO, *Narrow Roads to the Deep North and Other Travel Sketches* (Tokyo, Japan: Mushinsha Ltd., 1966). Note also R. H. Blythe (translations) Haiku. 4 Vols. (Tokyo: Hokuseilo, 1952).

Sumi-e

YASUICHI AWAKAWA, *Zen Painting* (New York: Kodanshi International, Ltd., 1970).

SADAMI YAMADA, *Complete Sumi-e Techniques* (Tokyo: Japan Publishing Co., 1971).

Koans, Mondos, Anecdotes

PAUL REPS, *Zen Flesh, Zen Bones* (Rutland, Vt: Charles Tuttle, 1958).

Zen in Japanese Culture:
General Introduction

D. T. SUZUKI, *Zen in Japanese Culture* (New York: Pantheon, 1959).

Swordplay, Archery

EUGEN HERRIGEL, *Zen in the Art of Archery* (New York: Pantheon, 1953).

TAKANO SHIGEYOUSHI, "Psychology of Swordplay," in *Zen and Japanese Culture*, N. W. Ross, Ed. (New York: Random House, 1960).

Tea Ceremony

KAKUZO OKAKURA, *The Book of Tea* (New York: Dover Publications, 1964).

Other General Readings on Zen

N. W. ROSS, Ed., *The World of Zen* (New York: Vintage Books, 1960). An excellent and fun collection of Zen writings by both Eastern and Western spokespersons.

HERMAN HESSE, *Siddhartha*, trans. Hilda Rosner (New York: New Directions Publishing Corporation and London: Peter Owen, Ltd., 1951). A beautiful poetic account by a Westerner of the life of Buddha.

Zen in the Modern Japanese Novel

YUKIO MISHIMA, *The Golden Pavilion* (Berkeley: Berkeley Publishing Co., 1969).

Y. KAWABATA, *A Thousand Cranes* (Berkeley: Berkeley Publishing Co., 1969).

Historical Background and Related Readings

E. CONZE, *Buddhism: Its Essence and Development* (New York: Philadelphia Library, 1951).

H. C. WARREN, *Buddhist Texts in Translation* (New York, Atheneum, 1969). The reader is also referred to other books mentioned in *Precision Nirvana* such as the *Baghavad Gita* (trans. F. Edgerton) (Cambridge, Mass: Harvard University Press, 1944); the *Upanishads* (trans. Max Mueller, 2 Vols. (New York: Dover Publications, 1962); Lao-Tze's *Tao-Teh Ching* (trans. Willer Bynner) (New York: John Day Co., 1944); also *The Way and The Power: A Study of the Tao Teh Ching* (trans. Arthur Waley) (London: George Allen & Unwin, Ltd., 1936); Chuang Tzu's *Basic Writings* (tr. Burton Watson) (New York: Columbia University Press, 1964); Confucius, *Analects*, trans, Arthur Waley (London: George Allen and Unwin, Ltd., 1938).

First-person Accounts

For the reader interested in first-person experiential accounts, let me suggest Roshi J. Kennett's *Zen is Eternal Life*, 2nd ed. (Emeryville, CA: Dharma Pub., 1976); the personal accounts in Kapleau's *Three Pillars of Zen* (Boston: Beacon Press, 1967); Janwillen Van De Wettering, *Empty Mirror* (Boston: Houghton Mifflin Co., 1975) as well as Eugen Herrigel's *Zen in the Art of Archery* (New York: Pantheon Books, 1953).

Journals

Journal of Humanistic Psychology
Journal of Transpersonal Psychology
Psychologia: An International Journal of Psychology in the Orient
Journal of Altered States
East-West Journal

On Social Learning Theory, Behavior Therapy, and Behavioral Self-management

General Principles of Social Learning Theory

ALBERT BANDURA, *Social Learning Theory* (Englewood Cliffs, N.J.: Prentice-Hall, 1977). The best general description of the social learning approach. Well-researched and documented.

ALBERT BANDURA, *Principles of Behavior Modification* (New York: Holt, Rinehart, Winston, 1969). A useful thoroughly documented reference book citing the research upon which behavior modification principles are based.

B. F. SKINNER, *Beyond Freedom and Dignity* (New York: Knopf, 1971). An easily read book in which Skinner explains why our contemporary way of thinking about ourselves limits our ability to be truly free individuals.

B. F. SKINNER, *Science and Human Behavior* (New York: Macmillan, 1953). A small book in which Skinner lays out most of his basic ideas.

B. F. SKINNER, *Walden Two* (New York: MacMillan, 1962). A fictional account of what a planned Utopia would be like.

WALTER MISCHEL, *Personality and Assessment* (New York: Wiley, 1968). A sophisticated, well-documented book that discusses the limits of trait concepts and traditional diagnostic tests. Lays the philosophical foundation for a social learning "personality theory."

WALTER MISCHEL, *Introduction to Personality*, 2nd edition (New York: Holt, Rinehart, Winston, 1976). An extremely useful guide to ways social learning theorists look at a variety of psychological phenomena, such as self-esteem, emotions, child development, etc.

W. WHALEY and R. MALOTT, *Elementary Principles of Behavior Modification* (Kalamazoo, Michigan). A useful introductory summary of behavioral terms.

General Texts on Behavior Therapy

K. DANIEL O'LEARY and G. T. WILSON, *Behavior Therapy: Applications and Outcomes* (Englewood Cliffs, N.J.: Prentice-Hall, 1975).

DAVID C. RIMM and JOHN C. MASTERS, *Behavior Therapy: Techniques and Empirical Findings* (New York: Academic Press, 1974).

J. WOLPE, *The Practice of Behavior Therapy* (New York: Pergamon Press, 1969).

A. LAZARUS, *Behavior Therapy and Beyond* (New York: McGraw-Hill, 1971).

L. P. ULLMAN, and L. A. KRASNER, *A Psychological Approach to Abnormal Behavior* (Englewood Cliffs, N.J.: Prentice-Hall, 1975). This book takes the standard psychiatric labels from the *Diagnostic and Statistical Manual II* and translates the labels into behavioral terms. An excellent and comprehensive book.

General Techniques of Behavioral Self-management

MICHAEL MAHONEY and CARL THORESEN, *Self-Control: Power to the Person* (Monterey, Cal.: Brooks/Cole, 1974). A useful introduction to the principles and techniques involved in behavioral self-management. The book also contains chapters by Kazdin on self-observation and by Meichenbaum on self-instructions which are particularly useful.

M. R. GOLDFRIED and M. MERBAUM, Eds., *Behavior Change through Self-Control* (New York: Holt, Rinehart and Winston, 1973). One of the first collections of readings on behavioral self-control.

FRED KANFER and A. P. GOLDSTEIN, (Eds), Helping People Change (New York: Pergamon, 1975).

Practical Self-help Guides:

General Applications

JHAN ROBBINS and DAVE FISHER, *How to Break Bad Habits and Make Good Ones* (New York: Dell, 1976).

CAROL FOSTER, *Developing Self-Control* (Kalamazoo, Michigan: Behaviordelia, 1974) (may be ordered from Behaviordelia, P.O. Box 1044, Kalamazoo, Michigan 49005).

Applications to Families, Children

JOHN and HELEN KRUMBOLTZ, *Changing Children's Behavior* (Englewood Cliffs, N.J.: Prentice-Hall, 1975).

GERALD PATTERSON, *Families* (Champaign, Ill. Research Press, 1971).

Assertiveness Training

SHARON and GORDON BOWER, *Assert Yourself* (Reading, Mass.: Addison-Wesley, 1976).

Weight

RICHARD STEWART, *Slim Chance in a Fat World* (Champaign, Ill.: Research Press, 1972).

Fears, Phobias

GERALD ROSEN, *Don't Be Afraid: A Self-Help Guide for Overcoming Fears and Phobias* (Englewood Cliffs, N.J.: Prentice-Hall, in press).

Insomnia

CARL THORESEN and TOM COATES, *How to Sleep Better* (Englewood Cliffs, N.J.: Prentice- Hall, 1977).

Specific Techniques:

Systematic Desensitization

WES WENRICH, HAROLD DAWLEY, DALE GENERAL, *Self-Directed Systematic Desensitization* (Kalamazoo, Michigan: Behavioradelia), 1976.

Contracting

WILLIAM DE REIS and GEORGE BUTZ, *Writing Behavioral Contracts: A Case Simulation Practice Manual* (Champaign, Ill.: Research Press, 1975).

Relaxation Exercises

G. HENDRICKS and R. WILLS, *The Centering Book* (Englewood Cliffs, N.J.: Prentice-Hall, 1974).

Ethical Considerations

REED MARTIN, *Behavior Modification: Human Rights and Legal Responsibilities* (Champaign, Ill.: Research Press, 1974).

Journals

Behavior Therapy

Behavior Research and Therapy

Journal of Behavior Therapy and Experimental Psychiatry

Journal of Applied Behavioral Analysis

Behavior Modification: A Quarterly Journal

On Existentialism

General Overview

WILLIAM BARRETT, *Irrational Man* (New York: Doubleday, 1958).

WALTER KAUFMANN, *Existentialism from Dostoevsky to Sartre* (New York: World Publishing Company, 1956).

Both these books give a clear and useful overview of existentialism. Barrett's book has a well-written section covering, in brief form, Kierkegaard, Neitsche, Heidegger, and Sartre. Kaufmann's book has readings from the original thinkers, plus his extensive comments.

Relationship to Psychology

ROLLO MAY, Ed., *Existential Psychology* (New York: Random House, 1961). A good introduction to different thinkers—May, Allport, Rogers—trying to define existential psychology.

ROLLO MAY, *Man's Search For Himself* (New York: W. W. Norton, 1953). An extremely moving earlier work, describing the existential condition of the modern person.

VICTOR FRANKL, *Man's Search for Meaning* (New York: Pocket Books, 1971). This book records Frankl's experiences in a concentration camp, telling how, from the midst of despair, he began the formulation of logotherapy, a school of therapy based on our human search for meaning in life.

JAMES BUGENTAL, *An Existential-Humanistic Approach to Psychotherapy* (San Francisco: Jossey-Bass, 1976). Bugental describes several cases from his own private practice, and shows how he uses existential and humanistic psychotherapy.

PETER KOESTENBAUM, *Managing Anxiety: On Knowing Who You Are* (Englewood Cliffs, N.J.: Prentice-Hall, 1974). Koestenbaum is a philosopher who has the ability to translate abstractions into useful, helpful knowledge. This book illustrates how an existential viewpoint can help in dealing with the anxiety that is our human condition.

Related Philosophical Religious Books

MAURICE FRIEDMAN, *To Deny Our Nothingness* (NewYork: Dell, 1967).

MICHAEL NOVAK, *The Experience of Nothingness* (New York: Harper, 1971).

RICHARD RUBENSTEIN, *After Auschwitz* (New York: Bobbs-Merrill, 1966).

MARTIN BUBER, *I and Thou* (New York: Scribner's, 1958).

SØREN KIERKEGAARD, *Either/Or* (New York: Doubleday, 1959).

PAUL TILLICH, *The Dynamics of Faith* (New York: Harper and Row, 1958).

ALBERT CAMUS, *The Myth of Sisyphus* (New York: Random House, 1955).

ALBERT CAMUS, *The Rebel* (New York: Random House, 1956).

JEAN PAUL SARTRE, *Being and Nothingness* (New York: Washington Square Press, 1966).

Literary

RAINER MARIA RILKE, *Notebooks of Malte Laurids Brigge* (New York: Capricorn Books, 1958).

FRANZ KAFKA, *The Trial* (New York: Modern Library, 1956).

FYODOR DOSTOEVSKY, *Notes from Underground Man* (New York: New American Library, 1961), *The Idiot* (New York: New American Library, 1969), *Crime and Punishment* (New York: Bantam Books, 1962).

JEAN-PAUL SARTRE, *The Words* (Greenwich, Conn: Fawcett Publications, 1966); *Nausea* (New York: New Directions Paperback, 1964).

ALBERT CAMUS, *The Stranger* (New York: Random House, 1946).

ALBERT CAMUS, The Fall (New York: Random House, 1956).

ALBERT CAMUS, The Plague (New York: Random House, 1962).

APPENDIX 6: CHAPTER NOTES

Preface

[1] I first heard the term "transpersonal behaviorism" used by Charles Tart at a conference I chaired on Ways of Healing, University of Santa Clara, 1976. Jim Fadiman suggested the term "Zen Behaviorism."

Part I

[1] From Paul Reps, *Zen Flesh, Zen Bones* (Rutland, Vt.: Charles Tuttle, 1958), p. 5.

[2] I first heard the term "Grand Conditioner" in a quote from Floyd Matson during a speech by Michael Mahoney at the annual meeting of the American Educational Research Association, 1974.

[3] For a useful elaboration of the different types of Zen, see Alan Watts, "Beat Zen, Square Zen, and Zen," in *This is It* (San Francisco: City Lights Books, 1959).

[4] It is important that the reader not confuse humanistic psychology, which believes in the innate, self-actualizing nature of the individual (as described by Goldstein, Rogers, Maslow, and others) with the American Humanist Association, which defines humanist as follows: "Any account of nature should pass the test of scientific evidence. . . . We find insufficient evidence for belief in the existence of a supernatural. . . . As nontheists, we begin with humans, not God, nature not Deity. (Humanist Manifesto 11. The *Humanist*, 1973, 33(5), 4-9.

For further readings on Humanistic Psychology, see Angyal, A *Neurosis and Treatment: A Holistic Theory* (New York: Wiley, 1965), Goldstein, K. *The Organism* (New York: American Book Co., 1939); Maslow, A., *Motivation and Personality* (New York: Harper & Row, 1954); Maslow, A., *Toward a Psychology of Being* (Princeton, Van Nostrand, 1968); Rogers, C., *Client Centered Therapy* (Boston: Houghton Mifflin, 1951).

Chapter 1

[1] This poem is quoted in Alan Watts, *The Way of Zen* (New York: Pantheon, 1957), p. 27.

[2] Herman Hesse, *Siddhartha*, translated by Hilda Rosner (New York: New Directions, 1951), p. 99.

[3] For a more detailed account of the different types of meditation, see Claudio Naranjo and Robert Ornstein, *On the Psychology of Meditation*

(New York: Viking, 1971), and Dan Goleman, *Varieties of the Meditative Experience* (New York: Dutton, 1977).

[4] Walpole Rahula, *What the Buddha Taught* (New York: Grove Press, 1959), p. 70.

[5] For a more thorough discussion of these five steps of meditation, see Deane Shapiro and Steve Zifferblatt, "Zen Meditation and Behavioral Self-Control: Similarities, Differences, and Clinical Applications," *American Psychologist*, 31 (1976), pp. 519-32.

[6] There may be a great variety of "altered states" produced by different self-regulation techniques (hypnosis, autogenic training) by drugs as well as by different forms of meditation. (See C. Tart, *Altered States of Consciousness* (New York: Wiley, 1968.) We are referring here to one type of altered state, described in detail in the text. This state may, to a greater or lesser degree, overlap with other so-called altered states. Neurophysiologically, we don't yet know enough to make that determination.

[7] Deane Shapiro, *Soaring* (unpublished novelette; available from author P.O. Box 2084, Stanford, CA. 94305), p. 59.

[8] Herbert Benson, *The Relaxation Response* (New York: William Morrow, 1975). For a discussion of the physiological changes during meditation, see also R. Woolfolk, "Psychophysiological Correlates of Meditation," *Archives of General Psychiatry*, 32 (1975), 1326-33. For a detailed review of the literature on meditation and its application to clinical concerns such as stress and tension, hypertension, the addictions, insomnia, as well as altered states of consciousness, see Deane Shapiro and David Giber, "Meditation: A Review of the Research on Clinical Applications and Altered States of Consciousness," paper presented at the American Association for the Advancement of Science, Pacific Regional Meeting, June 1976. *Archives of General Psychiatry*, in press.

[9] Deane Shapiro and Steven Zifferblatt, "A Clinical Combination of Zen Meditation and Behavioral Self-Management Strategies: Reducing Methadone Dosage in Drug Addiction," *Behavior Therapy*, 6 (1976), pp. 694-95.

[10] From *Maitraya-Brahmana Upanishad* trans. F. Max Muller. (New York: Dover Publications), 1962, p. 295.

[11] Eugen Herrigel, *Zen in the Art of Archery* (New York: Pantheon, 1953), pp. 57-58.

[12] Matsuo Basho, *Narrow Roads to the Deep North and Other Travel Sketches* (Tokyo, Japan: Mushinsha Ltd.)

[13] John Dollard and Neal Miller, *Personality and Psychotherapy* (New York: McGraw-Hill, 1950).

[14] *Chuang Tzu, Basic Writings*, trans. Burton Watson (New York: Columbia University Press, 1964).

[15] Cited in D. T. Suzuki, in *Zen Buddhism* (William Barrett, Ed.) (New York: Doubleday, 1956), p. 9. Original author unknown. Quote is often attributed to Bodhi-Dharma.

[16] For a more thorough discussion of right and left brain hemispheric specialization, see David Galin, "Implications for Psychiatry of Left and Right Cerebral Specialization," *Archives of General Psychiatry* 31 (1974), pp. 572-83; and Julian Davidson, "The Physiology of Meditation and Mystical States of Consciousness," *Perspectives in Biology and Medicine*, 1976, pp. 345-380 (see particularly the section on mystical experiences and hemispheric laterality).

[17] These poems were cited and discussed in D. T. Suzuki, "Lectures in Zen Buddhism," in *Zen Buddhism and Psychoanalysis* (New York: Harper & Row, Harper Collophon Books, 1960).

[18] In *Selected Writings of D. T. Suzuki*, Ed. William Barrett (New York: Anchor Books, 1956).

[19] Alan Watts, "The Sound of Rain," *Playboy*, April 1972.

[20] Cited by D. T. Suzuki in *Zen Buddhism* (W. Barrett, Ed.), 1956, p. 251. Originally cited in *The Transmission of the Lamp.*

[21] Akira Kasamatsu and Tomio Hirai, "An Electroencephalographic Study of Zen Meditation (Zazen)," *Folia Psychiatria et Neurologia Japonica*, 20 (1966), 315-36. Reprinted in Charles Tart, Ed., *Altered States of Consciousness* (New York: Wiley, 1969).

[22] Martin Buber, *I and Thou*, trans. Walter Kaufmann (New York: Charles Scribner, 1970), pp. 58-59.

[23] T. Lesh, "Zen Meditation and the Development of Empathy in Counselors," *Journal of Humanistic Psychology*, 10 (1970), 39-74.

[24] Cited in Suzuki, *Zen Buddhism* (W. Barrett, Ed.).

[25] See, for example, the writings of Abraham Maslow, *Religion, Values, and Peak Experiences* (Columbus: Ohio State University Press, 1964).

[26] Arthur Deikman, "Deautomization and the Mystic Experience," *Archives of General Psychiatry*, 29 (1966), 329-43.

[27] Y. Akishige, Ed., "A Historical Survey of the Psychological Studies on Zen," *Bulletin of the Faculty of Literature of Kyushu University* (1974), pp. 1-57. R. Ikegami's "Psychological Study of Zen Posture" appears in the same collection, pp. 105-35.

[28] Robert Ornstein, *The Psychology of Consciousness* (San Francisco: W. H. Freeman, 1972), p. 148.

[29] In *Selected Writings of D. T. Suzuki.*

[30] In Watts, "The Sound of Rain."

[31] Ornstein, *Psychology of Consciousness.*

[32] Arthur Deikman, "Experimental Meditation," *Journal of Nervous and Mental Disease*, 136 (1963), 329-43. Reprinted in Tart, Ed., *Altered States of Consciousness*, (New York: Wiley, 1969) p. 201.

[33] B. K. Anand, E. S. Chhina, and B. Singh, "Some Aspects of Electroencephalographic Studies in Yogis," *EEG Clinical Neurophysiology*, 13 (1961), 452-56. Reprinted in Tart, *Altered States of Consciousness*, p. 501.

[34] Rahula, *What the Buddha Taught*, p. 70.

[35] Watts, "The Sound of Rain," p. 220.

[36] Shapiro and Zifferblatt, *American Psychologist*, 31 (1976), p. 521.

[37] Rahula, *What the Buddha Taught*, p. 71.

[38] In Watts, "The Sound of Rain."

[39] From Paul Reps, *Zen Flesh, Zen Bones* (Rutland, Vt.: Charles Tuttle, 1958).

[40] Mondos are cited from D. T. Suzuki, *Introduction to Zen* (London: John Murray Ltd., 1949).

[41] From Sutra 63, Majjhima-Nikaya, cited in *Selected Writings of D. T. Suzuki.*

[42] D. T. Suzuki, *Zen Buddhism* (New York: Doubleday, 1956), p. 30.

[43] From *Selected Writings of D. T. Suzuki.*

[44] Bradford Smith, *Meditation, The Inward Trip* (Philadelphia: Lippincott, 1963).

[45] From *Selected Writings of D. T. Suzuki*, p. 285.

[46] Basho, *Narrow Roads to the Deep North.*

[47] Ibid.

[48] Unpublished collection of poems from the class Zen Buddhism, Stanford University, 1972.

[49] D. Shapiro and J. Shapiro, *A Daily Musing*, unpublished book of *haiku* and other poetry. Available from the authors, P.O. Box 2084, Stanford, CA. 94305.

Chapter 2

[1] Lao-tse, *Tao-Teh Ching*, trans. Arthur Waley (London: George Allen and Unwin, Ltd., 1936).

[2] Chuang Tsu, *Basic Writings*, trans. Burton Watson (New York: Columbia University Press, 1964).

[3] G. A. Miller, "The Magical Number 7 ± 2: Some Limits On Our Capacity for Processing Information," *Psychological Review*, 63 (1965), 81-97.

[4] See, for example, J. S. Bruner, R. R. Oliver, and P. Greenfield, Eds., *Studies in Cognitive Growth* (New York: Wiley, 1966).

[5] John Dollard and Neal Miller, *Personality and Psychotherapy* (New York: McGraw-Hill, 1950).

[6] Walter Mischel, *Personality and Assessment* (New York: Wiley, 1968). As Mischel notes, although trait formulations may be adaptive from a survival standpoint, there are some definite problems when we use traits as explanations of behavior. This will be discussed at greater length in Chapter 4.

[7] S. E. Asch, "Effects of Group Pressure upon Modification and Distortion of Judgment," in E. E. Maccoby, T. M. Newcomb, and E. L. Hartley, Eds., *Readings in Social Psychology*, 3rd ed. (New York: Holt, Rinehart and Winston, 1958).

[8] See Robert Sommer, *Personal Space* (Englewood Cliffs, N.J.: Prentice-Hall, 1974); and Adams and Biddle, *The Realities of Teaching* (New York: Holt, Rinehart and Winston, 1970).

[9] D. Bem "Self-Perception Theory," in L. Berkowitz, Ed., *Advances in Experimental Social Psychology*, Vol. 6 (New York: Academic Press, 1972), pp. 1-62.

[10] See, for example, S. Valins and R. E. Nisbett, *Attribution Processes in the Development and Treatment of Emotional Disorders* (New York: General Learning Press, 1971).

[11] S. Schachter, "The Interaction of Cognitive and Physiological Determinants of Emotional States," in C. D. Speilberger, Ed., *Anxiety and Behavior* (New York: Academic Press, 1966).

[12] Kahil Gibran, *The Prophet* (New York: Knopf, 1977).

[13] Hannah Green, *I Never Promised You A Rose Garden* (New York: New American Library, 1964).

[14] The elements of a fair contract are adapted from Lloyd Homme and D. Tosti, *Behavior Technology: Motivation and Contingency Contracting* (San Rafael, Cal.: Individual Learning Systems, 1971).

[15] For a discussion of progressive relaxation techniques, see Edmund Jacobson, "The Two Methods of Tension Control and Certain Basic Technique in

Anxiety Tension Control" in J. Kamiya, T. Barber, L. V. DiCara, N. E. Miller, D. Shapiro, and J. Stoyva, Eds., *Biofeedback and Self-Regulation* (Chicago: Aldine-Atherton, 1971).

[16] Adapted from a tape recording to teach relaxation by John H. Marquis, Ph.D., V.A. Hospital, Palo Alto, Calif.

[17] See Joseph Wolpe, *Psychotherapy by Reciprocal Inhibition* (Palo Alto, Cal.: Stanford University Press, 1958) for the most comprehensive first account of the development of this technique.

[18] The fear survey schedule has been revised and readapted many times. The one excerpted here is adapted from J. Wolpe, P. J. Lang, J. H. Geer, M. D. Spiegler, and R. M. Liebert. See J. Wolpe and P. J. Land, "A Fear Survey Schedule," *Behavior Research and Therapy*, 2 (1964) 27. See also J. Wolpe, *The Techniques of Behavior Therapy* (New York: Pergamon, 1969) Appendix 3, 283-86.

[19] I first learned of the "sandwich technique" from Lloyd Homme in a personal communication, 1972.

[20] D. Premack, "Reinforcement Theory," in D. Levin, Ed., *Nebraska Symposium on Motivation* (Lincoln, Nebraska: University of Nebraska Press, 1965), pp. 123-80.

[21] See, for example, W. G. Johnson, "Some Applications of Homme's Coverant Control Therapy: Two Case Reports," *Behavior Therapy*, 2 (1971), 240-48.

[22] From column on Arnold Palmer Method, in *San Francisco Chronicle*, 1976.

[23] Cited in Maxwell Maltz, *Psychocybernetics* (New York: Grossman and Dunlop, 1970).

[24] For descriptions and theoretical rationale for this model of stress and tension reduction, see D. Meichenbaum and R. Cameron, "The Clinical Potential and Pitfalls of Modifying What Clients Say to Themselves," in M. J. Mahoney and C. E. Thoresen, *Self-Control: Power to the Person* (Monterey, Cal.: Brooks/Cole, 1974); see also M. R. Goldfried, "Reduction of Generalized Anxiety through a Variant of Systematic Desensitization," in M. R. Goldfried and M. Merbaum, Eds., *Behavior Change through Self-Control* (New York: Holt, Rinehart and Winston, 1973).

[25] For a further discussion of "as if" see H. Vaihinger, *The Philosophy of As If* (London: Routledge & Kegan Paul, Ltd., 1924). Also see William James' discussion of "will" in which James chose to believe in free will. "My first act of free will shall be to believe in free will. For the remainder of the year, I will . . . voluntarily cultivate the feeling of moral freedom. . . ." William James, cited in R. B. Perry, *The Thought and Character of William James* (Boston: Little Brown, 1935) Vol. 1, p. 147.

[26] See, for example, J. Bugental, *An Existential Humanistic Approach to Psychotherapy* (San Francisco: Jossey-Bass, 1976).

[27] Jacobson, "The Two Methods of Tension Control," in *Biofeedback*, p. 475. (Italics mine.)

[28] J. M. R. Delgado, *Physical Control of the Mind* (New York: Harper & Row, 1969), p. 225.

[29] F. Kanfer and P. Karoly, "Self-Control: A Behavioristic Excursion into the Lion's Den," *Behavior Therapy*, 3 (1972), 398-416.

[30] B. F. Skinner, "Freedom and the Control of Man," *American Scholar* (1955), pp. 47-65.

Chapter 3

[1] For a discussion of ways in which we are conditioned without our awareness, the reader may wish to refer to selected studies in Walter Mischel, *Introduction to Personality* (New York: Holt, Rinehart and Winston, 1971); and in Bernard Berelson and Gary Steiner, *Human Behavior: An Inventory of Scientific Findings* (New York: Harcourt, Brace & World, 1964). See also the discussion of Gerald Davidson "Counter-Control and Behavior Modification," in *Behavior Change, Methodology, Concepts, Practice*, L. Hamerlynck, L. C. Handy, and E. J. Mash, Eds. (Champaign, Ill.: Research Press, 1973). For a summary discussion of the different theories of awareness and learning (nonmeditational, independent response systems theory, cognitive view, and reciprocal interaction theory), see A. Bandura, *Principles of Behavior Modification* (New York: Holt, Rinehart and Winston, 1969), pp. 566-68.

It should be noted, too, that although some learning can take place without awareness, we do learn faster once we become aware of the process: see W. Mischel, *Personality and Assessment* (New York: Wiley, 1968), p. 197.

[2] The underground man's poetic feelings are reflected in an article by H. M. Lefcourt entitled "The Function of the Illusion of Control and Freedom," *American Psychologist*, 28 (1973), 417-25. Lefcourt notes that "the sense of control, the illusion that one can exercise personal choice, has a definite and positive role in sustaining life. The illusion of freedom is not to be lightly dismissed without anticipating undesirable consequences."

[3] B. F. Skinner, *Science and Human Behavior* (New York: Macmillan, 1953).

[4] Herman Hesse, *Siddhartha*, trans. Hilda Rosner (New York: New Directions Books, 1951), pp. 77-81.

[5] *Ibid*, p. 83.

[6] Dustin Hoffman, in *Playboy* interview, ©1975, by *Playboy*.

[7] See discussion of M. Heidegger in W. Barrett, Ed., *Irrational Man* (New York: Doubleday, 1958), 206-39.

Chapter 4

[1] This may not be the exact translation of this poem, but I believe the content is true to the "spirit" of the original poem. Since I couldn't remember the original proper names, I made up names for the mountain and lake which I don't believe are in the original. I apologize to the poem's creator for this.

[2] Charles Tart, Ed., *States of Consciousness* (New York: Dutton, 1976).

[3] Claudio Naranjo and Robert Ornstein, *On the Psychology of Meditation* (New York: Viking, 1971).

[4] For a discussion of "outsight," see C. Ferster, "An Experimental Analysis of Clinical Phenomena," *Psychological Record*, 22, No. 1 (1972), 1-16; for the problems of reliability in self-observation, see Carl Thoresen and Michael Mahoney, *Behavioral Self-Control* (New York: Holt, Rinehart and Winston, 1974), pp. 48-63.

[5] From Paul Reps, *Zen Flesh, Zen Bones* (Rutland, Vt.: Charles Tuttle, 1958), p. 34.

[6] F. Dostoevsky, *The Idiot*, trans. Eva Martin (New York: Dutton, 1972).

[7] Victor Frankl, *Man's Search for Meaning* (New York: Pocket Books, 1971).

[8] Albert Camus, *The Myth of Sisyphus* (New York: Random House, 1955), p. 3.

[9] There are basically three different theories to explain motivation: id psychology, ego psychology, and social learning theory. In social learning theory terms, motivation is not seen as innate but rather influenced by social variables, cultural stereotypes, models, and other conditioning factors. Early psychodynamic theorists, such as Freud and the id psychologists, posited a drive reduction model of motivation in which there were certain instinctual drives which motivated an individual. Once these drives were reduced the individual was satiated (See J. Dollard and N. Miller *Personality and Psychotherapy*, New York: McGraw-Hill, 1950). Later dynamic formulations such as Hartman (Hartman, H. *Essays on Ego Psychology: Selected Problems in Psychoanalytic Theory*, New York: International University Press, 1964) suggested that the ego, rather than merely reacting to the id's impulses, may in fact be a "conflict freesphere"; and still later formulations, such as that of Robert White (White, R. "Motivation Reconsidered: The Concept of Competency." In *Functions of Varied Experiences*, edited by D. W. Fiske and S. R. Maddi Homewood, Illinois: Dorsey, 1961, Chap. 10) suggests that the ego may have an energy of its own: a drive towards competence (see also White, R. W. "Ego and Reality in Psycho-

analytic Theory: A Proposal Regarding Independent Ego Energies, *Psychological Issues*, 1963, 3, pp. 1-210.

With the ego psychologists came a new conception of the human potential. Writers such as Abraham Maslow pointed out that there were not only deficit motivations such as drive reduction (need for food, clothing, shelter) but also growth motivations, "self-actualizing qualities inherent in the organism." (Maslow, A., *Toward a Psychology of Being*, 2nd Edition, Princeton: Van Nostrand, 1968; Maslow, A., *Motivation and Personality*, New York: Harper and Row, 1954.

The ego psychological model was given some empirical support in both animal and human research. Experimental psychology showed that the tension reduction model of the id psychologists and Dollard and Miller was insufficient to account for all observable behavior in animals, and that there may be other motivators, such as curiosity, to account for such phenomena as "exploratory behavior." Other research, such as that by Berlyne (Berlyne, D., "Curiosity and Exploration," *Science*, 153, 1966, 25-33; Berlyne D., *Conflict, Arousal, and Curiosity*, New York: McGraw-Hill, 1960) showed that individuals tend to spend more time looking at new objects than they do at objects that are already known.

Let me suggest how the ego psychology view of motivation may be reconciled with social learning theory. First, if there is in fact an instinctual exploratory drive in an individual, there is every reason to believe that this drive would be strongly influenced by the person's learning history. For example, if a rat is shocked the first time it explores beyond its cage, there will be less likelihood it would engage in future exploration. Similarly, if each time a student tries to act creatively and outside the traditional framework of the school setting, he or she is punished or criticized, this will likewise influence the frequency of exploratory behavior. Finally, as we will further discuss in Chapter 5, it may be an irrelevant question whether or not individuals actually have an innate self-actualizing drive (ego psychology) or are choosing to follow the models of excellence that they would like to emulate (social learning theory). Both beliefs may lead to the exact same outcome.

[10] F. Nietzsche, *Beyond Good and Evil* (New York: Vintage Books, 1963), p. 43.

[11] See Soren Kierkegaard, *Fear and Trembling*, trans. W. Lourie (Princeton: Princeton University Press, 1971).

[12] Dostoevsky, *The Brothers Karamazov*, trans. A. MacAndrew (New York: Bantam, 1970).

Chapter 5

[1] From Carlos Castenada, *The Teachings of Don Juan* (Berkeley, Cal.: University of California Press, 1968).

[2] See Carl G. Jung, "The Structure and Dynamics of the Psyche." In *Collected Works*, Vol. 8 (Princeton: Princeton University Press, 1960).

[3] See C. R. Rogers, *Client Centered Therapy* (Boston: Houghton Mifflin, 1951); and Rogers, *On Becoming a Person* (Boston: Houghton Mifflin, 1961).

[4] David Reisman, *The Lonely Crowd* (New Haven: Yale University Press, 1950).

[5] From Paul Reps, *Zen Flesh, Zen Bones* (Rutland, Vt.: Charles Tuttle, 1958), p. 5.

[6] Two useful books on the nature of ordinary awareness are Robert Ornstein's *The Psychology of Consciousness* (San Francisco: W. H. Freeman, 1972) and Walter Mischel's *Personality and Assessment* (New York: Wiley, 1968). Ornstein's book gives more information on ordinary awareness in general; Mischel's book gives more information about the specific nature of trait formulations.

[7] See P. E. Meehl, "The Cognitive Activity of the Clinician," *American Psychologist*, 15 (1960), 19-27.

[8] D. Rosenhan, "On Being Sane in Insane Places," *Science*, 1973 (179) 250-258.

[9] Ibid., p. 255.

[10] B. F. Skinner, "Behaviorism at Fifty," in W. T. Wann, Ed., *Behaviorism and Phenomenology* (Chicago: University of Chicago Press, 1964).

[11] Mischel, *Personality and Assessment*, p. 68.

[12] See, for example, the discussions of Sartre and Heidegger in William Barrett, *Irrational Man* (New York: Doubleday, 1958), pp. 206-60.

[13] Cited in Suzuki, *Zen Buddhism* (W. Barrett, Ed.).

[14] D. T. Suzuki, in Erich Fromm, "Zen and Psychoanalysis," *Psychologia*, 2 (1959), pp. 79-99.

[15] D. T. Suzuki, *Zen Buddhism* (New York: Doubleday, 1956), p. 3.

[16] C. G. Jung, Conscious, Unconscious, and Individuation. In *Collected Works*. Vol. 9, Part 1 (Princeton: Princeton University Press, 1959). Originally published in English, 1939.

[17] R. M. Bucke, *Cosmic Consciousness* (New York: Citadel Press, 1970).

[18] Rogers, *Client Centered Therapy*, 1951; Maslow, *Toward a Psychology of Being*, 1968; Goldstein, *The Organism*, 1939.

[19] See, for example, Kanfer and Karoly's model of self-control involving self-observation, self-evaluation, and self-reinforcement. In the model of the mirror we are discussing here, there is only self-observation. (F. Kanfer and P. Karoly, "Self-Control: A Behavioristic Excursion into the Lion's Den," *Behavior Therapy*, 3 [1972], 398-416.)

[20] Paul Tillich, *Dynamics of Faith* (New York: Harper and Row, 1958).

[21] Claudio Naranjo and Robert Ornstein, *On The Psychology of Meditation* (New York: Viking, 1971), p. 194.

[22] In Shinru Suzuki Roshi, *Zen Mind, Beginner's Mind* (New York: Weatherhill, 1976).

[23] D. T. Suzuki, cited in Maupin, "On Meditation," in C. Tart, Ed., *Altered States of Consciousness* (New York: Wiley, 1969), pp. 181-91.

[24] See, for example, Edmund Husserl, *Cartesian Meditations*, trans. Dorian Cairns (Hague, Netherlands: Martinus Nijhoff, 1960).

[25] Teillhard de Chardin, *The Future of Man* (New York: Harper and Row, 1964).

[26] Albert Bandura, "Behavior Theory and the Models of Man," *American Psychologist*, 29 (1974), 859-69.

[27] See Chapter 2, Discussion of "as if."

[28] Tomio Hirai, *Psychophysiology of Zen* (Tokyo: Igaku Shoin Ltd., 1974).

[29] George Gallup, in a poll described in the *San Francisco Chronicle*, November 1976, noted that nearly 8 percent of the American population (16 million people) were involved in some way with Eastern disciplines and Eastern techniques such as meditation and yoga.

[30] See section on Heidegger in W. Barrett, Ed., *Irrational Man* (New York: Archer, 1962) 206-39.

[31] Quoted in *San Francisco Chronicle*, 1976.

[32] Quoted in *San Francisco Chronicle*, 1976.

[33] *Baghavad Gita*, trans. F. Edgerton (Cambridge, Mass.: Harvard University Press, 1964), Chap. 4, verse 18, p. 25.

[34] Ibid., 4.14.

[35] R. Linssen, cited in N. W. Ross, *The World of Zen* (New York: Random House, 1960), p. 220.

[36] Herman Hesse, *Siddhartha*, trans. Hilda Rosner (New York: New Directions Books, 1951), pp. 63-64.

[37] Eugene Herrigel, *Zen in the Art of Archery* (New York: Pantheon Books, 1953).

[38] D. T. Suzuki, in Erich Fromm, Ed., *Psychoanalysis and Zen Buddhism* (London: George Allen and Unwin Ltd., 1910), p. 7.

[39] See for example Carl Rogers, *On Becoming a Person* (Boston: Houghton Mifflin, 1961); Albert Ellis, *Reason and Emotion in Psychotherapy* (New York: Stuart, 1962). Carl Jung talks of removing the *persona*, the façade we wear, and turning inward to find our real "individuated" self, Jung, Collected Works, Vol. 8, 1960; Vol. 9, pt. 1, 1959.

[40] E. Fromm. *The Art of Loving* (New York:Harper and Row, 1956).

[41] K. Gibran, *The Prophet* (New York: Knopf, 1977), p. 16.

[42] Abraham Maslow, *Toward a Psychology of Being*, 2nd Edition (New York: Van Nostrand, 1968), p. 276.

[43] Fromm, "Zen and Psychoanalysis," p. 92.

[44] Karen Horney, *Neurosis and Human Growth* (New York: Norton, 1950).

[45] F. Kanfer and P. Karoly, "Self-Control."

[46] Claudio Naranjo and Robert Ornstein, *On the Psychology of Meditation* (New York: Viking, 1971), p. 108.

[47] Reed Martin, *Behavior Meditation: Human Rights and Legal Responsibilities* (Champaign, Illinois: Research Press, 1975).

[48] Alan Watts, *The Spirit of Zen* (New York: Grove Press, 1958), p. 108.

[49] Reps, *Zen Flesh, Zen Bones*, p. 18.

[50] Watts, *The Spirit of Zen*, p. 37.

[51] Frederick Spiegelberg, *Spiritual Practices of India* (New York: Citadel Press, 1962), pp. 46–47.

[52] Paul Reps, *Zen Flesh, Zen Bones*, pp. 22-23.

[53] From *Playboy* Magazine.

[54] F. Kanfer and D. Goldfoot, "Self-Control and Tolerance of Noxious Stimulation," *Psychological Reports*, 18 (1966), 79-85.

[55] Cited in Lesley Cole, *Remember Laughter* (New York: Knopf, 1976).

[56] D. T. Suzuki, *Introduction to Zen Buddhism* (London: John Murray, Ltd., 1949) p. 86.

[57] Kahil Gibran, *The Prophet* (New York, Alfred Knopf, 1977), p. 12.

[58] Reps, *Zen Flesh, Zen Bones*, p. 7.

[59] Gordon Allport, *Becoming* (New Haven: Yale University Press, 1955), p. 297.

[60] Allport, *Personality and Social Encounter* (Boston: Beacon Press, 1961), p. 160.

[61] It is possible that the phenomena of "detachedness," of removal of "emotional overlay" can be understood in terms of the psychological process of habituation and extinction.

[62] Carl Rogers, *On Becoming a Person* (Boston: Houghton Mifflin, 1961).

[63] See J. Breuer and Sigmund Freud, *Studies on Hysteria*, Standard Edition, Volume 2 (London: Hogarth Press, 1955). (First German Edition, 1895.)

[64] See Ferster, "An Experimental Analysis of Clinical Phenomena," and A. W. Staats, "Language Behavior Therapy: A Derivative of Social Behaviorism," *Behavior Therapy*, 3 (1972), 165-92.

[65] See E. Jacobson, "The two methods of tension control and certain basic techniques in anxiety tension control" in J. Kamiya, T. Barber, L. V. DiCara, N. E. Miller, D. Shapiro, and J. Stoyva, Eds., *Biofeedback and Self-Regulation* (Chicago: Aldine-Atherton, 1971).

[66] See A. Maslow, "Health as Transcendence," in *Toward a Psychology of Being* (New York: Van Nostrand, 1968), pp. 179-89.

[67] Roger Walsh, "Reflections on Psychotherapy," *Journal of Transpersonal Psychology*, 1976, 8, 100-111.

[68] See Staats, "Language Behavior Therapy" 165-92.

[69] Cited in A. Watts, *The Spirit of Zen.*

[70] Naranjo and Ornstein, *On the Psychology of Meditation*, p. 199.

Chapter 6

[1] The technique of having a client put self-instructing note cards on a cigarette carton was first used by M. Mahoney, "The Self-Management of Covert Behavior," *Behavior Therapy*, 1 (1970), 510-21.

[2] See Gordon Allport, "The Law of Reverse Effects," in *Becoming* (New Haven: Yale University Press, 1955).

[3] Walter Mischel, E. B. Ebbesen, and A. R. Zeiss, "Cognitive and Attentional Mechanisms in Delay of Gratification," *Journal of Personality and Social Psychology*, 21 (1972), 204-18.

[4] The role of focusing (our "mind") is just barely being explored. Studies range from the work on self-control by Mischel (above) to attempts to manage emotional aspects of malignant diseases, such as cancer. O. C. Simington and S. Simonton, "Belief Systems and the management of emotional aspects of malignancy" *Journal of Transpersonal Psychology*, 7 (1975), 29-48.

[5] This case study is cited in Ken Pelletier and Eric Peper, "The Chutzpah Factor in Altered States of Consciousness," *Journal of Humanistic Psychology*, 1977 (17) 63-73.

[6] Ibid. pp. 63-73.

[7] F. H. Kanfer and D. A. Goldfoot, "Self-Control and Tolerance of Noxious Stimulation," *Psychological Reports*, 18 (1966), 79-85.

[8] M. Evans and G. Paul, "Effects of Hypnotically Suggested Analgesia on Physiological and Subjective Response to Cold Stress," *Journal of Consulting and Clinical Psychology*, 35, No. 3 (1970), 362-372.

[9] B. K. Anand, E. S. Chhina, and B. Singh, "Some Aspects of Electroencephalographic Studies in Yogis," *EEG Clinical Neurophysiology*, 13 (1961), 452-56.

[10] M. L. Rilke, *The Notebooks of Malte Laurids Briggs* (New York: Capricorn Books, 1958).

[11] A. Camus, *The Plague* (New York: Random House, 1972).

[12] Ira Progoff, *The Personal Journal* (New York: Dialogue House Library, 1975).

[13] Ronald Bracewell, *The Galactic Club: Intelligent Life in Outer Space* (San Francisco: San Francisco Book Club, 1976).

Chapter 7

[1] J. Lilly in *Center of the Cyclone* (New York: Julian Press, 1972), p. 5.

Chapter Eight

[1] Herman Hesse, *Siddhartha*, trans. Hilda Rosner (New York: New Directions Books, 1951), p. 77.

[2] Chuang Tzu in *Basic Writings*, trans. Burton Watson (N.Y.: Columbia University Press, 1964).

[3] See, for example, R. Sperry, "A Modified Concept of Consciousness," *Psychological Review*, 76 (1969), 532-36.

[4] See David Galin, "Implications for Psychiatry of Right and Left Cerebral Specialization," *Archives of General Psychiatry*, 31 (1974), 572-83.

[5] See Julian Davidson, "The Physiology of Meditation and Mystical States of Consciousness," *Perspectives in Biology and Medicine*, 19 (1976), 345-80.

[6] Poem by Pao-tzu cited in Conrad Ayers, *Zen and the Comic Spirit* (Philadelphia: The Westminster Press, 1973), p. 81.

[7] From *Vajra Bodhi Sea*, 1, No. 3 (October 1970), 40. Used by the Ch'an Master Hsuan Hua to conclude a work of intense meditation.

Appendix 3

[1] This is a condensed and summarized version of the following article: D. Shapiro and S. Zifferblatt, "Zen Meditation and Behavioral Self-Management: Similarities, Differences, Clinical Applications," *American Psychologist*, 31 (1976), 519-32.

[2] See D. Van Nuys, "A Novel Technique for Studying Attention During Meditation," *Journal of Transpersonal Psychology*, 3 (1971), 125-33; also D. Shapiro and S. Zifferblatt, "An Applied Clinical Combination of Zen Meditation and Behavioral Self-Control: Reducing Methadone Dosage in Drug Addiction," *Behavior Therapy* (1976), 694-95.

[3] Walter Mischel, *Personality and Assessment* (New York: Wiley, 1968).

[4] See H. M. Lefcourt, "Internal Versus External Control of Reinforcement: A Review," *Psychological Bulletin*, 65 (1966), 206-20.

[5] See Tomio Hirai, *Psychophysiology of Zen* (Tokyo: Igaku Shoin, Ltd., 1974).

[6] See W. Luthe, "Autogenic Training: Method, Research, and Applications in Medicine," in C. Tart, Ed., *Altered States of Consciousness* (New York: Wiley, 1969).

[7] G. Paul "Physiological Effects of Relaxation Training and Hypnotic Suggestion," *Journal of Abnormal Psychology*, 74 (1969), 425-37.

[8] E. Jacobson "The two methods of tension control and certain basic techniques in anxiety tension control," in J. Kamiya, T. Barber, L. V. DiCara, N. E. Miller, D. Shapiro, and J. Stoyva, Eds., *Biofeedback and Self-Regulation* (Chicago: Aldine-Atherton, 1971). "The clinical potential and pitfalls of modifying what clients say to themselves," in M. J. Mahoney and C. E. Thoresen, *Self-Control: Power to the Person* (Monterey, CA: Brooks Cole, 1974), 263-91.

[9] J. Lesh, "Zen Meditation and the Development of Empathy in Counselors," *Journal of Humanistic Psychology*, 10 (1970), 39-74.

[10] D. Shapiro, "Behavioral and Attitudinal Effects Resulting from a Zen Experience Weekend and Zen Meditation," *Journal of Humanistic Psychology*, in press.

[11] See, for example, Dan Goleman, "Meditation as Metatherapy," *Journal of Transpersonal Psychology*, 3 (1971), 1-25; also F. Kanfer and P. Karoly, "Self-Control: A Behavioristic Excursion into the Lion's Den," *Behavior Therapy*, 3 (1972), 398-416. Note particularly the model of self-observation, self-evaluation, and self-reinforcement.

[12] See Wolpe, *Psychotherapy by Reciprocal Inhibition*, 1958.

[13] See Goldfried, M. "Reduction of generalized anxiety through a variant of systematic desensitization," in M. Goldfried and M. Merbaum, Eds., *Behavior Change Through Self-Control* (New York: Holt, Rinehart, Winston, 1973).

[14] F. Kanfer and D. Goldfoot, "Self-Control and Tolerance of Noxious Stimulation," *Psychological Reports*, 18 (1966), 79-85.

[15] B. K. Anand, S. Chhina, and B. Singh, "Some Aspects of EEG Studies in Yogis," *EEG Clinical Neurophysiology*, 13 (1961), 452-56.

[16] Boudreau, L., "Transcendental meditation and yoga as reciprocal inhibitors," *Journal of Behavior Therapy and Experimental Psychiatry*, 3 (1972), 97-98.

Appendix 4

[1] See, for example, Gerald Davidson, "Counter-Control and Behavior Modification," in *Behavior Change, Methodology, Concepts, Practice*, Hamerlynck et al., Eds. (Champaign, Ill.: Research Press, 1973).

[2] See, for example, Carl Thoresen, "Behavioral Humanism," in C. Thoresen, Ed., *Behavior Modification in Education* (Chicago: University of Chicago Press, 1972) and Roger Walsh, "On a Behavioral Definition of Mental Health, unpublished manuscript, Stanford University; 1. Homme and D. Tosti, 1971, Contingency Management, 1971.

[3] See Walter Mischel, *Personality and Assessment* (New York: Wiley, 1968), p. 263.

[4] See J. M. Grossberg, "Behavior Therapy: A Review," *Psychological Bulletin*, 62 (1964), 73-73.

[5] There are three primary contributions which the existentialists have made to the process of therapy. The first relates to the act of labeling (where appropriate) feelings of confusion and meaninglessness as "existential anxiety." As we pointed out in Chapter 2, the act of labeling helps us feel more in control of a situation, helps us feel we are making some order out of chaos. Second, the existentialists model a vision of the possibility of living an authentic life; further, they stress the importance for us to choose and take responsibility for our own lives. Third, they let us know that the confusion and difficulty of making a decision is a "natural" process and that we all, to a certain extent, face it. Further, they provide a shared camaraderie in our common struggle to make order out of chaos, in our search to find meaning in a meaningless universe (see Camus' *Rebel*, Sartre's *Nausea*).

[6] See Alan Watts, "Beat Zen, Square Zen," in *This Is It* (San Francisco: City Lights Book Store, 1959).

[7] There seems to be a fear that intellect and understanding may remove the mystery and beauty. If we only use intellect and analysis and never *experience*, this is a reasonable and justified fear. As we have pointed out in the book, there seem to be two modes of knowing. The intellectual mode, however, does not preclude the mode of the altered state. As Buber noted, we can learn to analyze a tree and learn to experience it as "thou." Analysis does not preclude experiencing—the beauty of the tree still exists, as long as we are able to perceive it.

[8] Like all therapists, we as humanistic/transpersonal psychologists have a vision of who we can become—our human potential. Whether we admit it or not, we try, in some way, to give our clients the skills to reach that vision. For example, C. Truax noted, when observing Carl Rogers, that even in client-centered therapy the therapist decides when to respond nonjudgmentally and when not to respond at all. (C. Truax, "Reinforcement and nonreinforcement in Rogerian psychotherapy," *Journal of Abnormal Psychology*, 71 (1966) 1-9.) Further, we may selectively reinforce the development of internal criteria of excellence in our clients. We need to be honest and recognize that we, too, are often trying to influence our clients toward the fulfillment of *their* human potential. This is as it should be. Let's just acknowledge it. Then, rather than pretending we don't use techniques, we can look for and develop and teach the best techniques available for our particular client's concern.

[9] See, for example, the review by D. Shapiro and D. Giber: "Meditation, a Review of the Clinical Literature," *Archives of General Psychiatry*, in press.

[10] See J. D. Nolan, "Freedom and Dignity: A Functional Analysis," *American Psychologist*, 29 (1974), 157-60.

[11] A. Maslow, *The Psychology of Science* (New York: Harper & Row, 1966).

[12] For problems with meditation, see D. Shapiro and Giber, "Meditation," in press & Smith, "Meditation as Psychotherapy," *Psychological Bulletin*, 82 (1975), 558-64; for problems with behavioral self-control, see C. Thoresen and M. Mahoney, *Behavioral Self-Control* (New York: Holt, Rinehart and Winston, 1974).

APPENDIX 7: GLOSSARY

Aikido: A Japanese martial art, meaning the "way of harmony." It is practiced like a dance, and there is an emphasis on being yielding and nonconfrontive, flowing with the other person's "energy."

Alpha Waves: One type of brain wave, considered to be a sign of relaxation.

Altered State (Satori, Nirvana, Kensho Samadhi): A state of awareness in which there is an absence of words, labels, evaluations, analysis; different from ordinary awareness.

Angst: A German word which refers to anxiety about one's place in the world and one's meaning in life.

Antecedent: That which comes before; determining behavioral antecedents is part of one's *Self-observation* skills.

Attachment: See *Nonattachment.*

Attribution: Refers to what we say causes a certain event to occur.

Behavioral Programming: Involves the way we reinforce and punish ourselves *after* a behavior has occurred.

Behavioral Self-management: Development of skills derived from *Social Learning Theory* principles that can help us take more control of our own lives.

Behavioral Self-observation: See *Self-observation.*

Behavior Modifier: Traditionally used as a term designating an individual who practices behavior therapy with clients. Used here to designate an individual who practices behavior therapy (behavioral self-management skills) on him/herself. (See *Grand Conditioner.)*

Behavior Therapy: A school of psychology that deals with human problems, growth, development; emphasis is on learning as the means by which we develop both our overt and covert behaviors. (Also called behaviorism, social learning theory, behavior modification.)

Choice Points: Points during a person's life, when there is an opportunity to *consciously* decide how one wants to act, rather than acting by habit and reflex.

Chronos: A Greek word referring to chronological time (hours, minutes, seconds, days, weeks, etc.).

Cognitive Avoidance: A term social learning theorists use to refer to a means by which an individual keeps from facing certain events or thoughts.

Concentrative Meditation: See *Meditation.*

Conditioning: Process by which our behavior is influenced by the environment (social, physical, internal).

Consequence: What happens after something has occurred; a causal relationship is implied. [See Punishment and Reinforcement]

Contingent: Performing one action (thought, feeling) based upon the occurrence of another action (thought, feeling).

Contingencies: Consequences for a given set of actions.

Contracting: An agreement employing negative and positive consequences for decreasing maladaptive and increasing adaptive behavior, entered into either with self or with other people; a *Behavioral Self-management* skill.

Cosmic Chuckle: Learning to attain a sufficient distance from life events so that they are seen as humorous; also, a quiet, joyous appreciation of the wonder and grandeur of life.

Covert: Internal, inside our heads (covert self-statements and covert images are those that occur in our thoughts, not necessarily expressed in words).

Covert Images: Images or pictures inside our heads, which may be used to influence our behavior.

Covert Self-modeling: Using an image of ourselves acting in a positive, constructive way to help teach us how to behave that way in real life.

Covert statements: Dialogue inside our head, which may be used either negatively or positively to influence our behavior.

Deautomization: Undoing the normal automatic ways of doing something (in this case, perceiving the world).

Desensitization: A process by which an individual learns to not let himself be bothered by fears and concerns. *Systematic Desensitization* refers to constructing a series of events about a specific fear or fears. *Global Desensitization* involves no structured series of events, but rather "what's on your mind at the time."

Detached Observation: Refers to the ability to observe oneself without feeling threatened; helps us gain a perspective on our own life.

Differentiate: To be able to see the difference between two things.

Discrimination: Ability to focus on one thing, attribute, etc., as distinct from the overall gestalt, larger group, etc.

Double-bind Situation: Situation in which a person receives two simultaneous, contradictory messages of equal importance.

Environmental Planning: A self-management strategy which takes place *before* the occurrence of the actual *Target Behavior.* The strategy may involve pre-arranging the antecedents (see *Stimulus Control*) or the consequences, in order to influence the target behavior in the desired direction.

Existential Psychology: A school of psychology that puts primary emphasis on the need for individuals to find meaning and purpose in life, and to choose who they want to become.

Generalization: The process by which we apply what we learn in one situation to other situations.

Global Desensitization: See *Desensitization.*

Global Reinforcement (the "Big Cuddle"): A type of general (non-contingent) reinforcement, not related to specific behaviors or actions.

Grand Conditioner: That person who knows the most about *Behavior Therapy* (conditioning theory) and who applies those principles to him/herself (*Behavioral Self-Management* skills). (See *Behavior Modifier.*) The term is a play on the phrase, "The Grand Inquisitor" from Dostoevsky's *The Brothers Karamazov.*

Habituation: Psychological term referring to a process by which a new stimulus, if repeated sufficiently, will cease to be perceived. For example, if you walk into a new room, you may notice the noise of a fan. However, if you remain in the room for a time, eventually your awareness of the fan's sound will disappear (i.e., you will *habituate* to the sound of the fan).

Haiku: A form of Japanese Zen poetry, consisting of seventeen syllables grouped in a 5-7-5 pattern.

High-probability Behavior: Something that you do a lot (and like).

Humanistic Psychology: A school of psychology that deals with the potential for human growth and development; assumes a positive view of the individual—a view in which human beings are seen as innately good and self-actualizing.

Jujitsu: An ancient Japanese art of weaponless fighting.

Judo: A Japanese sport developed from jujitsu that emphasizes the use of quick movement and leverage to throw an opponent.

Kairos: A Greek word referring to timelessness; eternity; opposite of *Chronos.*

Karate: An oriental art of self-defense in which force is met with force, and an attacker is disabled by crippling kicks and punches.

Kensho: A Zen term for enlightenment: seeing into one's own true nature.

Koan: A sentence upon which to meditate, given by the Zen Master to the pupil. The sentence makes no sense by conventional logic.

Kwat: A blow to a student who is failing to meditate properly, administered by the Zen Master.

Low-probability Behavior: Any behavior you don't do very often because it is not reinforcing to you (in the short term), but which you would like to do more often.

Mantra: A sacred word or syllable repeated to oneself or repeated out loud during meditation.

Meditation: An awareness technique in which you focus without evaluation and analysis, used in Eastern disciplines as a means to attain enlightenment. The *concentrative meditation* technique involves an intense focus on a single object. Other objects are blocked out. *Opening-up meditation* is a technique that involves keeping yourself aware of all objects, sounds, smells, sensations simultaneously. (See also *Shikan-taza; Mindfulness meditation.*)

Mindfulness Meditation: A type of meditation that involves discriminating and labeling all cues that come into awareness.

Modeling: Performance of any behaviors, or attitudes which are identified with by an observer and which then lead to the acquisition of those behaviors on the part of the observer.

Mondo: A series of questions and answers, between master and monk, that do not seem to make any sense by our ordinary conventional logic.

Mudra: The position of the hands during meditation.

Negative Reinforcement: Removal of an aversive stimulus. (See *Reinforcement.*)

Nirvana: The Eastern version of "heaven"; literally means "blow-up" or "extinction." A peaceful spiritual state of mind, a state of enlightenment and well-being.

Nonattachment: Ability to be nonpossessive, nonclinging; yielding of possessions (and people).

Ordinary Awareness: The way we have been taught by our culture to see things; involves labels, traits, analysis.

Opening-up Meditation: See *Meditation.*

Overt: Something that is visible; you can see it as it happens (as opposed to *Covert*).

Persona: A term used by Carl Jung, referring to a facade adopted by an individual, to keep from revealing his true nature to others (and to himself).

Positive Reinforcement: See *Reinforcement.*

Precision Nirvana: A way of thinking and living which enables us to integrate psychological and spiritual self-management techniques from both the East and West to attain a personal vision of excellence drawn from Eastern and Western values and goals.

Premack Principle: Refers to Premack's idea that a *High-Probability Behavior* can serve as a reinforcement for a *Low-Probability Behavior* upon which it is made *Contingent.*

Projection: That which occurs when we attribute our feelings (e.g., anger) to another (e.g., I feel fine, but I think he's angry).

Punishment: A consequence for behavior; decreases the likelihood that that behavior will occur again.

Reactive Effect: Refers to the fact that the very act of observing something, such as our own behavior, may cause that behavior to change. In *Meditation* this reactive effect seems to make us "stumble"; in *Behavioral Self-Observation* the reactive effect seems to move the behavior in the desired direction.

Reinforcement: Positive reinforcement refers to a positive event that occurs after a certain behavior, increasing the likelihood that that behavior will occur again (getting a big hug for helping a little old lady across the street). *Negative Reinforcement* refers to an event that occurs after an unpleasant behavior, and causes the unpleasant behavior to cease. For example, a mother is negatively reinforced for giving her child a bottle when it cries, for the crying stops. The child, however, is being positively reinforced, for its behavior of crying is getting a positive result. Negative reinforcement should not be confused with *Punishment.*

Repression: A psychoanalytic term referring to when an individual is unwilling to face certain events, and these events are stored in the unconscious. Social learning theorists refer to this as *Cognitive Avoidance.*

Samadhi: A Hindu term for Illumination; the goal of Yoga practice.

Satori: A Zen term for Enlightenment; seeing into one's true nature. See *Kensho.*

Self-modeling: Using images of the self in our mind to set an example for ourself of how we would like to be acting and feeling.

Self-instructions: Making statements to ourselves which encourage us to feel and act in the way we would like to feel and act. A *Behavioral Self-management* technique.

Self-observation: A *Behavioral Self-management* technique that helps us to carefully analyze the relationship between our actions and the environment.

Self-regulation: A term used to describe a variety of different techniques which individuals can learn to use to influence their consciousness and bodily processes.

Self-reinforcement: Reinforcement of a symbolic, material, or verbal nature, which we give to ourselves. See *Reinforcement.*

Self-statements: Dialogue by oneself, either overt or covert, which refers to the self.

Shikan-taza: A type of meditation in which one "just sits," focusing on nothing . . . neither Koan, nor breaths.

Social Learning Theory: A branch of psychology that puts major emphasis on the ways we learn to behave. (See *Behavior Therapy.*)

Stimulus Control: Refers to a way of arranging the environment to help us act the way we want to act. For example, if we want to cut down on eating unhealthy foods, we make sure we don't buy any when we go to the market. (See *Environmental Planning.*)

Successive Approximation: Proceeding toward our goals through accomplishment of a series of successively more complex subgoals.

Sumi-e: Japanese brush-stroke painting.

Systematic Desensitization: See *Desensitization.*

Tao: Refers to that which cannot be named; beyond words and labels—holistic one.

Target Behavior: The behavior that you choose to work on changing.

Thought Stopping: Deliberately making oneself stop negative thoughts, substituting positive ones; a *Behavioral Self-management* technique.

Time Out: Calling a halt when things seem to be getting out of hand, and removing ourself (or others) to a place that is quieter; a *Behavioral Self-management technique.*

Trait Description: A trait is a verbal label that is used to describe an individual's behavior across a variety of situations. When we use traits to describe behavior, sometimes we inappropriately use traits themselves as explanations for behavior.

Transpersonal Psychology: A school of psychology that deals with the "further" reaches of human growth and development and optimum human functioning. Eastern psychologies are included in this school.

Yoga: Literally a yoke, or discipline; a technique of meditation whereby an individual attempts to bring himself into unity with the one, ultimate reality of the Universe. There are five types of yoga; Gnana (path of knowledge); Karma (path of action); Bhakti (path of love); Raja (Royal Path—a synthesis of the other three); and hatha (consisting of complicated physical and psychic exercises).

Zen: A school of Buddhism which teaches that through *Meditation* (Zazen) one can learn to see one's true self. A *Zen Master* is one who has achieved a high level of inner freedom through use of the Zen philosophy.

Index